CONTOURS OF
A CAUSE

Theological Vision of the
Church of God Movement
(Anderson, Indiana)

By
Barry L. Callen

Published by
Anderson University School of Theology
Anderson, Indiana

Printed by
Old Paths Tract Society
Route 2, Box 43
Shoals, IN 47581

Contents

Chapter Five: Frontiers

Appendix: The Vision in Stained Glass

Select Bibliography

Dedication

To the pioneers of the Church of God movement, in all of its generations, who have seen the vision of a holy and united church, and have given their lives in its pursuit. Representing these visionary servants of Christ and His church, six leaders of this movement have been especially influential on this writer. Deep gratitude is expressed for the insight and faithfulness of Boyce W. Blackwelder, Lillie S. McCutcheon, James Earl Massey, Gene W. Newberry, Robert H. Reardon, and John W. V. Smith.

Dr. Barry L. Callen

Biblical Foundations

Church:

So then you are no longer strangers and aliens, but you are citizens with the saints and also members of the household of God, built upon the foundation of the apostles and prophets, with Christ Jesus himself as the cornerstone. In him the whole structure is joined together and grows into a holy temple in the Lord; in whom you also are built together spiritually into a dwelling place for God.

(Eph. 2:19-22 NRSV)

Holiness:

May the God of peace himself sanctify you entirely; and may your spirit and soul and body be kept sound and blameless at the coming of our Lord Jesus Christ. The one who calls you is faithful, and he will do this.

(1 Thess. 5:23-24 NRSV)

Unity:

"As you have sent me [Jesus] into the world, so I have sent them into the world. And for their sakes I sanctify myself, so that they also may be sanctified in truth. I ask not only on behalf of these, but also on behalf of those who will believe in me through their word, that they may all be one. As you, Father, are in me and I am in you, may they also be in us, so that the world may believe that you have sent me."

(John 17:18-21 NRSV)

Hope:

"Then I heard what seemed to be the voice of a great multitude, like the sound of many waters and like the sound of mighty thunderpeals, crying out, "Hallelujah! For the Lord our God the Almighty reigns. Let us rejoice and exult and give him the glory, for the marriage of the Lamb has come, and his bride has made herself ready; to her it has been granted to be clothed with fine linen, bright and pure"—for the fine linen is the righteous deeds of the saints.

(Revelation 19:6-8 NRSV)

Introduction

Christian theology seeks to interpret the human story in light of the divinely-inspired story of God with us in Jesus Christ.[1] The critical question is: What guides the process of interpreting and embodying this story of redemption? The Church of God movement (Anderson, Ind.) had sought to advance church renewal by a return to the Bible as authority and to the Spirit as the enabler of the Bible's interpretation and application.

The Christian faith presents as its center the ultimate paradox that is said to be good news indeed. Time and eternity have been united in the God-man, Jesus Christ. The resulting human task is less to *find* and *systematize* truth and more *to be found* by a gracious God and then *to live* the truth of Jesus Christ in obedience and joy.

Since the late nineteenth century, the Church of God movement has issued a vigorous call for the life-changing integrity of personal faith in the perverting face of denominational preoccupations, creedal rigidities, and the widespread abandonment of true holiness. Contrary to the excessive individualism of much American revivalism, this movement also has had a vision for the integrity and wholeness of the church itself. The movement's journey has been a quest for the holiness of each believer (sanctification) and the holiness of the church (unity in the Spirit).[2]

The Church of God movement is a body of Christian

---

[1]Alister McGrath, *Understanding Doctrine* (Grand Rapids: Zondervan, 1990), 36.

[2]See the narrative history of the Church of God movement by John W. V. Smith, *The Quest for Holiness and Unity* (Anderson, Ind.: Warner Press, 1980).

believers that has sought to recover and be informed by the whole of Christian truth, especially "apostolic" truth narrated in Scripture. This movement has declared itself open to the cumulative theological wisdom of God's church in all times and places. By conscious intention, it always has been "orthodox," standing in the mainstream of Christian believing over the centuries. It also has been "radical" when necessary by its commitment to truth's proper application in the face of stagnant, suffocating, and divisive church institutions, creedal traditions, and the church's tendency to accept the world's values in place of genuine discipleship. The movement aspires to be "catholic" and "protestant," belonging to the whole and standing against all that distracts from the fullest truth or disrupts the unity of the church that is required for effective mission in the world.[3]

Whatever the special emphases made and prominent problems addressed, a basic characteristic of the teaching tradition of this Church of God movement is the conscious rejection of being *innovators* in either Christian doctrine or practice. To the contrary, the call is to a fresh commitment to the foundational beliefs and practices inspired by God, recorded in the Bible, and interpreted by the Holy Spirit. This call is driven by a sense of urgency, the conviction that the movement shares in a divine commission to represent and encourage the whole church toward the modern restoration of apostolic faith, experience, practice, fellowship, and mission. The longing is to return to the original essence of Christianity, casting aside the tangle of churchly debris that has accumulated over the centuries in the forms of competitive structures, divisive creeds, and human usurpings of Christ as head of the church. To what Christ has defined and

---

[3]It is admitted that this stance of openness and wholeness, while persisting in principle, has not always been exhibited in practice. The prophetic voice of the movement often has been muted as it has gotten caught in its own isolationism and occasional arrogance.

commanded this movement wishes to be true. To this it would add nothing; from this it would drop nothing.

A central paradox should be noted. On the one hand, this movement always has been committed to biblical truth. Doctrinal preaching and writing have even respected highly and a concern for theological correctness has been apparent in most local situations. From almost the beginning of the movement around 1880, there has evolved a rather well-defined and generally understood *consensus of thought* concerning the basic outline of what constitutes accurate and thus acceptable Christian teaching. This general focusing of opinion on a given pattern of biblical interpretation, shifting slightly at points over the decades and never quite formalized, undoubtedly has helped to give this relatively small and (by usual standards) quite unstructured group of Christians the corporate identity and cohesiveness needed for it to relate meaningfully and work fruitfully.

On the other hand, a central part of this traditional theological consensus has been a persistent opposition to the tyranny of theological creeds and to the development by the movement of its own "denominational" characteristics. There has been a *holistic emphasis*, a vision of all of God's people, a reaching toward all of the truth in Christ, knowing always that no one person or creedal statement (limited as they are and well-intentioned as they may be) will ever be in a position to become the final authority. The only recognized boundary of the Christian fellowship has been the *experience of salvation*, actually being a Christian.

Thus the paradox. Participants in the Church of God movement have functioned together with a rather clear set of goals and, for the most part, with basic theological agreement.[4] At the same time, they have been committed in principle to resisting the

---

[4]For an anthology of the teachings of the Church of God movement, including key selections from a wide range of its writers and institutions, see Barry Callen, *The First Century*, vol. 1 (Anderson, Ind.: Warner Press, 1979), 241-456.

narrowing effects of traditional denominationalism. Living with this paradox has been judged hypocritical by some Christians who continue to see denominationalism as unavoidable. They have seen the movement's consensus of thought as clearly denominational in character. Other Christians have studied the movement's vision and life and have used words like *admirable* and *idealistic*. They have judged it to be most commendable, even if destined to inevitable frustration. Admiration is elicited by a vision of the church (1) that is divinely oriented, (2) that by intent is inclusive of all true Christians without regard to affiliation, nationality, race, gender, or current biblical understanding, (3) that always is open to more of the truth, and (4) that refuses to recognize human standards and organizations as legitimate fences that often are allowed to divide Christians from each other. But such an admirable vision has made this Church of God movement unusually vulnerable to criticism when the movement's own functioning has proven to be less than the ideal for which it stands and toward which it strives. Even so, this vision is vigorously maintained because it continues to commend itself to this movement as God's will for the church.

So, focusing on this theological vision, its beginnings, boundaries, foundations, fruits, and frontiers, is the purpose of this book. Despite the special attention given to this one church movement, especially in light of the vision in question, the reader should know that no slavish imitation of this tradition's theological particulars is envisioned as necessarily ideal—nor would such a thoughtless pursuit be consistent with this movement's own stated goals. One must not be distracted by what sometimes are only the passing incidentals of a group's time and place in history or by the awkward aberrations that occasionally arise in its midst. In this particular tradition, nonetheless, there are theological roots, clues, and directions worthy of careful note during these transitional and troubled times for the church and world.

This present focusing on the Church of God movement is in the spirit of Carl Braaten when he points favorably to his Lutheran tradition. Writes Braaten: "It is not our intention to push the Lutheran tradition for its own sake. When Lutheranism achieves its goal of reforming the church, it goes out of business as a confessional movement. Otherwise it lingers on as a sect. And that is a fate we would wish to avoid at all costs."[5] Likewise, the Church of God movement understands its mission as enhancing the fuller health of the whole church, not its own upbuilding or perpetuation.[6] Truth, transformation, and mission are the core concerns. The goals are hearing, embodying, and telling the whole world the wonderful story of God in Christ. Holiness of life, the wholeness of the church, and dedicated discipleship are ever-present keynotes.

How can contemporary Christians acquire an adequate understanding of the Christian faith and then engage in its effective embodiment in this world? How can the substance of the faith become a driving force in the service of the church's mission? How can believers live in the reality of *now,* with adequate faith roots in the church's *yesterday*, roots that are inspired by hope in the coming *tomorrow*, and out of that past and hope provide the proper vision for a *transformed today*?

The intention of this theological exploration of the vision of one movement is to encourage the whole church toward a fuller integrity of thought and action, belief and mission. Christian theology is "to inquire about the nature of the gospel, and to ask whether the praxis [actual current practice] of mission truly

---

[5]Carl Braaten, *Principles of Lutheran Theology* (Philadelphia: Fortress Press, 1983), xi.

[6]See below for a recent statement of the mission of this renewal movement.

reflects the faith."[7] What is the good news and is it being lived out and shared effectively in our time? Highlighting the tradition of the Church of God movement is justified in part by this particular movement's distinctive commitment to making *visible* in our time the classically identified attributes of the true church, its unity, holiness, catholicity, and apostolicity.

Such attributes were championed by the Protestant reformers of the sixteenth century in their attempts to address the abuses that had appeared from inappropriate human innovations in conflict with the Bible. The church has difficulty functioning in human history in a pure form. Martin Luther, for instance, retained Augustine's distinction between the *visible* and *invisible* church as a way of explaining the church's appearance in history as less than she ought to be. The Church of God movement has appreciated Luther's vision and caution. However, it also has been so committed to the intended present integrity and mission responsibility of today's church that it chooses not to resort to "invisibility" as the means of explanation.

Holiness means genuine transformation, true and obvious set-apartness for God. Believers are called to be holy as God is holy (Lev. 20:26). Unity among believers also appears to be God's intent (John 17). Oneness among Christ's disciples is enabled by the dynamic of holiness and is directed toward mission. Mission means making the church very visible indeed! While full arrival of realized holiness and unity may yet be a great distance off, the focus of the Church of God movement remains on nothing short of the full and final destination.

Believers not acquainted with the theological vision of the Church of God movement can profit from a consideration of what this particular tradition hopes to offer the whole church. It is an option that may be a way around some of the perennial

---

[7]Carl Braaten, *The Flaming Center: A Theology of the Christian Mission* (Fortress Press, 1977), 11.

impasses of the "ecumenical" movement and a corrective to some of the pitfalls experienced by today's "evangelical" community. Believers now a part of this movement, but nonetheless relatively unaware of its rich theological heritage, need to become immersed in that which has given the movement cohesion, vision, and relevance for over a century. May it remain so as a new century soon will dawn.

An extensive bibliography is provided at the conclusion of this work for the reader who wishes to explore further the many facets of the theological vision of this particular renewal movement. To begin the exploration, however, the focus and changing flavor of this movement can be caught, in part, by noting two brief self-identifications from its history.

1. This vigorous affirmation is found on the masthead of the earliest issues of the *Gospel Trumpet*, the movement's influential periodical (1881 onward):

> DEFINITE, RADICAL, and ANTI-SECTARIAN, sent forth in the name of the Lord Jesus Christ, for the publication of full Salvation, and Divine Healing of the body, and Unity of all true Christians in "the faith once delivered to the saints."

2. The following statement of mission for the movement was endorsed by the Executive Council and General Assembly of the Church of God (Anderson, Indiana, June, 1988), and "commended to the church as a resource and working document in the pursuit of its multi-faceted ministries":

> The mission of the Church of God is to be a caring community of God's covenant people under the Lordship of Jesus Christ and the leadership of the Holy Spirit:
>
> > a. To proclaim the love of God, through Jesus Christ, to all persons;

b. To enable persons throughout all the world to experience redemptive love in its fullest meaning through the sanctifying power of the gospel and know Jesus Christ as Saviour, Master, and Lord;

c. To call persons to holiness and discipleship;

d. To equip persons to be servants of Christ in the world;

e. To live as citizens of the Kingdom of God here and now, work for justice, mercy and peace, and abide in the Christian hope;

f. To build up the whole body of Christ in unity.

CHAPTER ONE

Beginnings

In 1809 Thomas Campbell delivered his famous *Declaration and Address* in Washington County, Pennsylvania. Soon it would be the centerpiece of a vigorous Christian "restorationist" tradition in America.[1] In this historic declaration, Campbell questioned: "Why should we deem it a thing incredible that the Church of Christ, in this highly favored country, should resume that original unity, peace, and purity which belong to its constitution, and constitute its glory?"[2]

Rather than incredible, time and place then favored such an attempted resumption. The earliest colonists in America, those pilgrim pioneers of a "new world," sensed in the air a fresh potential for real freedom. The period after the American Revolution brought the "democratization" of American Christianity.[3] The power of elite religious establishments slowly crumbled, to be replaced by movements like the Methodists, Baptists, and Disciples. Ordinary people were taking matters of faith into their own hands. There arose a rugged individualism, a distinctly American lifestyle that often featured a mistrust of institutionalized authority. People increasingly were prone to think for themselves and often founded new denominations that they could shape and control.

---

[1]This tradition later would be known as the Disciples of Christ, with major branches now called the Christian Churches/Churches of Christ and the Churches of Christ (non-instrumental).

[2]Leonard Allen and Richard Hughes trace this impulse for a restorationist idealism back to the Renaissance of the fourteenth and fifteenth centuries (*Discovering Our Roots: The Ancestry of Churches of Christ*, Abilene, Tx.: Abilene Christian University Press, 1988, chapter 2).

[3]Nathan Hatch, *The Democratization of American Christianity* (Yale University Press, 1989), chaps. 1, 3, 4.

In significant ways, such a vision of radical reform of the established churches with roots in Europe reflected the influential ethos of the times. Historian Sidney Mead identifies three religious ideas that drove denominational developments in the young American nation. They were: "the idea of pure and normative beginnings to which return was possible; the idea that the intervening history was largely that of aberrations and corruptions which was better ignored; and the idea of building anew in the American wilderness on the true and ancient foundations."[4]

Given this vigorous young nation and these powerful motivating ideas, a new movement like the Stone/Campbell (Disciples) has been judged "the quintessential American denomination."[5] The Disciples movement, embodying well the ethos of the times, grew rapidly. Thomas Campbell, for instance, insisted in his *Declaration and Address* that the one hope for religious renewal in America lay in a return to "simple evangelical Christianity, free from all mixture of human opinions and inventions of men." The old institutions and traditions could be abandoned in favor of the freeing and purifying air of the broad and beckoning American frontiers.

The theological perspectives of today's Church of God movement (Anderson, Ind.) are influenced greatly by these perceptions, characteristics, and ideals of the early American period. This movement was shaped by the time and place of its own formative period, the final decades of the nineteenth century. It inherited the restorationist ethos of the Disciples' movement and the general American mentality within which that ethos emerged. It also drew on the maturing of a "pentecostalism" pattern that had come to penetrate large segments of many

---

[4]Sidney Mead, *The Lively Experiment: The Shaping of Christianity in America* (Harper & Row, 1963), 111.

[5]Mark Toulouse, *Joined in Discipleship* (St. Louis: Chalice Press, 1992), 22.

denominational bodies by the 1880s. This pattern had evolved in large part from themes in the Methodist tradition, themes themselves shaped by experiences of the churches and the young nation, especially after the Civil War.[6]

As historian John Smith once said about the Church of God movement, "the foundations of this reformation were fashioned in the crucible of real life," not "out of a new philosophy nor even out of a new interpretation of Christian theology."[7] The time of Civil War aftermaths was a time when the nation was expanding rapidly and traditional understandings of particular Christian doctrines were being reshaped significantly.[8]

Visions of Freedom and Restoration

Jürgen Moltmann identifies helpfully two conflicting visions that dominated and clashed in the nineteenth century.[9] The increasing prominence of the first over the second created much of the environment in which movements like the Church of God arose, and out of which much of twentieth century Christian theology has developed.

The first of these visions was the *vision of freedom* symbolized well by the French and American revolutions. This invigorating new freedom vision encouraged people to insist on seeing themselves as *free citizens,* not *controlled subjects.* In this view,

---

[6]See Donald Dayton, *Theological Roots of Pentecostalism,* rev. ed. (Peabody, Mass.: Hendrickson Publishers, 1987, 1991).

[7]John Smith, *Truth Marches On* (Anderson, Ind.: Gospel Trumpet Co., 1956), 18.

[8]To find descriptions of these times and how they formed an immediate context for the beginnings of the Church of God movement, note Barry Callen, *Guide of Soul and Mind: The Story of Anderson University* (Anderson University and Warner Press, 1992), 7-18, and Callen, *She Came Preaching: The Life and Ministry of Lillie S. McCutcheon* (Anderson, Ind.: Warner Press, 1992), 14-27.

[9]Jürgen Moltmann, *Theology Today* (Philadelphia: Trinity Press International, 1988), 1-6.

society should be more egalitarian, with religion a private and not a state established, sponsored, or otherwise controlled thing. People began claiming the right to direct their own futures. Through the progress of science, the process of evolution, and, if necessary, the disruption of revolution, a wholly new and better future was thought to lie ahead, one that should be created anew rather than being limited by restrictive beliefs and institutions of the past.

One theological manifestation of this aggressive and optimistic attitude was the pervasive "pentecostalism" of early revivalism in America. Drawing on the Wesleyan theme of overcoming evil in this life (personal and social sanctification), prominent voices like Charles Finney, Henry Cowles, and the Oberlin College faculty in Ohio saw the church able, through its own faithfulness to God's grace and power, to make progress in Christianizing the nation and thus bringing about the Kingdom of God prior to Christ's eventual return.[10] In eschatological terms, this was the era of post-millennialism.[11] Such a cultural outlook was the "party of hope" and Alexander Campbell of the Disciples tradition was a leading representative.[12]

---

[10]Dayton, *op. cit.,* 153-157. While the vision of freedom was consistent with the free-church nature of the Believers' Church tradition, not consistent was the tendency to become deeply involved in public institutions with the intent of reshaping and expressing the faith through them. The Church of God movement, arising later in the nineteenth century, championed an optimism of grace (John Wesley's influence), but saw the personal and social implications of grace being fulfilled in purified believers and a purified church more than in a reclaimed society (Believers' Church influence).

[11]See Stanley Grenz, *The Millennial Maze* (InterVarsity Press, 1992), chap. 3.

[12]Richard Hughes, "The Apocalyptic Origins of Churches of Christ and the Triumph of Modernism," *Religion and American Culture* 2:2 (Summer, 1992), 183-184.

The second vision noted by Moltmann was a reaction to the first. It was "God, King and Fatherland," a conservative resurgence that saw in the freedom-vision's attempt at extensive uprooting of the past "an apocalyptic downfall of the world."[13] Surely the result of such innovative human arrogance would be atheism, religious anarchy, and rampant individualism. This "modern spirit," an invasion of the sacred by the secular outlook of the Enlightenment, must be resisted by a new insistence on what is unchangingly right, properly ordered, clearly revealed, and absolutely established by God.

The primary concern, argued this reacting conservative mentality, should not be our human "rights" and freedom to think, believe, associate, and act however we judge best. Truth is truth! Within the Christian community, this meant that truth from God is to be obeyed, not altered and recreated to suit some modern mood. What once was truth still should be accepted gladly as truth. There are limits to frontier freedoms!

Toward the end of the nineteenth century it had become clear that the Christian community was not succeeding in bringing in the Kingdom of God through progressive social and moral programs. Rapid industrialization and urbanization were powerful and often humanly destructive forces. Moral compromise lay on every hand. The dominance of an optimistic post-millennialism had been replaced by a more pessimistic pre-millennialism. An ideal time of God's reign on earth would have to wait to be initiated by the dramatic return of Christ.

---

[13]Hughes (*op. cit.*, 184) calls this the "party of memory." Participants were generally pessimistic about progress on "modern" terms and often were "profoundly apocalyptic." Barton Stone was a good example. The irony is that the Campbell and Stone movements merged in 1832 based on a range of similarities (both using the rhetoric of restoring primitive Christianity and seeking Christian unity), but their worldview differences later brought rupture (see C. Leonard Allen, "Stone the Builders Rejected," in Anthony Dunnavant, ed., *Cane Ridge in Context,* Nashville: Disciples of Christ Historical Society, 1992, 52).

The resulting theological landscape of the last quarter of the nineteenth century, then, was mixed, even volatile. Church divisions were common and often ugly. There were restorationist schemes of the "hope" and "memory" types, but also a growing pessimism that tended to mute all idealism. The bourgeois spirit of the modern vision of freedom was taking a strong hold through the emergence of "liberal" theologies. But soon this kind of "enlightened" approach to theology would be countered by the vigorous reaction of a "fundamental" theology that would insist on a rigid return to the authoritarian principle. Much of twentieth-century Christian theology is "still preoccupied with the problems of churches and Christians in adapting themselves to developments in the nineteenth century."[14]

Combining the Visions

Beginning about 1880, one such "adapting" effort was the Church of God movement. In the dynamics of this late nineteenth-century context, this growing body of believers emphasized a definite vision of freedom coupled closely to a vigorous, conservative, "pentecostal" call for all Christians to return to the apostolic roots of the faith. The dynamic to make this return possible was identified as the Spirit of God who alone sanctifies, unifies, gifts, empowers, and sends.

Here was a movement seeking to incorporate in its own distinctive way both of the competing visions of the time. The visionary Christians comprising this movement hoped to pioneer a better way. They felt directed by God in that particular setting to champion their "catholic" identity as members of the church universal rather than to limit their loyalty to any divisive denominational body inappropriately called a "church." They were convinced that formalized and official creeds tend to blunt the primacy of biblical authority in the church's life and encourage sectarian division. This was the freedom part of the vision.

---

[14]Jürgen Moltmann, *op. cit.*, 8.

Likewise, early adherents of the Church of God movement insisted on a return-to-the-foundation. Freedom from everything "man-made" in the church was to be disciplined by an apostolic anchor. Church organizations, it was judged, usually lead to an erosion of the leadership of the Holy Spirit. Therefore, these "radical" reformers sensed and soon championed a divine commission to be formed themselves by the ancient apostolic faith. They then hoped to help the whole church recover that ancient foundation as narrated in the New Testament and centered in Jesus. These visionary pioneers were determined to fulfill the evangelistic mission of biblical faith in an open and free fellowship of sanctified and unified believers. These emphases were understood to be central in the Christian past and especially right for the times.

One caution is in order. Movements seeking dramatic reform often view the presumed apostasy of the church's past in very negative and virtually absolute terms (one of those formative American ideas). Sometimes they believe or at least give the impression that they themselves are a new reality on the scene, original, fresh, and alone authentic.[15] In fairness, it should be noted that vigorous calls for freedom from the follies of denominationalism and a resumption of the power and priority of biblical faith had been prominent in numerous Anabaptist, Pietistic, and then Pentecostal circles from at least the sixteenth century.

---

[15]In *Illusions of Innocence* (University of Chicago, 1988), Leonard Allen and Richard Hughes explore this common tendency. In time, of course, the Church of God movement became more aware and accepting of the complex reforming heritage of which it is a part. Note the movement's church historian Charles Brown in his *When the Trumpet Sounded* (Anderson, Ind.: Warner Press, 1951), 23-41, and the later historian John Smith in his doctoral dissertation, "The Approach of the Church of God (Anderson, Indiana) and Comparable Groups to the Problem of Christian Unity" (University of Southern California Graduate School of Religion, 1954).

Increasingly, however, such calls had become newly prominent in America in the decades immediately preceding the rise of the Church of God movement. Reforms have precedents, even if unrecognized.

The Stone-Campbell movement (the Disciples), for instance, from early in the nineteenth century had perceived most of the same dilemmas and proposed some of the same solutions that later would characterize the Church of God movement.[16] God clearly was at work, often in circles larger than those readily recognized. One important circle was a movement initiated by John Winebrenner (1797-1860).

John Winebrenner[17] and the reforming movement he spawned held its first General Eldership meeting in 1849. This reforming body, later to be related directly to the beginnings of the Church of God movement through its relationship to Daniel Warner,[18] had "abandoned the Calvinist stance of the German Reformed church and declared themselves to be Arminian. Intensely biblical, they adopted no written creed but affirmed that the Word of God was their only rule of faith."[19] Winebrenner believed that there is only one true church, the church of God, and that it is the duty of God's people to belong to it and to none else.

---

[16]For broad perspective on the Stone-Campbell movement that spanned almost all of the nineteenth century and remains significant yet today, see Louis and Bess White Cochran, *Captives of the Word* (Joplin, Mo.: College Press Pub. Co., 1987, original 1969); Henry Webb, *In Search of Christian Unity* (Cincinnati: Standard Publishing, 1990); Mark Toulouse, *Joined in Discipleship* (St. Louis: Chalice Press, 1992); and James North, *Union In Truth* (Cincinnati: Standard Publishing, 1994).

[17]An excellent biography is that by Richard Kern, *John Winebrenner, Nineteenth-Century Reformer* (Harrisburg, Pa.: Central Publishing House, 1974).

[18]See Barry Callen, *It's God's Church! The Life and Legacy of Daniel Warner* (Anderson, Ind.: Warner Press, 1995).

[19]John Smith, *The Quest for Holiness and Unity* (Anderson, Ind.: Warner Press, 1980), 38.

John Winebrenner loomed large in Daniel Warner's mind "as a spiritual father." Warner's "self imposed course of private biblical and theological studies, his first two marriages, his library collection, his diaries, his ministerial career, his religious journalism, and his very mental furniture bear the Winebrennerian stamp."[20] What was the theological nature of this stamp? It focuses on a five-point theological transformation experienced by Winebrenner across the 1820s that by 1830 led to a rupture in his relationship with the German Reformed Church in Harrisburg, Pennsylvania.

This transformation was encouraged by Winebrenner's involvement in revivalism and his interaction with leaders of groups like the United Brethren in Christ that reflected roots in German Pietism and other "radical" elements of the Protestant Reformation that had been transplanted to America. The transforming theological points were:

1. The Bible is the Word of God, the only authoritative rule of faith and practice. This "only" left no place for church tradition, including human inventions like creeds, catechisms, rituals, etc.;

2. Spiritual regeneration, being born again, always is necessary for a person to become a real Christian and church member. Thus the Christian faith is rooted in the Bible and in such spiritual experience;

3. Humankind possesses free moral agency and the ability, with the Spirit's assistance, to repent, believe, and be saved. Thus denied were the Reformed doctrines of predestination, providence, and perseverance;

4. Baptism and the Lord's Supper became seen as symbolic "ordinances" rather than grace-conveying "sacraments." Baptism necessarily is to be preceded by belief and

---

[20]L. Leon Long, "To What Extent Was Warner a Winebrennarian?" in *The Church Advocate* (February, 1976), 6.

regeneration and is best administered by immersion (eliminating the appropriateness of infant baptism); Feetwashing also joined the list of the church's ordinances;

5. Regarding the church, the only requirement for membership in a local congregation is having been born again and the true biblical name for a local congregation or for the Body of Christ as a whole is "Church of God."[21]

Daniel Warner experienced conversion in a revival held near Montpelier, Ohio, in 1865. The evangelist was a minister of the General Eldership of the Churches of God (Winebrennarian). Warner then received his ministerial license from the West Ohio Eldership in 1867, having absorbed such theological emphases as listed above. Soon, however, he came to view them through the eyes of the Wesleyan holiness experience. These eyes focused on the purifying love of God that could be the dynamic needed to restore the unity of the church. In a little booklet called *The Church of God*, Warner restated many of these Winebrennarian themes, but now in light of his own Wesleyan experience of "entire sanctification."[22]

There also was the Evangelical United Mennonite church that operated a publishing house in Goshen, Indiana, in the 1870s.[23] Daniel Warner (1842-1895), the most prominent pio-

[21]J. Harvey Gossard, "John Winebrenner: Founder, Reformer, and Businessman" in *Pennsylvania Religious Leaders* (Historical Study No. 16, The Pennsylvania Historical Association, 1986), 89-90. For an elaboration of these and other beliefs as held currently by the Churches of God: General Conference (Winebrennerian), see the booklet *We Believe* (Findlay, Ohio: Churches of God Publications, 1986).

[22]Daniel Warner, booklet *The Church of God* (1885). This writing reflects key themes of Thomas Campbell's *Declaration and Address* (1809) and bears close resemblance to John Winebrenner's booklet *The Church of God* (1829, rev. ed. 1885, Harrisburg, Pa.: Board of Publication, General Eldership of the Churches of God).

[23]This was the publisher of the first book emerging from within the Church of God movement, *Bible Proofs of the Second Work of Grace* by Daniel Warner (1880).

neer of the Church of God movement, had intimate contact with this body, providing him with an influential exposure to the emphases of the general Anabaptist tradition.[24] Included among these emphases were "believers' baptism, voluntary submission to Christian disciplines, the rejection of 'worldliness,' the dual authority of the Bible and the Holy Spirit, the Church as a holy community with its members committed to a life-embracing discipleship, and strong emphasis on the eschatological dimension for life on earth and hereafter."[25]

There had evolved a significant "pentecostal" consensus on the broader evangelical scene in America following the Civil War.[26] This cluster of four doctrinal emphases, the "foursquare gospel," comprised much of the theological ethos in which the Church of God movement first emerged. These emphases were personal salvation, physical healing, baptism in the Holy Spirit, and the second coming of Christ. The elements of this distinctive theological cluster had roots in Anglicanism, Pietism, and Puritanism, especially as these were taught by John Wesley and then reshaped somewhat in revivalistic America.[27] Donald Dayton traces carefully the Methodist-related theological roots of these four doctrines of the pentecostal consensus, observing how each became Americanized, radicalized, and placed in a particular restorationist framework. Together they provided a vigorous context for fresh reformation as the nineteenth century came to an end.

A Free-Church Stance

John Yoder, prominent Mennonite theologian, reflects helpfully on one Christian tradition that has provided a set of sturdy

---

[24]Warner's personal journal entry for September 26, 1879, refers to "these beloved brethren" with whom "our hearts are wonderfully knit together in love."

[25]John Smith, 1980, 39.

[26]This consensus did *not* highlight a gift of "speaking in tongues," something to be characteristic of much Pentecostalism in the twentieth century.

[27]Donald Dayton, *op. cit.*, 38.

shoulders on which the Church of God movement stands. He identifies an approach referred to variously as free church, believers' church,[28] and radical reformation. These phrases seek to describe a common view of Christian faith and life that differs significantly from much usually referred to as the Protestant Reformation, and what more recently has become known as "evangelicalism."[29]

"Reformation," explains Yoder, "means standing in judgment on what has come of Christianity over time."[30] Poor "forms" have evolved, whether lifestyle, organizational, or doctrinal formulations. The needed re-formation should be "radical," should go to the root and avoid superficial analyses and corrections. Emphasis on "believers" makes plain that the biggest correction needed is to reverse the "Constantinian" compromise of inclusivism in the constituency of the visible church.[31] The church should be reformed on the basis of con-

---

[28]The current highlighting of the "Believers' Church" tradition began with a series of conferences so-named that originated with the vision of Johannes Oosterbaan. His experience at the New Delhi Assembly of the World Council of Churches (1961) convinced him of a circumstance needing correcting. While the denominations growing out of the mainstream Protestant reformation are rich in official documents and institutions through which they enter ecumenical discussions on a substantial base, representatives of the "radical reformation" are, by intent, diverse and relatively unorganized. Soon a major conference on the concept of the Believers' Church was convened at Southern Baptist Seminary (June, 1967). Others followed, including one at Anderson University School of Theology (Church of God) in June, 1984 (see Merle Strege, ed., *Baptism & Church: A Believers' Church Vision*, Grand Rapids: Sagamore Books, 1986).

[29]See chapter five for explanation of the approach of evangelicalism and how it contrasts with the vision of the Church of God movement.

[30]John Yoder, "Thinking Theologically From a Free Church Perspective," in J. Woodbridge, T. McComiskey, eds., *Doing Theology in Today's World* (Grand Rapids: Zondervan, 1991), 251.

[31]See Stanley Hauerwas and William Willimon, *Resident Aliens* (Nashville: Abingdon Press, 1989), 17-18. When the Roman Emperor Constantine embraced Christianity and even established it as "official" in the Empire (c315 C.E.), the faith is said then to have "fallen."

sciously committed adult believers. "Free" focuses on liberation from state control so that the church again can be God's and God's alone, not coterminous with, but "resident aliens" within any nation or culture.

The critiquing, liberating, radical (not superficial corrections, but back-to-the-root) elements of this free church stance entered directly into the theological bloodstream of the Church of God movement. The result has been an unrelenting commitment to truth, God's truth, truth released from compromise, establishment control, and uncommitted adherents. The Believers' Church tradition asks if the only options for pursuing truth are coercive uniformity and tolerant inclusivism. Yoder says that the free church responds with this claim: "There are ways to disavow coercion without giving up on the truth; namely, through binding dialogue under the rule of Scripture."[32]

In the early intentions of the Church of God movement there was no preoccupation with developing a final "systematic" theology around some particular ideology of the times. After all, it seemed to these "saints" in the 1880s that time itself was short. Christ would return soon and the then-dominant ideologies were part of the problem, not a vehicle for the solution. There were important things to be done. The times called for action, for radical reformation. What was needed was an urgent coming out of churchly apostasy and a faithful coming to the church of Christ's intent and final gathering. Therefore, many sensitive saints set out, not to capture and systematize another divisive doctrinal "system," but to be captured themselves by life-changing and church-changing truths that they did not control or fully comprehend. Once captured, they felt compelled to become a "flying ministry," excited agents of such wonderful truths. They were orthodox, and yet radical, more like frontline gospel sol-

---

[32]John Yoder, in Introduction to Merle Strege, ed., *Baptism & Church* (Grand Rapids: Sagamore Books, 1986), 7.

diers than ivory-tower theologians. They were caught up in the story of what God was understood to be doing in "these latter days."

These movement pioneers were anxious to reintroduce the rightful role of authentic spiritual experience into the Christian truth-knowing process. They were aware, however, that they must not become mired in a world of subjective chaos. After all, an unchecked yielding to spiritual experience could result in each Christian pushing whatever "truth" that person perceives, leading to more chaos of a very human and destructive sort.[33]

The crucial need was understood to be centered in Christians being willing to return to *divine* truth, gifts, agendas, and ways, abandoning the usual church preoccupations with *human* thinking, creed making, church organizing, and constituency choosing and regulating. Admittedly, distinguishing between divine and human is difficult indeed. What was clear was at least

----

[33]John Wesley offers an appropriate caution here. On the one hand, he was the man whose "heart was strangely warmed" and who sought and testified to the internal "assurance" of the Spirit regarding his own salvation. On the other hand, reports Lowell Ferrel: "Wesley was very much a prophet of both the Reformation and the Age of Enlightenment. From the former, he inherited a high view of Scripture which grounded revelation in objective reality. From the latter he gained an appreciation for reason as an alternative to primitive superstitions and vain imaginations" ("John Wesley and the Enthusiasts," *Wesleyan Theological Journal,* Spring/Fall, 1988, 182). While committed to the important role of religious experience in Christian knowing and living, Wesley opposed the "enthusiasts" of his time who seemed to set reason and discipline aside in favor of merely subjective impressions. While he gave priority to biblical authority, Wesley recognized that "all truth is existentially perceived and appropriated. . . . This is not a subjectivizing of the biblical revelation, but a frank acknowledgment that all truth is mediated in a larger context, rather than merely through a logical and rationalistic framework" (Laurence Wood, "The Wesleyan View," in Donald Alexander, ed., *Christian Spirituality,* Inter-Varsity Press, 1988, 95).

the focus of commitment. The time was right for God to be honored as the Lord of the church and the core of truth itself! How theologically appropriate is the prayer of E. Stanley Jones:

> O Saviour, You do not only save me, You save truth—save it from being a proposition and made it into a Person. You did say, "I am the truth," and lo, Truth is lovable and livable and not a dry-as-dust proposition. I am at Your feet, Gracious Truth. Amen.[34]

A radical, free-church vision rests in reliance on the sovereignty of God. This sovereignty "relativizes *all* human concepts, institutions, and activities. Human claims to truth stand under judgment of the One who alone is holy, the One who transcends all of our projects and explanations—a realization to which Scripture testifies on practically every page"[35] (e.g., Isa. 55:8-9; Acts 17:24-25, 28). Existing together are God, who is the truth, and the partial human understandings of God's being and Self-revelation. The first two of the ten commandments say it plainly. Commandment one calls for human commitment to the one and only God. Commandment two cautions that the human comprehension of God is limited and that we dare not short-circuit our limitation by idolizing anything. Pride in premature claims to full comprehension or embodiment is idolatry.

Authentic spiritual life is found in God alone. Gathering around God alone is the essential meaning of the true church. Obedience to God alone is the only way to gain personal holiness, church unity, and effective Christian mission. To be self-centered or denominationally-centered is the way of subtle idola-

---

[34]E. Stanley Jones, in *The Word Became Flesh,* as quoted by Bob and Michael Benson, compilers, *Disciplines for the Inner Life,* rev. ed. (Nashville: Thomas Nelson, 1989), 313.

[35]Michael Kinnamon, *Truth and Community: Diversity and Its Limits in the Ecumenical Movement* (Grand Rapids: Eerdmans, 1988), 19.

try. Rather than truth as "me," or "us," Christ is the truth. Believers move closer to truth and to each other only as they move closer to Jesus Christ.

Truth is apprehended best as believers together seek it in mutual humility and in the direct light of Christ. There is a corporateness about truth's fuller apprehension, so that the whole truth requires the whole church as context for the quest. Theologian Hans Küng writes: "A Church which truly desires to find unity with other Churches must be a lover and follower of truth, completely devoted to truth. It must be a Church which knows in all humility that it is not the manifestation of the whole truth, that it has not fulfilled the whole truth, a Church which knows that it must be led anew by the spirit of truth into all truth."[36]

If truth is not the sole domain of any one church body, neither is it the lowest common denominator among them. The early "saints" associated with the Church of God movement, while sounding arrogant at times about their own grasp of the full truth, certainly were not suggesting that they had achieved control of the total truth. Nor were they prepared to reduce their proclamation of divine truth to whatever generic level would include all so-called Christians—thus offending none. That would be a tragic and very human way to seek Christian unity at the expense of Christian truth. Truth, when known to be from God, certainly is understood to be non-negotiable. Before establishing any doctrinal positions in shifting theological sands, movement leaders insisted that the very nature and role of divine truth in the church's life needed to be understood anew.

Sterile theological confessions and restrictive denominational structures for too long had been human obstacles placed in the path of God's intentions. God's agenda now was understood to be calling for Christian truth to be fully received, deeply

---

[36]Hans Küng, *The Church* (Garden City, N. Y.: Image Books, 1976), 376.

loved, and cooperatively shared. No longer was it to be manipulated, frustrated, and dominated by human agendas. Announced the editors of the *Herald of Gospel Freedom* in 1879:

> It [*Herald*] believes in raising men to the Bible standard of holy living by leading them into the Bible measure of grace. It advocates a salvation that lifts men above the regions of mere duty and places them in such sweet and perfect harmony with God that they delight to do his will; a salvation that constrains to every good work by the infinite power of perfect love, and not by the lash of the law.[37]

Getting at the "pure" truth, however, is a difficult task indeed, even when the Bible is held up as final authority. Robert Lyon speaks with concern about "evangelical" Christianity in the United States today. He notes "a failure of nerve to remove filters that both history and tradition have laid over the reading of Scripture. Evangelicals believe the Scriptures are the Word of God. . . . But they must become more aware of the obstacle tradition poses to the hearing of the Word."[38] Clark Pinnock has the same concern and illustrates it by addressing the struggle of many Bible-believing Christians to interpret the creation texts of Genesis 1-2. Conservative Christians are "understandably nervous about existential hermeneutics, but that is no reason to overreact and make the Bible a victim. . . . The lesson to be learned here is the principle of allowing the Bible to say what it wants to say and not impose our imperialistic agendas onto it, squeezing it into our molds."[39]

---

[37]Daniel S. Warner and I. W. Lowman, editorial statement, *Herald of Gospel Freedom* (forerunner of the *Gospel Trumpet*), 1879.

[38]Robert Lyon, "Evangelicals and Critical Historical Method," in W. McCown and J. Massey, eds., *Interpreting God's Word for Today* (Anderson, Ind: Warner Press, 1982), 135, 154, 156.

[39]Clark Pinnock, "Climbing Out of a Swamp," *Interpretation* (April, 1989), 154-155.

Church of God movement theological leaders since the nineteenth century have sought to affirm unadulterated biblical truth by removing the interpretive filters (a proper ideal, but always achievable only in part).[40] They have sought to dismiss all claims other than biblical authority so that the truth, whatever it wants to be and say, can be controlling and transforming truth again. Such a radical stance fueled the launching of a vibrant tradition that features opposition to the tyranny of all merely human traditions! There was an urgent call sounded by this new movement for Christians to "come out" of all that walled them away from each other and from God's truth, gifts, and will. The church is to be whole again. It takes a whole church to realize and embody credibly for the world the whole truth of God.

Rejection of the Status Quo

The Church of God movement came to share most of the pentecostal and free-church emphases, including much of their general restorationist frameworks. Exceptions were the premillennial form of the second-coming expectation and any unusual stress on public gifts of the Spirit, especially the "speaking in tongues" that emerged just after the beginning of the twentieth century. In these regards, the early movement was closer to the original teachings of John Wesley who, while certainly a theologian of the Spirit, nonetheless cautioned against irrational "enthusiasms"[41] and was optimistic about what could be accomplished in this world by the working of the Spirit of God through faithful souls (not waiting on a millennium).

In Pentecostalism the increasing focus was on the affective and miraculous presence and working of the Spirit. In Wes-

---

[40]Since removing all interpretive filters is only an ideal, at least existing filters are to be identified and compensated for to the degree possible. Caution and humility always are in order. An educated self-insight is crucial. Being open to the scrutiny and correction of the larger body of Christ is essential.

[41]See Lowell Ferrel, *op. cit.*, 180-187.

leyanism the focus was more on the regenerating and sanctifying work of the Spirit and less on the dramatic "signs and wonders" that the Pentecostals came to insist should and would follow. For the Church of God movement, influenced much by revivalistic Wesleyanism, in place of an unusual stress on *gifts* restoration was the "catholic" vision of a Spirit-enabled *unity* restoration. Such a realizing of the unity intended by Jesus for his disciples (John 17) was understood to be possible in the context of the experience of Christian holiness and by a separation from the denominational chaos that had intensified in America toward the end of the nineteenth century.[42]

A key event happened in April, 1881, as Daniel Warner was conducting a revival meeting in Hardinsburg, Indiana. As the event was characterized later, he "saw the church." Warner had been troubled for years about the inconsistency of his repudiating "sects" in principle and yet continuing to belong to organizations like the Indiana State Holiness Association that insisted on basing its membership on formal sect recognition. How, pondered Warner, could one oppose the divisive evils of the sect system within the church and remain supportive of a body requiring that its members be faithful denominational adherents?[43] For Warner the struggle inherent in this dilemma had to end.

---

[42]In its earliest decades the nature of this unity included the expectation that denominational walls would crumble, resulting in an open fellowship of all Christians in the power of the Spirit.

[43]The usual approach of the Holiness Movement did not generate this dilemma. The general intent of the many holiness associations was to be a trans-denominational renewal force. Their primary concern was not denominationalism as such, but nominal Christianity. Their expectation was that participants in the holiness associations would be loyal members in their respective denominations so that they could be renewed by the holiness emphasis and return to their denominational homes to broaden the renewal impact. As established denominations rejected the holiness-reform efforts, however, the inclination among holiness people toward separatism (come-outism) increased. Daniel Warner pioneered an actual implementing of this inclination. See Melvin Dieter, "Primitivism in the American Holiness Tradition," in *Wesleyan Theological Journal* (Spring 1995), 78-91.

Ending the dilemma produced the dynamic needed to launch the new Church of God movement (not Warner's immediate intent). To use an expression of Parker Palmer, it was the decision to be "divided no more."[44] The power comes when one steps outside the logic of the establishment, no longer tolerating the diminishment of one's self by honoring one reality inwardly and obeying another outwardly. Warner finally chose to champion an integrated life. In this integration was the only integrity he could conceive. No longer would he condone the disjunction between his holiness-generated unity vision and the standard acceptance of sect division. At stake in a failure to act would be the diminishment of the church itself and its mission in the world.

Warner tried and failed to get the Indiana Holiness Association to open its membership "to all true Christians everywhere" (whether denominational adherents or not). The time had come for him to withdraw or lose the integrity of his own vision. In his view, a free and unified fellowship of sincere Christian believers would be a natural, corporate expression of the renewing grace of God that had been experienced personally. He therefore declared freedom from the whole arena of division, intending to create no more himself.

Later that same year (October, 1881) Warner's pattern of withdrawal became complete. He confronted the Northern Indiana and then Northern Michigan Elderships of the Churches of God (offshoots of the Winebrennerian movement) with proposals whereby they might "conform more perfectly to the Bible standard with reference to government." He preferred that preachers be recognized by their fruits rather than by formal licenses, so he sought a congregational membership not restricted by denominational standards, but open to all persons experiencing and evidencing new life in Christ.[45]

---

[44]Parker Palmer, lecture at Anderson University, January 29, 1993.
[45]John Smith, 1980, 44-45.

Warner's proposals were rejected in both Beaver Dam, Indiana, and Carson City, Michigan. In both places, then, he and others with him departed "sect Babylon," adhering, as the withdrawing Michigan group said, "to no body or organization but the church of God." Here was an overt challenge to the whole denominational system, a radical declaration of oneness with all of God's true people, a oneness that hoped to be unencumbered by human standards and structures that divide.[46]

A radical reformer-restorer, Warner rejected the status quo of denominationalized American Christianity. He intended to participate only in a "movement" of God, not start another denomination.[47] He grasped or, better, he had been grasped by the vision of a "church beyond division."[48] Seen in such a grand view was a sovereign God doing a wonderfully new thing among and through sincere disciples. No longer would the obscenity of a sectarian Berlin Wall remain to divide one people. No longer would Christians set their own standards for who could be church members. The control of human hands would be released so that the church again could function visibly as the church *of God*, the church that is the gathering of God's redeemed children, *all of them,* abiding together as the church belonging only *to God.*

Warner's line of thought, he judged, was clear and compelling. Here is his logic in brief:

---

[46]See the "Carson City Resolutions" in Barry Callen, *The First Century,* vol. 1 (Anderson, Ind.: Warner Press, 1979), 295-96.

[47]Time has shown this to have been more of a theological vision of the ideal than an immediately practical theological stance. The persistent question is how one rises above being "denominated" as a group, even when a group's platform is opposition to division among Christians. Is merely being denominated the core of the real problem? See the helpful discussion by James Earl Massey in his *Concerning Christian Unity* (Anderson, Ind.: Warner Press, 1979). Also see chapter four of this book.

[48]See Charles Brown's *The Church Beyond Division* (Anderson, Ind.: Gospel Trumpet Co., 1939).

1. The division of the Church into sects is one of Satan's most effectual, if not the very greatest means of destroying human souls;

2. Its enormous sin must be answered for by individual adherents to, and supporters of sects;

3. The only remedy for this dreadful plague is thorough sanctification, and this is only wrought by a personal, individual contact with the blood of Christ through faith;

4. The union required by the Word of God is both a spiritual and visible union;

5. The divisions of the Church are caused by elements that are foreign to it, . . . by deposits of the enemy, which exist in the hearts and practices of individual members, involving their responsibility and requiring their personal purgation.[49]

According to the heritage of the Church of God movement that grew from this vision, the task of "doing theology" requires that one first get inside this lived story and come to share the pain and passion of visionary believers like Warner. One must sense his dilemma, be jolted now by the joy he found then. Consequently, theology comes to be understood as something beyond an impersonal, intellectual quest. It does not begin with some set of philosophic abstractions and then work deductively to a broad range of doctrinal conclusions. Instead, theology begins with a divine-human encounter, a life-changing experience of sheer grace, a regeneration in Christ, and a shared holiness that issues in a vision of the one church in its intended purity and true catholicity.

The theologian is more an artist and poet than a metaphysician and dogmatist. The biblical story is to be *our* story. The church is the community of the life-receivers and the vision-

_____

[49]Daniel S. Warner, *Bible Proofs of the Second Work of Grace* (Goshen, Ind.: E. U. Mennonite Publishing Society, 1880), 431-32.

sharers. Theology is "the mirror in which today's church is confronted with her potential convictions, the mirror which asks if . . . she recognizes herself not as she is but as she must be."[50] Church of God movement pioneers understood themselves to be holding up a mirror and calling the church to be what God intends.

Warner and the growing body of "saints" around him saw what to them is God's intention for the church. Seeing and claiming this intention means being set free and becoming united in the Spirit. This vision is radical, truly apostolic,[51] genuinely catholic, and thus fully orthodox in a rooted and yet freeing sense. Indeed, it is the framework in which all theological thinking is to proceed. It is the naming and then the dismantling of a destructive human monarchy that had been choking God's people. Compromise was to be exchanged for questing after the ideal. Required would be the courage to reject the stagnation of the religious status-quo.

Such intentional withdrawal from all human monarchies and false alliances lies at the heart of the Anabaptist or "radical reformation" tradition. This "Believers' Church" approach views the church as the gathering of those who belong by an act of faith. The church is not state owned, supported, and operated. Rejected is the old society-religion synthesis of the Roman emperor Constantine. Championed instead is the church as a new social reality. It is God's living body, formed by a distinctive vision and value system, normed by Jesus Christ, and existing by grace as a prophetic witness to any host society. In the case of the Church of God movement's application of this radical Christian tradition, the fractured arena of the troubled Chris-

---

[50]James McClendon, *Systematic Theology: Ethics* (Nashville: Abingdon Press, 1986), 33, 35.

[51]See chapter three for discussion of what is meant by being "apostolic" today.

tian community itself was seen as a sterile and unacceptable human establishment that had to be rejected. Human strangle-holds on church life, whether by state or church leaders and systems, have to go!

A Distinctive Theological Mix

About 1880, then, a vigorous and quite spontaneous new movement emerged among God's people in North America. The Church of God movement, as it eventually came to be known, intended to be newly faithful to the divine redemption story reported and interpreted in Scripture. By God's guiding grace it also intended to be prophetic to its troubled time and place. This movement soon came to understand itself as a fresh instrument in God's hands, one that was meant to function fruitfully through current participation in and embodiment of the ancient apostolic faith. It intended to be part of a church reformation by the power of the Spirit and in light of the church's apostolic foundation, all seemingly so distant from common belief and practice.

The theological vision that has and continues to emerge in the Church of God movement provides valuable insight for all Christians as they seek to conserve, communicate, and visibly embody the gospel of Christ in today's world. This is not to say that times are unchanged, requiring no difference in the particular outcomes of analysis, approach, or application. Rather, it affirms that a certain vision and cluster of commitments, formed over a century ago and still forming, have an inherent dynamic, an ongoing "movement" quality that keeps them distinctive and significant, while encouraging adjustments as external changes and fresh biblical understandings warrant. It is an approach to faith that, in vision at least, remains riveted to the foundation (the Bible) without needing to get rusty for lack of ongoing reflection and refinement (work of the Spirit).

Albert Outler maintained a lifelong conviction that the evangelical and ecumenical resources of John Wesley's theology, originating in the eighteenth century, had yet to be claimed fully by the heirs of the Wesleyan tradition.[52] Similarly, the theological resources resident in the tradition of the Church of God movement, originating in the ninetcenth century and indebted in large part to the Wesleyan and the Believers' Church (free-church) traditions, have yet to be realized fully by the movement itself or appreciated adequately by the larger Christian community. A current retelling of the biblical story of salvation in Christ is served well by occasional reference to the vision this movement has sought to present and embody.

John Wesley stimulated a significant reformation of the Christian faith community that he found in eighteenth-century England. He came to insist, for instance, on "heart religion" in place of nominal orthodoxies and liturgical routines that easily become separated from vital faith. In the late nineteenth century, the new Church of God movement saw the need to repeat much of the same reforming process in the denominationalized American scene, often among now nominal Wesleyans!

This movement is aspirational in nature. A biblically-rooted religion of the heart is seen as having dramatic implications for understanding the nature and achieving the intended unity and mission of the church. This particular reform movement has sought to offer a theological approach committed to Christian basics and yet open to the inspired insights of all Christians as life is lived in changing circumstances. "New light" on truth always is to be welcomed from any source as long as that light is consistent with the biblical story of God in Christ.

While open in principle to all available sources of Christian truth, particular sources have been prominent in their influence on the Church of God movement to date. The movement has

---

[52]Albert Outler, "The Wesleyan Quadrilateral in John Wesley," in T. Oden and L. Longden, eds., *The Wesleyan Theological Heritage* (Grand Rapids: Zondervan, 1991), 21.

been shaped significantly by (1) Martin Luther and other "magisterial"[53] reformation leaders and (2) the "restorationist" and "Anabaptist" free-church traditions.[54] It also has been nourished by the many theological resources found in the "holiness" heritage going back especially to the work of John Wesley in eighteenth-century England[55] and appearing prominently in the American Holiness Movement of the last decades of the nineteenth century. These several informing traditions had been joined by a "pentecostal" emphasis that features the present gifting and empowering of the Spirit of God.[56]

John Wesley's teachings seldom have been examined from the perspective of the Anabaptist or Radical Protestant tradition. Since that tradition is providing one of the "primary paradigms" for church renewal today, and since the crucial events in Wesley's life from 1738 to 1740 "pushed him in directions parallel to

---

[53]Leaders like Martin Luther, Huldrych Zwingli, and John Calvin sometimes are called "magisterial" because their reform movements were endorsed, even established by ruling civil authorities. By contrast, Menno Simons ("Mennonites"), an Anabaptist and more "radical" reformation leader, was a non-establishment reformer often at odds with civil authorities.

[54]Timothy George, *Theology of the Reformers* (Nashville: Broadman Press, 1988), serves as a good introduction to the thought of the "magisterial" reformers. See Henry Webb, *In Search of Christian Unity: A History of the Restoration Movement* (Cincinnati: Standard Publishing, 1990), and James North, *Union In Truth* (Cincinnati: Standard Publishing, 1994), for recent histories of the restorationist (Disciples) tradition. A classic work on the Anabaptist tradition is Donald Durnbaugh, *The Believers' Church*, 1985 ed. (Scottdale, Pa.: Herald Press).

[55]For substantive presentations of Wesleyan theology, see H. Ray Dunning, *Grace, Faith & Holiness* (Kansas City: Beacon Hill Press, 1988) and Randy Maddox, *Responsible Grace: The Practical Theology of John Wesley* (Nashville: Kingswood Books, Abingdon Press, 1994).

[56]The Church of God movement has not been representative of the "tongues-speaking" brand of pentecostalism that has become prominent in the twentieth century. For clarification, see Donald Dayton, *Theological Roots of Pentecostalism* (Peabody, Mass.: Hendrickson Publishers, 1987).

Radical Protestantism," such examination can yield valuable insight.[57] Being radically apostolic and sensitive to the Believers' Church tradition, especially when these are filtered through key aspects of a Wesleyan lens, is important historical perspective on theology as generally understood and taught in the Church of God movement.

The resulting mix (reformationist/restorationist/holiness/free-church) is a theological model that is biblical and dynamic, traditional and contemporary, both pointedly apostolic and potentially authentic in any present. It is "radical" and "orthodox," "protestant" and "catholic."[58] It brings its own perspective to the very motive for focusing on serious theological development. This perspective highlights the experiential and the practical. It tends to focus on genuine personal transformation, insist on Christ-like discipleship, and initiate fundamental church renewal. It calls for an abrupt departure from the status-quo of the institutional church, highlighting: (1) the root, the radical, the apostolic Christian past; (2) the mainstream, the orthodox, the classic church tradition; and (3) the incarnational present, the mission, the radical in the sense of being distinct from any civil authority or human establishment seeking to supplant the church of the Spirit.

Incarnational, in fact, is one appropriate adjective for the vision of the Church of God movement. Creation is understood

---

[57]Howard Snyder, *The Radical Wesley* (Downers Grove, Ill.: Inter-Varsity Press, 1980), 110. Snyder explains how John Wesley was himself a "restorationist radical" in the midst of his high-church Anglicanism. Also see Luke Keefer, Jr., "John Wesley: Disciple of Early Christianity," *Wesleyan Theological Journal* (Spring, 1984), 23-32.

[58]Note Frederick Norris, *The Apostolic Faith* (Collegeville, Minn.: The Liturgical Press, 1992). Norris suggests that a tradition similar to the Church of God movement is described well as "free-church catholic" (xxvii). This phrase probably was originated by Alfred DeGroot, *Disciple Thought: A History* (Fort Worth: Texas Christian University, 1965).

from the Bible to be real and good apart from sin. God has chosen graciously to enter the sordid stream of human history, even
revealing to and identifying with humans in the fleshly life of
Jesus, an actual man who also was God among us. The church,
the Kingdom community of Christ's faithful disciples, is called
to make known, visible, and concrete, to enflesh now the new
creation as a sign of God's coming future. What a privilege and
challenge!

This demanding incarnational perspective is a dynamic
mixture of Apostolic and Anabaptist, Mennonite and Methodist.
It seeks to be creatively "catholic," "evangelical,"[59] and
"reformed," much like Thomas Langford's description of the
United Methodist's understanding of its place in the wider Christian community:

> *Truly catholic* points to our heritage in the larger Christian
> tradition; we align ourselves with all those throughout the
> ages who are aligned with Jesus Christ;
>
> *Truly evangelical* points to our emphases on the gospel, on
> the centrality of grace, and on personal conversion;
>
> *Truly reformed* indicates our conviction that the Church
> must undergo continual renewal and be constantly vigilant
> about its faithfulness to God.[60]

Radicals like the Quakers usually have not been inclined
toward abstract theological speculation. Typically they have
resisted thinking about Christian faith apart from actually experiencing that faith. As Wilmer Cooper summarizes: "Beliefs tes-
tify to our inner experience of the Spirit working in our lives.
Thinking of our beliefs in this way keeps them alive and fresh

---

[59]Note the discussion in chapter five about how the Church of God
movement differs in some ways from contemporary "evangelicalism."

[60]Thomas Langford, *God Made Known* (Nashville: Abingdon Press,
1992), 48.

and helps to avoid the ossification of our faith."[61] Theology for the Christian is not to be detached, a merely intellectual exercise. Instead, it should grow out of a vital and deeply held faith, one actively in search of understanding and application, of proclamation and incarnation.

Like John Wesley, judged by some a "practical" or "folk" theologian, theology in the Church of God movement has been conceived out of the joy of Christian experience and in the service of the church's actual life and mission. Writing Christian theology never has been viewed as an isolated academic priority. The intent has been to address helpfully, from the beating heart of the biblical revelation, the immediate needs of individual believers and of the church. Wesley produced theology much like the Apostle Paul, writing instructional and troubleshooting letters, sermons, and essays in the process of active Christian mission and needed church reform. While such a process may be seen as lacking in detached sophistication, it nonetheless is concrete, timely, mission-oriented, biblically-disciplined, discipleship-focused, and probably theology at its best.

Early shapers of theological thought in the Church of God movement often were called "flying ministers," evangelists rushing about the countryside with urgent concerns and timely good news. In the history of this movement, one does not find numerous works of systematic theology, particularly ones attempting to be highly academic, philosophic, or exhaustive in nature.[62] There have been few attempts to define and then defend a set confessional stance apart from the experienced reality and cur-

---

[61]Wilmer Cooper, *A Living Faith: An Historical Study of Quaker Beliefs* (Richmond, Ind.: Friends United Press, 1990), xiii.

[62]The three that have been developed across the twentieth century have been Frederick G. Smith, *What the Bible Teaches* (1914), Russell R. Byrum, *Christian Theology* (1925), and Albert F. Gray, *Christian Theology,* vols. I & II (1944-1946).

rent embodiment of the implications of the living faith itself. The dynamic of the biblical revelation is "radical" in contrast to the many sterile forms in which it often comes to be expressed and established.

What one does find in the teaching tradition of the Church of God movement are theological "tracts for the times," all thoroughly "orthodox" and often quite prophetic in their critical view of current denominationalized church life. Here is an important kind of theology—freshly faithful to a foundational past and newly determined to translate that past into the life of the present, without fear or favor. There is a consistent interest in Christian theology, but only as it functions to direct Christian discipleship, informs the crucial role of evangelistic preaching, and sheds divine light on prominent problems in the life and mission of the church. The orientation is "radical" in that new life and costly discipleship always are primary considerations.

In spite of the "practical" orientation, it would be wrong to classify someone like John Wesley as anything other than a serious theologian. It also would be a mistake to dismiss leading thinkers of the radical reformation as persons relatively uninterested in theology just because of their emphasis on Christian experience and current discipleship obligations. "Praxis" always is a centerpiece of authentic theology. One should *be* as well as analyze and explain; one should *do* as well as preach or publish about what should be done.

Leaders in the Church of God movement typically have been theologically concerned and truth conscious. They have been guided by a vigorous and wholistic, if not a philosophic or "systematic" theological vision. Their approach has provided creativity, cohesion, and a sense of urgent cause for individual Christians and for the life of the movement itself. Often their vision has focused on practical issues that were especially evident in the American church of the late nineteenth and early twentieth centuries. Many of these issues are still crucial to the viability of the church's mission in our "postmodern" time. Idealistic-sounding pronouncements by prophetic voices should not be dismissed merely because their practical applications are not yet complete, even in the lives of the prophets.

When apostasy and disillusionment shape the church scene, when there is "the jarring clash between the unique genius of the church as the community of God's people and the tranquilized, traditionalized, institutionalized and often secularized reality that goes under the name 'Christian church,' "[63] radicalism naturally emerges. It can take various forms. The particular form that has taken shape as the Church of God movement is our interest here, especially as it offers potential for renewal of the whole church.

Beginning, then, in the final decades of the nineteenth century and moving across the entire twentieth century, there has been within the Church of God movement a special message to be shared, a perception of some obvious wrongs to be righted, new life to be found, ancient truth to be revived, divided Christians to be re-related by the Spirit. No responsible leader of this movement has dared to assume (in theory at least) that she or he had the last word biblically or theologically. Still, there has been an urgency born of belief that God's plan for redeeming and regathering a people is moving forward. Faithful disciples are being called to holiness, that is, being changed into God's likeness. They also are being called to a unity in the Spirit that will enhance God's mission in this world. The Church of God movement since the 1880s has dreamed of participating in the fulfillment of this divine call.

[63]Howard Snyder, *The Radical Wesley & Patterns for Church Renewal* (InterVarsity, 1980), 109.

CHAPTER TWO

Boundaries

Chapter one explored the historical context and original character of the theological vision of the Church of God movement. This chapter begins a closer analysis of the elements essential to this vision. The issues of immediate concern here focus on the idea of "boundaries."

Michael Kinnamon has probed helpfully the thesis that "the vision behind the modern ecumenical movement involves a necessary tension between truth and diverse community." The central question that faces the ecumenical community, then, and also the Church of God movement, is "how to determine the limits of acceptable diversity."[1] We, therefore, examine the nature of "truth" and the roles of spiritual experience and creedal formulations in defining truth and exercising control in the church's life.

An All-Truth Vision

Welcome indeed has been the arrival in recent generations of a humility long needing to be evidenced by denominations of Christian believers. With the coming of the ecumenical age,[2] the churches finally "have set aside their absolutism, the conviction that they alone possess the truth of Christ, and their triumphal-

---

[1]Michael Kinnamon, *Truth and Community: Diversity and Its Limits in the Ecumenical Movement* (Grand Rapids: Wm. Eerdmans, 1988), vii.

[2]An active search for a more adequate realization of Christian unity has been a prominent characteristic of the worldwide Christian community, beginning especially with the Edinburgh Missionary Conference in 1910. This led to the founding of the World Council of Churches in 1948. "Ecumenical," coming from the Greek meaning "the inhabited earth," is now used commonly to describe the concern among Christians for realizing more fully the unity of the church and all things in Christ.

ism, the attitude that they themselves are already 'heaven on earth.' "[3] From its earliest days the Church of God movement has longed for just such a setting aside of human arrogance, and at times has had to resist itself becoming more of this inappropriate triumphalism. Sinful tribalism is so tempting in the religious arena. This movement has sought to remove human barriers that artificially divide Christians from each other.

Daniel Warner increasingly understood himself in the 1880-1895 period to be a pioneering part of a company of faithful Christian "saints" being raised up by God. Their divinely given mission was understood to center in the courage to stand on the platform of "all truth" as it is in Christ Jesus, free of the entanglements of things of human origin.[4] Warner's understanding was based on a powerful Christian vision, key aspects of which are crucial for all Christians in all times. These aspects are responses to a particular reading of God's revelation. They form elements of any adequate construction of Christian theology in these "latter days."[5] Christian people are to be carriers of good news initiated by God's action. This news is known best in Jesus Christ, spawns a faithful church formed by the news, and nourishes a commitment to "the truth" as it is in Christ, is biblically recorded, and is discerned by the ministry of the Spirit of God. Generating this commitment is a vision that "calls for the renunciation of [human] creeds and dogmas that all Christians may be free to believe and obey all of the Bible."[6]

---

[3]Jürgen Moltmann, *Theology Today* (London: SCM Press, 1988), 44.

[4]As quoted in Barry Callen, *A Time To Remember: Teachings* (Anderson, Ind.: Warner Press, 1978), 22. Also see Callen, *It's God's Church! Life and Legacy of Daniel Warner* (Anderson, Ind.: Warner Press, 1995).

[5]Warner and others in the new Church of God movement used this phrase and, on a rare occasion, even were confused with the Latter-day Saints and the Book of Mormon. In 1898 A. T. Rowe clarified such a total misidentification (*Gospel Trumpet,* January 6, 1898).

[6]Albert Gray, "Distinctive Features of the Present Reformation," *Gospel Trumpet* (February 23, 1922).

The movement associated with Warner is a visionary people hoping to assist the wider Christian community to be at its best as God's people in today's world. The concern is for present realization of the authentic and enduring in the Christian tradition and mission. This movement of the Church of God stands committed to whatever is true, whatever possesses the stamp of God's will and way, whatever yields the life of the Spirit and propels forward the Spirit's mission. In short, here is a people seeking to be in love with God's truth, whatever it is, costs, or demands.

The early leaders of this movement judged aspects of the life of the Christian community known to them in the late nineteenth century to be riddled with abuses of divine intent and infiltrated with serious deviations from the biblical revelation of divine truth. Such abuses and deviations had brought disastrous consequences to Christians over the centuries. There had been a widespread breakdown of spiritual life and a chaotic division among Christians. The resulting loss of true holiness and visible unity, obviously being set apart by God for God's purposes, had seriously undermined the ability of Christians to be a credible witness in the world. A problem of this dimension cried out then and cries out now for correction.

Although seldom by direct design, and usually with much inconvenience to themselves, many sensitive Christians in the years around 1880-1900 began moving with courage into the vacuum of this perceived spiritual wasteland.[7] In fact, with a

---

[7]See especially: Daniel Warner, *Bible Proofs of the Second Work of Grace* (Goshen, Ind.: E. U. Mennonite Pub. Society, 1880); John Brooks, *The Divine Church: A Treatise on the Origin, Constitution, Order, and Ordinances of the Church: Being a Vindication of the New Testament Ecclesia, and an Exposure of the Anti-Scriptural Character of the Modern Church or Sect* (Columbia, Mo.: Herald Pub. House, 1891); and Seth Rees, *The Ideal Pentecostal Church* (Cincinnati: The Revivalist Office, 1897). Warner was the most prominent pioneer of the Church of God movement. Brooks, an influential pastor in the Methodist Episcopal Church, became a central figure in the more "radical" sector of the holiness movement. Rees, a Quaker pastor and evangelist, co-founded the Apostolic Holiness Union in 1897 (later became the Pilgrim Holiness Church).

sense of humble joy and sheer amazement, increasingly they came to judge that God was freshly at work in their time and that they had become privileged to be a direct part of the divine plan! They wanted to follow God's lead and "come out" into the light of God's truth. They felt favored with the sight of "early morning light"[8] beginning to shine again in this late and crucial stage in the history of God's gracious dealings with humankind.

The "saints," as Church of God movement adherents soon were known, did not move forward with a philosophically refined and intellectually driven agenda. Rather, they began to proclaim a biblically-based, experience-enriched, and church-reforming set of theological perspectives. Theirs was to be a continuing "quest for holiness and unity,"[9] a comprehensive quest that, by their intent and by the Spirit's enlightenment and power, sought to embrace all of God's truth[10] and fulfill all of God's will. This quest stood on the shoulders of many earlier reformers and soon was being referred to by some as "the last reformation."[11] It centered in re-claiming and re-living *the truth.*

[8]See Robert H. Reardon, *The Early Morning Light* (Anderson, Ind: Warner Press, 1979). This phrase refers to authentic Christianity as seen especially in the earliest church. See Charles E. Brown, *The Apostolic Church* (Anderson, Ind.: Warner Press, 1947).

[9]See the movement's most recent narrative history, John Smith, *The Quest for Holiness and Unity* (Anderson, Ind.: Warner Press, 1980).

[10]The exact content of "all of God's truth" resided in a vision that drew vigorous commitment in principle, without the assumption that at any point a believer would achieve full and final comprehension of or control over God's truth. See the section "Comprehensive and Idealistic" in chapter three.

[11]See the book *The Last Reformation* by F. G. Smith (Anderson, Ind: Gospel Trumpet Co., 1919). The meaning of "last" was based both on the assumption that the second coming of Christ was not far off (thus no time for another reformation) and that, being open to all truth, in addition to that already restored by Martin Luther, John Wesley, etc., meant that no additional reformation would be necessary, only the fuller realization of this one.

This truth typically has been perceived by leaders of the Church of God movement in the context of a series of theses about truth itself. Truth (1) has a relational dimension, (2) is not to be separated from active discipleship, (3) cannot be captured in static intellectual formulae, (4) provides boundaries without eliminating frontiers, and (5) calls for the end of all idolatries in church life. The balance of this chapter is devoted to exploring these aspects of Christian truth.

Truth in Relationship and Action

In tracing the central theological thrusts of this reformation movement of the Church of God, a good place to begin is the same place that a witness typically begins when giving testimony in the courtroom. Emphasis is to be on *the truth,* the whole truth, and nothing but the truth, so help us God! The truth, divinely revealed truth, all of it and nothing else, surely has been the goal of this movement and presumably of the whole church. The point of the reformation effort is that the present integrity of truth is to be restored and honored as the shaping, the boundary-setting force in the church's life.

Warren Roark once wrote the following in reference to the Church of God movement: "We seek to be different from others only in this: While others build a fence or creed around the present truth which they hold, we remain open for new truth. The only creed we have is that which is found in the Bible, and we are open to the leadership of the Holy Spirit. . . . That is what makes us the Church of God. We are not afraid of truth."[12]

Christians are to be more lovers of and seekers after divine truth than final definers and constant protectors of what portion of it they are blessed with to date. The church is to be a truth-seeking and truth-affirming body of pilgrims who have found the

---

[12]As in Barry Callen, ed., *The First Century,* vol. 2 (Anderson, Ind.: Warner Press, 1979), 730.

way (Christ), but who know nonetheless that they have not yet arrived. They are to reach out their hands vulnerably in love rather than build walls of creed and tradition, gender and race, walls that divide them inappropriately from their Christian brothers and sisters. A common statement of resolve within the Church of God movement is, "We reach our hands in fellowship to every blood-washed one." The challenge always is to move from this admirable slogan to its functioning reality.

Truth is to be on the church's center stage. It is to be God's truth, not ours, all of God's truth, not merely the piece we prefer or the portion we currently happen to understand. We Christians are called to love the truth if ever we are to be formed, united, and sent by it. The love of truth always will send on a journey since full comprehension is the goal, never the present achievement. Being on journey speaks against the rise and dominance of restrictive establishments among God's people.

But what is truth? "Truth" in the full biblical sense means more than a body of factual information. It is not a collection of doctrinal statements that in themselves are the last word. Biblical truth carries the connotations of trustworthiness, covenant relationship, and authentic life involvement. In the Gospel of John a close relationship is assumed between life, freedom, and truth. Jesus is the way, the truth, and the life (14:6). He is the true bread (6:32) who comes from heaven to give life to humanity (6:33). "You will know the truth, and the truth will make you free" (8:32). But, again, what is the "truth"?

To the Greek mind John 8:32 would suggest that freedom is to be found through an intellectual apprehension of reality now said to be rooted in Jesus. If, however, John's Gospel is understood best in light of its Hebrew background, then of primary significance is the Hebrew concept of truth as faithfulness and trustworthiness.[13] The truth is related to the character of God's

---

[13]George Eldon Ladd, *A Theology of the New Testament*, rev. ed. (Grand Rapids: Eerdmans, 1974, 1993), 300.

actions in relation to divinely chosen people. God can be trusted to provide consistent caring for the people of the covenant. Those who reverence God are called the people of "truth" (Ex. 18:21; Neh. 7:2) when they respond faithfully to the faithful God. Truth involves right relationship between God and people, all of which now culminates in Jesus.

The covenant love and steadfastness that God displayed to Israel became incarnate. "The Word became flesh and lived among us, and we have seen his glory" (1:14). When Jesus said, "I am the way, and the truth, and the life" (14:6), he meant the full embodiment of God in fulfilling faithfulness to those who will be faithful in return. To know the truth (8:32) means to be aware of and favorably related to God's saving purpose embodied in Christ. The "Spirit of truth" (14:17) bears faithful witness to Christ, who is the truth (15:26), guiding disciples into all truth (16:13). In the Johannine setting, this does not indicate so much "an intellectual apprehension of theological truths as a full personal apprehension of the saving presence of God that has come to humanity in Jesus."[14] Such apprehension necessarily involves intimate personal relationship and responsible action. "But those who do what is true come to the light" (3:21; cf. 1 Jn. 1:6). In summary, "truth" in the Gospel of John is a salvation concept. The Story of God's redemptive work comes to full focus in Jesus. To "know" God is to be related rightly to God through Jesus Christ and to be engaged rightly in God's present purposes.

Knowing is not complete if it is only an intellectual exercise. Truth, to be fully itself and really apprehended and genuinely transforming, must be found in covenant communion and lived out in faith's worldly risking. In fact, God's truth is never really "known" until the aspiring knower is committed personally to the God of truth and to a course of action that applies the implications of the truth. Being *doers* rather than mere *hearers* is

---

[14]Ibid., 304.

required for the gaining of intimate understanding (James 1:22-25). Beyond merely engaging the truth with the mind, believers are to relate to it with the whole person. Life involvement precedes abstract speculation and doctrinal description. The early Christians "began not with creedal speculation about the metaphysics of the Incarnation. . . . They began with stories about Jesus, about those whose lives got caught up in his life."[15] The truth dawns upon us as we both hear and do the dramatic biblical story of God with us in Christ.

The Apostle Paul prayed for the Colossian Christians to be "filled with the knowledge of God's will in all spiritual wisdom and understanding." Why? It was "so that you may lead lives worthy of the Lord, fully pleasing to him, as you bear fruit in every good work and as you grow in the knowledge of God" (Col. 1:9-10). Knowledge of God involves the gift of spiritual wisdom and inevitably is linked to fruit-bearing lives. Knowing is a dynamic complex of revelation, relationship, and incarnation (Christ's and ours). Christian faith is not reducible to a cold set of theological propositions to be embraced only intellectually.

Christian faith assumes that certain perceptions of reality are true in actual fact. But what is truth? Thomas Langford says:

> Our language about God is a reach for truth, an effort to express truth. But our language never fully grasps truth; our language can never claim to capture all of the truth about God, for God is mystery. God is true and only God can speak the truth. And God has spoken in a person, in Jesus Christ. So, for Christian faith, truth is a person. Truth is Jesus Christ.[16]

Truth is received by faith through the biblical witness and the Spirit's work. There is a Word of God that is "objective" and

---

[15]Stanley Hauerwas and William Willimon, *Resident Aliens* (Nashville: Abingdon Press, 1989), 55.

[16]Thomas Langford, *God Made Known* (Nashville: Abingdon Press, 1992), 30.

exists prior to human experience of it. This Word is never encompassed by human experience, but breaks into our experience, informing and reshaping it. It always remains something divine, apart from and beyond human subjectivity. Rather, a divinely initiated (inspired) revelation comes from outside human experience. We humans can look more than inward where there is despair, but outward where there is hope. We look to the God whom we are told by the biblical narrative has acted in past history for our redemption. Faith comes by hearing the story of redemption (Rom. 10:8-9; 1 Cor. 1:21). Salvation comes "not from a teacher who draws truth out of us (as in Plato and Socrates), but from the Jews (Jn. 4:22), from God's decisive intervention in a particular history and a particular people."[17]

According to the Bible's consistent witness, human knowledge of God begins with God's self-disclosure. God comes, speaks, promises, judges, reveals. Therefore, the subject matter and criteria for Christian theology rest primarily in the being and initiatives of God, the One biblically presented. Ever since Friedrich Schleiermacher (1768-1834), the experience of receptive believers has been exalted widely as the essential content and criterion of theology.[18] Such exaltation is of value, but only

---

[17]Donald Bloesch, *A Theology of Word & Spirit* (InterVarsity Press, 1992), 206-07.

[18]Schleiermacher went too far in seeing truth essentially as an intuitive depth awareness of human dependence on the supporting divine. His influence is still significant. Reared a Pietist, he connected revelation to the experiences of the heart. Revelation is seen as a transformation of human consciousness, not a breaking in upon us from without that involves the conveyance of some "content" given by God, some dependable substance of truth. The neo-orthodox reaction to this subjectivistic "liberalism" was a neo-liberal approach. In this case revelation is said to exceed the universal human capacity for mystical experience. There is revelation, God's Word to be encountered; but such revelation cannot be captured in doctrinal propositions or human experience. Truth lies in the

if kept in the context of the historically based biblical story of God in Christ. The story is not to be lost in a subjectivism that shuns reason, culture, and church tradition, and even avoids responsible discipleship in the world.

Human awareness of the divine does originate in the *experience* of divine revelation, whether it be direct encounter or through the witness of others (cf. Ex. 10:1-2; 18:8-11). The knowledge gained thereby is not as much theoretical as it is transformingly personal. God seeks through revelation to make possible a renewed covenant relationship, a divine-human encounter in which "knowledge" is intimate and compelling. The result is knowledge by acquaintance rather than by rational argument or scientific equation. It is knowing God, not merely knowing about God. It is person-to-person more than proposition-to-intellect. The power is less in particular biblical words and more in the biblical narrative and salvation message.

The ancient Hebrews "knew" God because they had encountered God in the historical activity of the divine. God was recognized as having acted to free them from Egypt, led them in the wilderness, and given them a vision of life and a promised land. By divine choice Israel had come to know God as the freeing, guiding, giving One who called them to obedient response. God had chosen to "know" them and had offered the opportunity for them to "know" God in return. To accept this knowing relationship constituted their "salvation." It did not imply the gaining of intellectual mastery over the mysteries of God or open the door for any manipulation of the divine (a constant human desire and temptation). It did include a mode of knowing from the heart

---

divine-human encounter, necessarily expressed in existential and paradoxical ways. Conservative theologians have both appreciated the Neo-Orthodox reaction to classic liberalism and insisted that the reaction resembles too much the problem it seeks to correct.

that makes the believer "wise unto salvation" (2 Tim. 3:15, KJV).[19]

The essence of biblical faith is *right relationship*. The ethical command to love God and neighbor is more important than burnt offerings and sacrifices (Mic. 6:1-8; Mk. 12:28-34). Theological truths are important in biblical teaching, but they are not central, not first-order considerations. The Hebrews "did not view a life of true piety and godliness as an impersonal relationship to a structure of thought, but as a personal relationship renewed each day with the living God." The center of this relationship "was not found in an array of dogmas or cultic regulations, but in the response of one's whole person in love and total obedience to the Creator."[20] In the wholeness of the biblical witness, Judaism bequeathed this relational and practical vision to the followers of Jesus.

Karl Rahner summarizes: "Revelation is not the bringing of what was once unknown into the region of what is known, perspicuous and manageable; it is the dawn and the approach of mystery as such."[21] In humility, the task of Christian theology is to receive the gracious approach of God, be changed by it, then

[19]One of the more dramatic recent witnesses to a "knowing from the heart" conversion to Christ is that of Brennan Manning. Speaking of the personal relevance of the cross of Jesus, he says: "I had known that before, but in the way that John Henry Newman describes as 'notional knowledge'—abstract, faraway, largely irrelevant to the gut issues of life, just another trinket in the dusty pawnshop of doctrinal beliefs. But in one blinding moment of salvific truth it was real knowledge calling for personal engagement of my mind and heart. Christianity was being loved and falling in love with Jesus. . . . This is the movement from belief to experience via the bridge of faith" (*The Signature of Jesus,* Portland: Multnomah Press, 1992, 27-28).

[20]Marvin Wilson, *Our Father Abraham* (Grand Rapids: Eerdmans and Center for Judaic-Christian Studies [Dayton, O.], 1989), 320.

[21]Karl Rahner, *Theological Investigations* (Baltimore: Helicon Press, 1966), 4:330.

translate this encountered reality into concepts and language that are both fair to the unmanageable reality of God and yet meaningful to those who hear, read, and need to be changed by the potential of such a relationship.

Because it refers to the sovereign God, theological language tends to be paradoxical. Concepts of God that are adequate to the fullness of divine reality often have to yield to the limits of rational formulations. God has come to us; and yet God still eludes being captured by our categories and descriptive words. While in human history and genuinely available to be "known" by us in a transforming way, God nonetheless remains God. There is more than has been revealed, or that we humans could understand if it were revealed. Biblical and current language about God necessarily leans toward the analogical, poetic, paradoxical, and parabolic. It is a reporting of unimagined and finally inexpressible good news, not a catalog of religious equations, creeds, and divine dictates.

This, however, does not mean that theological language lacks objective reference or is not really true.[22] It only means

---

[22]Clark Pinnock warns that "the Word of God is not a bare existential address but includes objective truths about the gospel and ourselves. Paul made it clear that the gospel he preached was a communication full of content, centering upon the vicarious death of Christ for sinners and on his bodily resurrection from the dead (1 Cor. 15:1-19). This goes directly against a strong tendency in modern theology to affirm revelation as a transforming experience but not to affirm a message full of content and truth given in intelligible speech and language. . . . The loss of confidence in revelation as cognitive led to a great crisis in theology, and it is important to recover this confidence if we hope to make an effective proclamation of the gospel in our generation" (*The Scripture Principle*, S.F.: Harper & Row, 1984, 14). Even if overstated, Carl Henry and Ronald Nash repeatedly have sought to make this very point. We are proposing here that the cognitive content lies more in the biblical salvation story than in a wooden approach to the words of the text or in the fragile nature of rational formulations about the text's teaching.

that human language about God is necessarily metaphorical. Such language finds historical rootage and substantive meaning as it emerges from within and is interpreted by reference to the biblical narration of God's acting among us for our salvation.

In recent years the American holiness movement, one key setting from which the Church of God movement emerged, has engaged in something of a paradigm shift in its use of religious language. Earlier it was common for it to employ "objective" language that, for instance, spoke of *what* God would give to us in an experience of "holiness" and *what* ("inbred sin") would be removed from us by that experience. More recently there has been a search for fresh metaphors and more "relational" language. The shift, not agreed to by all, has been from the older categories of static substance to the newer ones of positive process.

Since believers are to be "holy as God is holy" (Lev. 11), holiness should be seen as participation in the life of God, a genuine change in human life made possible by acceptance of the offer of a restored divine-human relationship. Holiness, not as a *thing* to be had or a doctrine to be formulated abstractly, is the reality of God's character with which we are privileged by grace to relate transformingly. Believers become *like* God only as they *relate* to God in responding obedience—even though they never fully understand and certainly never control the divine.[23]

Experience the Power

Early leaders of the Church of God movement believed that the integrity of Christian identity calls for Christian faith to be understood as more than a prescribed set of sacred ideas. The

---

[23]See Stephen Seamands, *Holiness of Heart and Life* (Nashville: Abingdon Press, 1990), who develops the dimensions of true holiness by reviewing the perceptual and relational changes emerging from Isaiah's dramatic encounter with God (Isaiah 6:1-8).

essence of Christianity lies in *experiencing* and then *living* the truth revealed by God. This is orthodoxy in radical perspective, standard thought become new life and immediate mission. Testifies Charles Naylor (1874-1950) in one of his best-known choruses:

> I have read within the Bible,
> What His favor will impart:
> And, o glory! I have proved it,
> Now 'tis true within my heart.[24]

The reality that is prior to a theological system, creed, or doctrine is said by movement leader Earl Martin to be "religious." "For religion has to do with experience, and when one begins to explain that experience he has a theology, or doctrine. . . . Religion is spiritual experience, and theology is the rationale or explanation of that experience." Moving to the stage of formal theology is a tentative and humbling process, a very human enterprise. The situation, says Martin, is said to be as follows:

1. God is the ultimate Reality;
2. Religion is humankind's experience of God;
3. In experience, one never gets the total of that which is to be experienced;
4. In thought, one never gets the total of what one has experienced;
5. One never gets in words the total of what one has thought;
6. Yet men and women do rationalize their experiences, and this gives rise to theology or doctrine.[25]

For the Christian, faith is significantly experiential. As the Protestant Reformation of the sixteenth century reaffirmed, justi-

---

[24]Found in *Select Hymns* (Anderson, Ind.: Gospel Trumpet Company, 1911).

[25]Earl Martin, *Toward Understanding God* (Anderson, Ind.: Gospel Trumpet Co., 1942), 16-17.

fication of the sinner before God is by the personal experience of grace through faith. As was typical of revivalism in nineteenth-century America, confessional and liturgical approaches to gaining Christian identity are to be preceded (not wholly replaced by) the necessity of a life-changing conversion experience. There should and can be the personal assurance of sins forgiven and a wonderful new relationship with God.

A gospel song soon was written within Church of God movement circles to witness to such conversion:

> I'm redeemed, praise the Lord!
> I'm redeemed by the blood of the Lamb;
> I am saved from all sin, and I'm walking in the light,
> I'm redeemed by the blood of the Lamb.[26]

"Experience the Power!" was the theme for the 107th International Convention of the Church of God ("Campmeeting"), convened in Anderson, Indiana, in June, 1993. The program book interpreted this theme by focusing on the divine "dunamis" as was promised in Acts 1:8: "You will receive power when the Holy Spirit has come upon you." The Convention was opened with the national premiere of the praise concert "Alleluia!"[27] This theme and concert highlighted the way Church of God people tend to approach the Christian life.

The program folder prepared for the 10,000 people attending "Alleluia!" that evening said that the hope of creators Bill

---

[26]Joseph Fisher, "I'm Redeemed" in *Worship the Lord* (Anderson, Ind.: Warner Press, 1989), 569.

[27]The original version had been written twenty years earlier and also was premiered at an Anderson Convention. Said the Gaithers of the twenty years of use of the original version: "Not only has this work been performed in churches of nearly every denomination and size, but it has been translated into many languages, toured by traveling choirs, and used to bring communities together who had never worshiped as one body before" (as in the program folder, June 13, 1993). This illustrates one way of implementing the Christian-unity vision of the Church of God movement.

and Gloria Gaither was "to create a corporate worship experience . . . that would show through real life witness what God has been 'up to,' not only historically, but in the lives of women and men today. . . . It was our [Gaithers'] hope that no one could leave the place without being confronted with the amazing fact that the Jesus of the Scriptures is alive and at work in our lives today." Aliveness, real life, God experienced as active historically and presently, these are crucial relational themes guiding worship and theology in the tradition of the Church of God movement. They have solid biblical rootage and immediate experiential and theological importance.

Eugene Sterner and Samuel Hines, beloved movement leaders, were invited to preach at the International Convention in Anderson one summer. Each received in advance from the chair of the program committee a cordial letter that contained this caution for their sermon planning: "Please don't be too theological." Later, Rev. Hines authored the book elaborating the theme of the 1993 Convention. He recalled the earlier caution and said that his book was "primarily aimed at capturing the minds of serious Christian readers and escorting them into real encounters with the dynamic power of God, with the emphasis being more upon *practicing* the faith than upon *pronouncing* it. I am attempting to speak about our personal relationship with God without getting 'too theological.' "[28]

For this movement, emphasis typically falls on the experiential, relational, and implementational. "The importance of this experiential understanding of salvation in the minds of the pioneer leaders of the Church of God," concludes historian John Smith, "can hardly be overemphasized. It was related to all other

---

[28]Samuel Hines, *Experience the Power* (Anderson, Ind.: Warner Press, 1993), 1-2. Heard here is the traditional stress of the Believers' Church and Pietist traditions on the centrality of changed lives that participate in Christian discipleship, a *practicing* in life of what is *pronounced* in theology. Emphasis added.

aspects of their faith and practice, and especially to their view of relationships to each other, to the world, and to other Christians."[29] Often such witness soon was accompanied by the affirmation of the experience of "full" salvation, the claim to being "sanctified."

A prominent testimony has been preserved in the private journal of Daniel Warner, prominent pioneer of the Church of God movement. Recorded there is one of those rare moments of Christian insight and inspiration. In its own quiet way this testimony brought a turning point in the church's contemporary history. The day was December 13, 1877. A spiritually hungry and seeking Christian man took a walk in the woods to commune with God. His name was Warner.[30] Who he was, however, is less important than what happened next.

Warner thought much on that mild and fair day about the meaning of a person making a covenant with God. God already had acted, provided, invited. Now it was the turn of repentant women and men like himself to enter into a wonderfully available, divine-human agreement that would change and direct all of life. As he lingered reflectively in an isolated place, Warner recalled those words of divine promise found in Jeremiah 31:33, "They shall be my people." His response? Somehow it just burst with joy and new resolve out of the depths of his tender soul. "Amen, Lord, I am forever thine!"[31]

That indeed was a sacred moment. Soon it led to a fresh wave of evangelistic sharing and the sacrificial founding of the

[29]John Smith, *The Quest for Holiness and Unity* (Anderson, Ind.: Warner Press, 1980), 88.

[30]For a current biography of Daniel Warner, including numerous references to his private journal, see Barry Callen, *It's God's Church!: Life and Legacy of Daniel Warner* (Anderson, Ind.: Warner Press, 1995).

[31]As found in Andrew Byers, *Birth of a Reformation* (Anderson, Ind.: Gospel Trumpet Co., 1921, reprint 1966 by Faith Publishing House, Guthrie, Ok.), 159.

Gospel Trumpet, a little paper edited by Warner. Beginning with its first issues in the 1880s, this Christian publication carried a note of urgency and the weight of a major mission. That mission grew directly out of the editor's radical covenant with a holy God who had called and changed him and now was enabling this servant to live a humble, yet bold life of holiness. Warner knew himself privileged to participate in the life and thus the mission of God.

The "religious" beginning, then, of Christian theology is affirmed as personal encounter with the coming, self-revealing, and graciously covenant-making God. "Since," as Martin observes, "God is the supreme fact of existence, there can be nothing more important than to know him and, knowing him, to love him and better understand him. For if we understand him better we will love him more and serve him more zealously."[32]

Henri Nouwen laments that Christian theology has elevated its rational side to become one academic discipline alongside others. True theology, he counters, surely centers in spiritual union with God. He calls for a reclamation of "the mystical aspect of theology so that every word spoken, every advice given, and every strategy developed can come from a heart that knows God intimately." Being securely rooted in such Divine-human intimacy makes it possible for Christians "to remain flexible without being relativistic, convinced without being rigid, willing to confront without being offensive, gentle and forgiving without being soft, and true witnesses without being manipulative."[33]

Revelation does involve knowledge of "the heart." There is a complex mixture of the objective and subjective. Christian revelation has a "bipolar structure," with neither pole to be dis-

---

[32]Martin, *op. cit.,* 24.
[33]Henri Nouwen, *In the Name of Jesus* (N. Y.: Crossroad, 1989), 30-32.

missed in favor of the other. Established religious traditions often tend to highlight "the propositional nature of revelation at the expense of the existential, whereas contemporary liberal thought certainly stresses the inner, subjective dimension. One jeopardizes the vitality, the other, the noetic content of revelation."[34] A classic statement of proper balance is by P. T. Forsyth:

> The experimental religion of true faith is not based on experience, but on revelation and faith. It is *realized* by experience, it proceeds in experience; but it does not proceed *from* experience. Experience is its organ, but not its measure, not its principle. What we experience we possess, but faith is our relation not to what we possess, but to what possesses us. Our faith is not in our experience, but in our Saviour.[35]

Convictional, Not Creedal

If the heart of Christian identity and discipleship necessarily involves *experiencing* and then *living* the truth revealed by God in Israel and especially in Jesus Christ, then there will be strong conviction without oppressive creeds that are humanly developed and thus limited.

There was a public announcement for the Church of God camp meeting in Moundsville, West Virginia, scheduled for June, 1902. It began by saying: "A cordial invitation is given to all lovers of the truth to this general convocation of the children of God, on the campground at the Trumpet Home in the northeast part of the city." "Truth" was a central preoccupation of this community of believers. Many of this movement's adherents read closely what was being published by the Gospel Trumpet

---

[34]Clark Pinnock, *The Scripture Principle* (S.F.: Harper & Row, 1984), 5. See Donald Bloesch, *The Crisis of Piety* (Colorado Springs: Helmers & Howard, 1988), 122-123.

[35]P. T. Forsyth, "Christian Perfection," in his *God the Holy Father* (London: Independent Press, 1957), 108.

Company that was located in Moundsville at the turn of the century.[36] Surely, they believed, God has spoken and divine speech always is to be taken as prior to all other claims to wisdom. In Jesus Christ we humans have been encountered by God, and by God's fullest truth.

Often quoted among these "saints" was the New Testament verse, "Sanctify them in the truth; your word is truth" (John 17:17). This verse was not seen as a pretext for casting God's truth in another set of propositional theological statements that then could be claimed to have captured in so many words a full understanding of divine truth. Truth certainly was understood to point to objective reality; it also was judged to be personal, relational, dynamic, and contextual. Christian truth is restricted by the limits of human understanding and too often is distorted by the distracting weight of intellectualized and mandated human traditions.

Responding to "the truth" was believed by these sincere Christians to represent the potential of a new day for the whole church. God's light was beginning to shine again and lovers of truth were being called and privileged to "walk in the light" as God enables believers to see it. Soon these "saints" would come to sing vigorously and with joy and deep commitment:

> When the voice from heaven sounded, warning all to flee
> From the darksome courts of Babel back to Zion free;
> Glad my heart to hear the message, and I hastened to obey,
> And I'm standing *in the truth* today.[37]

One published summary of the history of the Church of God movement is titled *Truth Marches On,*[38] an appropriate way

---

[36]This company is now Warner Press. It moved to its present location in Anderson, Indiana, in 1906.

[37]"The Reformation Glory," verse 2 (emphasis added), by Charles Naylor and Andrew Byers, in *Worship the Lord* (Anderson, Ind.: Warner Press, 1989), 311.

[38]John Smith (Anderson, Ind.: Gospel Trumpet Co., 1956).

of characterizing a central burden of this movement. There has been a questing for the full truth as it is in Christ, not a crusading for any theological finality. Historian Merle Strege identifies helpfully key theological assumptions of the Church of God movement. They tend to be imbedded in the simple, yet profound phrase "lovers of truth."[39] These assumptions have much wisdom to share as followers of Christ from all traditions move into the twenty-first century. Two of these assumptions are that Christian truth is to be *experienced* and is *progressive*.

Leaders of the movement did not reduce Christianity "to a series of belief statements. . . . The real essence of Christianity was *experiencing* the truth, and that lay beyond belief." Much later than that 1902 meeting in West Virginia, the following slogan would come to be accepted widely as a brief way of identifying many congregations of this movement: "Where Christian Experience Makes You a Member."[40] Such a phrase does not intend to de-emphasize the theological content of faith. The purpose is to highlight the necessity of being involved personally in radical, life-changing obedience to the call of God, the source, focus, substance, and end of all true doctrine.

When the Christian faith is reduced to a matter of intellectual awareness and mechanical assent at the rational level, real understanding is compromised. To apprehend Christian faith adequately, one first must approach and embrace it with all of oneself. Then, by an enabling divine grace, one continues in the understanding process through embodying the faith in the realities of this present world. The knowing process is far more than

---

[39]See the article "Lovers of Truth" by Merle Strege in *Vital Christianity* (August 24, 1986), 22-23.

[40]"A united church for a divided world" is another common self-designation of this movement, used for years on the movement's national radio broadcast in the United States and Canada, the Christian Brotherhood Hour.

memorized creeds. It is life and mission, believing and questing, all in constant interaction.

So the theological focus of this movement has tended to be on direct change in one's life rather than on any isolated, routinely repeated, and often arid confessional formulation of Christian faith. In fact, the usual process by which Christian communities have written and confessed formal creeds has been criticized and avoided by the movement. In part this is because the severely divided Christian community has tended to use such theological formulations in institutionally protective ways that shields many believers from real life change and significant social impact.[41] It also is because such formulations often become tools to justify and maintain the dividedness of some Christians from others whose creeds or practices differ even slightly.

Church of God people seek to be clearly convictional without being narrowly and prematurely creedal. They are conservative, to be sure, but they seek to avoid being "denominationalists" in their view of the church or "fundamentalists" in their theological method. There is an appreciation for process and a disposition to be committed to the whole of truth that lies beyond the apprehension of any one tradition within the Chris-

---

[41]"Fundamentalism" is the common term for a rigid and protective theological stance. Martin Marty says that the base theological feature of modern fundamentalisms is "oppositionalism." Their agenda is "set by what they feel or calculate demands their resistance, by what they most contend against" (in Hans Küng, Jürgen Moltmann, eds., *Fundamentalism As An Ecumenical Challenge,* London: SCM Press, 1992, 3). Today that target is "modernism" in its many forms. An irony is that the rationalism of modernism (the Enlightenment influence) is used extensively by Christian fundamentalists in their vigorous defense of the truth as they see it. The current fundamentalistic phenomenon is not limited to Christianity, but also is seen in Judaism and Islam, e.g. Note the multi-volume study underway by Martin Marty and R. Scott Appleby (vol. 1 is *Fundamentalists Observed,* Chicago, 1991).

tian community. Thus, "catholic" is an important addition to any "free church" designation of this movement.[42]

Pioneer leaders of the Church of God movement recognized that truth, beyond needing to be *experienced,* tends to be *progressive.* New light had begun to shine on the gathered darkness of church life and surely there yet would be "more light." All such light had been and always would be thoroughly biblical in its substance, but human understanding of it inevitably is partial and always should be growing. While there is only one biblical revelation on which the faith is founded, that revelation grows on us and we in it. In this sense, it is progressive (not that it evolves, changes, and is added to over time).

The essential relationship of Christian experience, the process of knowing truth, and the related stance of openness to "new light" should not be misunderstood. These commitments are not intended to encourage movement leaders to be rash and individualistic, stepping outside the mainstream of Christian faith by exhibiting theological novelty in their thinking, believing, or acting. No one has sought or claimed any new divine revelation that surpasses what is available to all Christians or is not wholly consistent with traditional, "orthodox" thought. No "prophet" has received revelation from God that in any way has added to the substance of the salvation story found in biblical revelation. The task is to reform in light of the enduring biblical truth, not to extend and change that truth. This movement "is not committed to ecclesiastical standards or doctrines repugnant to

---

[42]These descriptive phrases, while fairly descriptive of the movement's aspirations, were rarely used by the movement of itself. At first there was little focus on church history other than as the arena of apostasy. Thus the "free-church" tradition as such was little known prior to the work of Charles Brown in the 1940s and 1950s. Since Roman Catholicism was viewed as a prime example of falsely institutionalizing the church by human hands, the word "catholic" understandably has been avoided as a primary movement self-description.

human reason. We do not believe in extremism or fanaticism of any kind. We have no sympathy for strange or freak doctrines that are maintained only with subtle arguments or with forced and unnatural interpretations of Scripture."[43] There is no rash novelty, only commitment to taking seriously what is authentic, enduring, and essential to Christian life and mission.

How does the authentic, enduring, and essential become known? Jesus is reported to have called God's Spirit "the Spirit of truth" (Jn. 14:17; 15:26; 16:13). The Spirit of God is linked closely by the New Testament record with the truth of what was being accomplished in the life of Jesus. Jesus is inseparable from the Spirit who communicates truth, especially the truth that is in Jesus himself. Those who worship the Father are instructed to do so "in spirit and truth" (4:23-24)—and Jesus is "the truth" (14:6), the truth conveyed to us by the Spirit.

The real challenge, movement leaders have insisted for generations, is to walk constantly in the light as God gives light, not ever canonizing the spot on which one stands or institutionalizing the perception one may hold at any given time. Faith always is a pilgrimage, a journey guided by the Spirit toward more and more light. These hymn lyrics express it well:

We limit not the truth of God, to our poor reach of mind,
By notions of our day and sect, crude, partial, and confined.
No, let a new and better hope, within our hearts be stirred:
The Lord hath yet more light and truth,
To break forth from the Word.[44]

Faith's focus should be on a Person more than on any proposition, even one respectfully drafted about that Person. Jesus Christ is himself the truth (John 14:6). Advice was given

---

[43]F. G. Smith, *Brief Sketch of the Origin, Growth, and Distinctive Doctrines of the Church of God Reformation Movement* (Anderson, Ind.: Gospel Trumpet Co., 1927).

[44]Verse one and refrain of "We Limit Not the Truth of God," words by George Rawson (1807-1889), based on parting words of Pastor John Robinson to the Pilgrim Fathers, 1620.

to Timothy so that he might be able to "fight the good fight, having faith and a good conscience (1 Tim. 1:18-19). It was made clear that God's intent is that everyone "come to the knowledge of the truth" (2:4). How is that truth identified? It centers in the belief that "there is one God; there is also one mediator between God and humankind, Christ Jesus" (2:5).

With Christ as central and the biblical revelation as the normative source for understanding Christ, the Christian life is a humble walking together as a maturing community of faith, always being shaped by the Christ Story, in the midst of searching, sharing, and living the Story. Believers are to be open to each other, resources to each other, continuing to think and experience, always inspired by the Spirit who is the conveyor of the divine light of Christ. Never without guiding, truth-full convictions, Christ's disciples also should never be without a large sail unfurled to capture any new breeze of God's ever unfolding truth.

Theological conviction always should be accompanied by an appropriate humility. The direction is clear. The foundation is firm. The biblically narrated revelation is set. The Person is known. The future is open, full of challenge, both on a sure path and in process toward our fuller understanding and increasing participation in the unfolding will of God. One day, it is promised, we will see the fullness of truth itself (1 Cor. 13:12).

The early Church of God "saints" were a theologically paradoxical people, at once clearly committed, yet deliberately dynamic about any final formulations of the faith. Balance, clarity, and doctrinal fullness are not necessarily to be seen in any one of the movement's respected teachers and writers in a given generation.[45] The instinct for integrity and wholeness and the

---

[45]This is not to say that at times there have not been attempts within the movement to codify and control "accepted" Christian doctrine. Once there even was a failed attempt to have judged as "standard literature" of the movement certain materials published prior to a given year in the 1920s, thus avoiding widespread acceptance of certain new ideas not acceptable to some leaders.

persistent "movement" openness are group aspirations believed essential to the increasing understanding of the fullness of truth over time. Here is a whole-church vision, not a closed-group operation. It is the championing of a process of joyful discovery rather than an establishment approach to theological questions.

Early movement theologian Russell Byrum (1889-1980) writes about the qualities of mind needed for a competent Christian theologian. One quality identified is a love for truth. Explains Byrum:

> Love for truth will keep one from opposite extremes of conservatism and progress. Extreme conservatism makes much of the "old paths" whether they are right or not, and persistently holds to the way which it happens to be even though the Spirit of God is endeavoring to lead into a rich and deeper spiritual life than that yet attained. . . . But proper love for truth will lead one to seek for greater light and at the same time cause him to hold fast all he has received that is really truth.[46]

The prevailing judgment of leaders of the Church of God movement is that attempts to standardize Christian truth in formal and final definitions binds to some degree the work of the Holy Spirit, retards in important ways the emerging of the fuller truth, and thus artificially stagnates the life of God's people. It is believed that God has and will continue to take the initiative in making truth known. No organizational pattern or restrictive creedal statement, no human desire or activity should be accepted if its impact is to impede the free flow of God's creating, organizing, informing, and commissioning of the church, the body of all God's redeemed. In short, Daniel Warner maintained that he had simply discovered a central spiritual principle, "the identification of the visible and invisible church in a spiritual congregation of

---

[46]Russell Byrum, *Christian Theology,* rev. ed. (Anderson, Ind.: Warner Press, 1925, 1982), 13-14.

Christians from which no Christian was excluded by any man-made rules or corporate forms of organization."[47]

Here are believers with a conviction that they (and all Christians) are to represent on a worldwide scale the modern restoration of apostolic faith, fellowship, and mission. Their longing is to return to the essence, purity, and power of New Testament Christianity. They declare themselves prepared to cast aside completely the web of theological compromise and the tangle of churchly debris that has accumulated over the centuries. Apostasy brought to the body of Christ quite the opposite of holiness and unity. The time of apostasy now should end for the sake of the church's mission.

For too long and for far too many people there has been a usurping of the roles belonging only to God. Beginning in the 1880s, movement pioneers rejoiced that a "new day was sweetly dawning." To what Christ had defined and commanded these saints would be true. To the biblical foundation they would add nothing; from it they would drop nothing. This movement wishes to be identified with no special doctrine. Instead, as Albert Gray says, "it seeks to unite all truth held by Christians and to ascribe to each the degree of prominence given it in the Bible." The Church of God movement "does not claim to be the originator nor sole custodian of the truths that it holds, but accepts light as it is revealed and stands committed to the full truth."[48]

Even so, alongside this universal attitude and resistance to human innovation is a certain distinctiveness in theological per-

---

[47]Wrote Warner in his personal Journal (March 7, 1878): "On the 31st of last January the Lord showed me that holiness could never prosper upon sectarian soil encumbered by human creeds and party names, and he gave me a new commission to join holiness and all truth together and build up the apostolic church of the living God. Praise his name! I will obey him."

[48]Albert Gray, "Distinctive Features of the Present Movement," *Gospel Trumpet* (February 23, 1922), 5.

spective. Historian John Smith prefers "distinguishing" to "distinctive" as the better adjective to describe the movement's doctrinal emphases since such emphases are not unique to the movement. "All of them," he says, "are thoroughly Christian and all are based on Scripture."[49]

In principle the movement has been open and anxious to draw from all segments of the Christian tradition that evidence God's revelation and the Spirit's presence rather than human apostasy and restrictive standards. Two streams from Christian history, however, have fed prominently into the movement's theological life since its beginning in the late nineteenth century. The movement's distinctiveness may be seen in part in the resulting and rich confluence of the *Wesleyan* and *Believers' Church* ("radical reformation") theological heritages.[50] Each, in differing settings and ways, seeks apostolic authenticity and contemporary relevance.

Featured in this resulting distinctiveness is the central concern for Christian *holiness* and *unity*. In fact, John Smith has presented the whole history of the movement as "a quest for holiness and unity."[51] The aliveness and ongoingness of the word "quest" is a deliberate designation. Focus on the doctrines of holiness and unity is judged experientially, theologically, and

---

[49]John W. V. Smith, *I Will Build My Church: Biblical Insights on Distinguishing Doctrines of the Church of God* (Anderson, Ind.: Warner Press, 1985), 4.

[50]Related traditions also have been influential in varying degrees. They include the Pietist, especially through the Churches of God: General Conference (Winebrennarian), and the Restorationist (Disciples) tradition, especially through the "Open Forum" dialogue that in recent years has been conducted between the Church of God movement and the Independent Christian Churches/Churches of Christ.

[51]John W. V. Smith, *The Quest for Holiness and Unity* (Anderson, Ind.: Warner Press, 1980).

missionally crucial. Both holiness and unity have been understood to be divine gifts and human achievements, wonderful things both possible and necessary for Christian mission. Each is understood to be definite *and* dynamic. They are real and distinctly Christian in nature. Holiness surpasses mere human effort at goodness. Unity reaches beyond the compromises characteristic of nominal Christians and denominational "unions." Both call for and alone enable *Christian integrity* for individual Christians and for the whole church.

Holiness and unity, the distinguishing emphases of this movement, are in-process realities about which believers can rejoice and for which believers yet must seek. The resulting theological vision is much too "orthodox" to get lost in the quicksands of an undefined and uncontrolled spirituality, and much too "radical" to get trapped in the premature prisons of inflexible church structures or rigid and regulating theological propositions. This vision is rooted biblically and is radical experientially. It is at the very heart of the movement's approach to knowing, living, and loving "the truth."

Boundaries and Frontiers

The teaching tradition of the Church of God movement now spans more than a century of time. At its heart one encounters a subtle, central, and probably inevitable paradox. On the one hand, the movement always has been committed to biblical truth. Doctrinal preaching and writing have been respected highly and a concern for theological orthodoxy usually has been apparent. On the other hand, a central part of the movement's traditional theological consensus has been a persistent opposition to the tyranny of theological creeds and any development by the movement of its own "denominational" characteristics. There has been a *holistic* emphasis, a catholic disposition, a vision of all God's people, an intention to reach toward all the truth. A persistent conviction has been that no one person or creedal statement (limited as they are and properly motivated and helpful as they can be) ever will be in a position to become the final authority. The only recognized boundary of the Christian fellowship is the life-changing and church-constituting experience of the new birth in Christ.

Clearly the Church of God movement has sought to chart a daring and difficult middle path in theology between a mechanical, fundamentalistic propositionalism and a rootless, "liberal" faddism. It has attempted to implement an *orthodox-radical idealism*.[52] This approach gladly apprehends revealed and experienced truth, while always realizing that in this life one never will comprehend fully the many mysteries in Christ. There has been a deliberate avoidance of employing tentative insights and theological formulations as assured means of judging others and thus building walls to divide Christian individuals or bodies from each other. Sad examples to the contrary are available even in the movement's own history. They do not, however, outweigh the movement's clear instinct and intent in this regard.

Within a movement such as the Church of God, there naturally has emerged over the years a particular network of personal acquaintances and teaching emphases, even special terms that soon became "in-house" language. Language tends to distinguish, if not denominationalize. Robert Reardon once collected a small glossary of such distinguishing terms and phrases used widely in the early decades of this movement's life. They are interesting, revealing, and now often dated.

One phrase was "taking your stand." Believers were urged to renounce sectism and take their stand for the truth. And "the truth," reports Reardon, came to mean "the cumulative interpre-

---

[52]Note Barry Callen, "The Church of God Reformation Movement: A Study in Ecumenical Idealism," masters thesis, Asbury Theological Seminary, 1969.

tation of Scripture by early pioneers in the movement such as D. S. Warner, E. E. Byrum, F. G. Smith, and H. M. Riggle."[53] This truth vibrated with excitement about what God was believed to be doing. So the movement sometimes saw itself as "this *present truth.*"[54] An early movement song of joyous testimony says:

> When a voice from heaven sounded, warning all to flee,
> From the darksome courts of Babel back to Zion free;
> Glad my heart to hear the message, and I hastened to obey,
> And I'm standing *in the truth* today.[55]

These pioneers, although they felt that they had been given a fresh grasp of truth, were careful to add caution to their grasp. They were trying to avoid building a new denominational mindset or structure around themselves and their own insights.

Reviewing Galatians 2:11-16 helps clarify a delicate and crucial tension with which this movement has chosen to live. Some forms of group uniformity (rigid following of Jewish customs in this case) become obsolete, distorting, and dangerous to the Christian gospel after knowledge of the universal and liberating Christ has come. The tendency to return to "the old ways" can be wise conservatism or costly retreat.

---

[53]Robert Reardon, "A Glossary of Church of God Terms," in Barry Callen, *The First Century,* vol. 2 (Anderson, Ind.: Warner Press, 1979), 615-616.

[54]There is a fine line between pioneer persons who are inspired by God on behalf of the whole Body of Christ and those who become fanatical about their own religious ideas and thus are inappropriately divisive in the Body of Christ. In the case of Daniel Warner of the Church of God movement, for instance, his radical commitment to a vision of holiness and unity brought freedom and joy to thousands, but eventually was denounced by his own wife as fanatical (see detail in Barry Callen, *It's God's Church! The Life and Legacy of Daniel Warner,* Anderson, Ind.: Warner Press, 1995), 107-112.

[55]Charles Naylor and Andrew Byers, "The Reformation Glory," verse 2, in *Worship the Lord* (Anderson, Ind.: Warner Press, 1989), 311.

We learn in this passage that the Christian community is to be a "moving" community, crossing geographic, racial, gender, and theological frontiers with liberating good news about Christ. This good news is community-building and unity-producing, and it is not always accompanied by a uniformity of thought about all related matters in the past, present, or future. Sometimes there does need to be the courage of persons like Paul who confront obvious error, even though it is wrapped in pious language and sanctified by centuries of church tradition (the "conservative" Jews of Jerusalem in this instance). Sometimes, like in Peter's dramatic new insight stimulated by the vision of Cornelius (Acts 10), one should be open to whole new understandings and relationships.

First Corinthians 8:1-13 is a key passage for exploring the limits of Christian freedom in the midst of diversity of perception, conscience, and practice. Believers who are "strong" should learn a theology of mutuality in which all members of the church exercise their gifts and freedom with a view to the wholeness and well-being of the body of Christ. This is yielding to the way of the cross where power disciplines itself to function in weakness, avoiding coercion in favor of empowerment. Every member is to be taken seriously. This Pauline text, however, does not say that an issue like the eating of food offered to idols should be skirted because someone might object to its being addressed. The cross is a way to address issues, not avoid them. Rather than catering to the whim of every moralist or legalist in the church, Paul's letters consistently argue for the church to be a serious forum of moral discourse.

How can the essential elements of truth be upheld in the church without demanding of all persons more uniformity of belief and practice than is legitimate, without destroying the God-given liberty of individual Christians, and without restricting the continuing ministry of the Holy Spirit? How are "legalistic" sisters and brothers to be fellowshipped and learned from without letting them turn the family of God into yet another restrictive denomination? How are "liberal" brothers and sisters to be fellowshipped and learned from without letting them lead the body into heretical theological territory? How can Christians be faithful to the redeeming and liberating gospel of Christ without imprisoning it in yesterday's outdated traditionalisms or perverting it by today's hedonistic values and religious fads? The proper path is very narrow, with significant dangers readily available on both sides.[56]

Galatians 2:11-16 at least begins to address such significant questions. Paul makes clear that a Christian is one who is justified by faith in Jesus Christ and not by observing the law—the law of the Jews or anyone else's. A Christian also is one who is prepared to act in line with the truth of the gospel and not necessarily in line with the preferences and sometimes the demands of even the most pious promoters of their own versions of the gospel. To be accepted fully in the ranks of the Church of God

---

[56]Michael Kinnamon explores such questions in *Truth and Community: Diversity and Its Limits in the Ecumenical Movement* (Grand Rapids: Eerdmans, 1988). He seeks to counter the common critique by "evangelicals" of the work of the World Council of Churches by insisting that there is more balancing of diversity and truth in this work than is usually recognized by critics. Said the Council's first assembly (Amsterdam, 1948), "there is no gain in unity unless it is unity in truth and holiness" (quoted by Kinnamon, 8). Kinnamon concludes by insisting, much like the classic idealism of the Church of God movement: "At their best, ecumenical Christians should be so committed to living the whole truth of the Christian faith that they readily confess that this truth is far greater than any of their separated witnesses" (10). Unfortunately, the Church of God movement and conservative Christians in general, while readily making such a confession in principle, often has struggled to live out such a principle in practice. Rather than being intentionally open to the whole of Christ's body, with the anticipation of enrichment to itself, the Church of God movement, for instance, usually has resisted wider involvements in fear that its own witness would be weakened in the process.

movement, for instance, must one believe everything that was taught by R. R. Byrum or F. G. Smith, influential writers of an earlier generation? Must one act within the precedents set by the Gospel Trumpet Family in Anderson, Indiana, in 1910 or agree to some statement from the movement's current Leadership Council or General Assembly?[57] Clearly the answers are firm negatives, however wise, commendable, and helpful such precedents and statements may be. The movement means to offer a stimulus toward truth-full freedom, not an anchor that traps a believer in another stultifying tradition that becomes weighty and restrictive. This freedom applies even to any binding tradition of the movement's own making.

An open dialogical process has characterized the Church of God movement's World Conferences (beginning in Germany in 1955) and International Dialogues on Doctrine (beginning in the United States in 1980). No one believer or national church body ever is in position to view the whole. Thus, these international events "do not seek the indoctrination of anyone." Since the movement consistently has said that it has no creed but the Bible, it appears to be committed by choice to "conversational church 'style.' "[58]

Dialogical sharing, guided by the enlightening wisdom of the Spirit, is very different from the establishment of some mandatory group uniformity. It is an open door and not a closed room. Historian Merle Strege judges rightly that this movement illustrates the "populist Christianity" that tends to reflect "a hostility to traditional forms of authority like ecclesiastical struc-

---

[57]For a presentation of all such statements from 1917-1991 (General Assembly of the Church of God, United States and Canada), see Barry Callen, *Thinking and Acting Together* (Anderson, Ind.: Warner Press, 1992).

[58]Merle Strege, "A Dialogical Church" in *Vital Christianity* (August 2, 1987), 4-5.

tures, formal theological training, and the like."[59] Such a style and emphasis, with obvious connections to the ethos of the time and place of the movement's origin, are more than a mere reflection of the late nineteenth century.

The human temptation always is there. George Tasker, an early Church of God missionary serving in India, wrote from Calcutta to the North American movement in 1924 to oppose any "standard literature mentality." When special reverence is accorded the movement's founders or appeals are made to "what the church believes" in a narrow and restrictive sense, Tasker was troubled. Such reverence and appeals sounded to him "altogether too much like the language of the apostasy, when men began to defend their own ecclesiastical views instead of trying them constantly and ruthlessly by the Word and Spirit of the Lord."[60] The true standard is the Bible—and even the movement had not then and, of course, still has not achieved a full and final interpretation of the Bible's meaning. Otto Linn would be identified later "as one of those people in the movement who have been captured by our notion that the truth may be *pursued* more than *possessed*. He firmly opposed authoritarian control of some minds by other minds."[61]

The theological vision of the Church of God movement, then, has been one of a delicate and yet essential balance. It is believed that there is both *boundary* and *frontier* at the heart of the Christian life and in the midst of the Christian's theological work. Christians "see through a glass darkly," genuinely seeing, and yet always seeing partially and needing to press on humbly.

---

[59]Merle Strege, *Tell Me the Tale* (Anderson, Ind.: Warner Press, 1991), 116. Note his reference to Nathan Hatch who sees such a strain of Christianity reflecting the democratizing forces at work early in the American culture generally (*The Democratization of American Christianity*, New Haven: Yale University Press, 1989).

[60]George Tasker, "An Appeal to the Free and Autonomous Churches of Christ in the Fellowship of the Evening Light" (Calcutta, 1924), 30.

[61]Merle Strege, *Tell Me the Tale*, 56.

There is a tension between theological commitment (boundary) and theological questing (frontier). Ideally, both the *substance of faith* and the *setting of freedom in Christ* exist in the life of the church. Both are necessary if that life is to be healthy, whole, and open to the entire Christian community, to all truth, and to the present work of the Holy Spirit.

Faith *substance* and *freedom style* are to co-exist in the church. The name "Church of God," for instance, has been used by the movement because it is understood to relate closely to the faith's substance. The name appears to be biblical and refers to all Christians rather than taking its lead from humanly conditioned things like a person (Lutheran), practice (Baptist), or polity (Presbyterian). The idea of "movement" has been intended to emphasize a divine dynamic within the whole, the deliberate avoidance of denominating some believers and thus distancing them from all others.[62] The resulting reformation movement sometimes has pictured itself as a leaven seeking to diffuse itself through the whole of God's people, rather than being another "church" among "churches."[63]

---

[62]In a similar way, the early Methodist movement was conceived as a transdenominational renewal effort. Note Albert Outler's view of Methodism as an "evangelical order" within the church catholic ("Do Methodists have a Doctrine of the Church?" in *The Doctrine of the Church,* ed., Dow Kirkpatrick, Nashville: Abingdon Press, 1964, 11-28). Note also Geoffrey Wainwright's statement that the mission of the Methodist movement is an "ecumenical vocation" as a holy people ("Ecclesial Location and Ecumenical Vocation" in *The Ecumenical Moment: Crisis and Opportunity for the Church,* Grand Rapids: Eerdmans, 1984, 189-221). Such descriptions of Methodism are close to the "movement" identity to which the Church of God movement aspires.

[63]In recent years some congregations of the movement have abandoned the name "Church of God" because of the use of this name by other groups in highly denominationalized ways. Some retain the use, feeling it is biblical and not optional regardless of possible confusion in public perception (including with "tongues speaking" advocates using this name). Others have moved to "community church" or local geographic names, hoping to avoid all real or perceived "denominational" designations.

— 81 —

Andrew Byers provides a classic summation. "It is not assumed that Brother Warner was right on every point of doctrine or in every application of a scriptural text, but that the movement . . . possesses that flexibility and spirit of progress by which it adjusts itself as God gives light."[64] Byers lists five movement characteristics that enable such flexibility as more light on truth might emerge:

> 1. It [the movement] teaches the scriptural process of salvation, by which people may obtain a real deliverance from sin and have the Holy Spirit as a witness to their salvation;

> 2. The truth only, and obedience thereto, is its motto; and it recognizes the rule of the Holy Spirit in the organization and government of the church;

> 3. It [the movement] does not assume to possess all the truth, but stands committed thereto, holding an open door to the entrance of any further light and truth;

> 4. The spirit of the movement is to acknowledge good wherever found and to regard no door into the church other than salvation and no test of fellowship other than true Christianity possessed within the heart;

> 5. Thus its basis is as narrow as the New Testament on the one hand, and as broad as the New Testament on the other.[65]

Here is a theological vision with clear boundaries and expansive frontiers. It is a vision *orthodox* to the core and *radical* to the end. It is "protestant" in its impatience with less than the ideal and "catholic" in its vision of all of God's people on journey together in search of and as servants of all the truth.

---

[64]As quoted by Barry Callen, *A Time To Remember: Teachings* (Anderson, Ind.: Warner Press, 1978), 76.

[65]Andrew Byers, *Birth of a Reformation* (Anderson, Ind: Gospel Trumpet Co., 1921, reprint, Guthrie, Ok.: Faith Publishing House), 24.

The End of Idolatry

Since the sixteenth century the Protestant denominational system has featured groupings of Christians carrying their distinctive names, highlighting their particular interpretations of the faith, and usually employing their distinguishing marks as means of promoting group loyalty. Each has tended to argue that it holds to "the truth" as opposed to the misguided notions of other believers. In conscious contrast, the Church of God movement, trying to avoid the divisive effects of concentrating on "our distinctives" or "Church of God doctrine," has hoped to set forth the unifying goal of emphasizing in a balanced manner all of God's truth as incarnated in Christ, contained in the Bible, and revealed by the Holy Spirit.[66] Here is an "all truth" ideal, a comprehensive approach designed to neglect no major doctrine and to keep each doctrine in proper relation to all others. This always is a quest, the ideal focus, never a proclaimed accomplishment.

Being lovers of truth above all else obviously is a visionary and daring way to live as an individual or to be as a people. Christians, like the Jewish community long before, are resisters of idolatry (though sometimes guilty of it) and affirmers of all revealed truth (though never fully comprehending it). They dare to believe that there is truth that has come to them, not out of them. They also understand that such truth, while graciously available in their midst, never comes under their human control. Christian faith centers *on God!*

Unfortunately, we "moderns" have sought subtly to make God subservient to ourselves. Like the earlier Jewish tradition, the Christian faith often has been trivialized by limiting God to given times and places, shaping God in human images, and focusing the view of God's will on the satisfaction of "our needs." The role

---

[66]See John W. V. Smith, *I Will Build My Church: Biblical Insights on Distinguishing Doctrines of the Church of God* [Anderson] (Anderson, Ind.: Warner Press, 1985), v-5.

given to God is that of being useful to what we feel we need or, worse yet, just want. This preoccupation with selfish pragmatism is the church's current slavery in Egypt, its painful exile in Babylon, its persistent temptation in the wilderness of today's rootless anxiety, loss of community, and material grasping. Pragmatism sits in many pews and absorbs resources through a wide range of church programs that go under the names of "being relevant" and "speaking to where I am." Idolatry can be very subtle.

Various modern concepts of God appear to reduce God to little more than an expression of the world itself. Such accommodation to the world does little justice to divine transcendence as biblically narrated. Delwin Brown makes clear that, while unfortunately such excessive accommodation does occur, "conservatives" share the guilt. His point is that "reductionism is everybody's problem. . . . It is difficult for me [Brown] to imagine a more worrisome attempt to exploit the Christian God than one finds in current equations of God's will with American foreign policy, capitalist economics, patriarchal social policies, racist illusions, and a few other favorite themes of conservative sermonizing."[67]

The Reformed Christian tradition maintains strong commitment to the centrality of the being and work of God in relation to all of human life. B. B. Warfield (1851-1921), for instance, says that a Calvinist is one who "sees God behind all phenomena and, in all that occurs, recognizes the hand of God working out His will; who makes the attitude of the soul to God in prayer its permanent attitude in all its life-activities; and who casts himself on the grace of God alone, excluding every trace of dependence on self from the whole work of his salvation."[68] While this tradition

---

[67]Clark Pinnock and Delwin Brown, *Theological Crossfire* (Grand Rapids: Zondervan, 1990), 93.

[68]B. B. Warfield, *Calvin as a Theologian and Calvinism Today* (Philadelphia: Presbyterian Board of Publications, 1909), 23-24.

needs complemented with certain qualifications,[69] it surely is a right place to begin. Israel did not discover and then adopt God as its own, as though it were in charge of the process. God introduced the divine presence to Israel and offered a covenant relationship as an act of sovereign grace.[70] Seen as central to the thrust of Scripture is the humble confession that "from him and through him and to him are all things. To him be the glory forever. Amen" (Rom. 11:36).

Glorifying God is an important biblical theme. It should not, however, be made a virtual absolute as in much of the theology that is based on the teaching of John Calvin. Calvinism views the glory of God as the primary cause for God's creation, "whereby for his own glory he hath foreordained whatsoever comes to pass."[71] But, concluding that a major portion of all human creation will be eternally lost—by God's choice not to extend an opportunity for the acceptance of saving grace— surely is an inappropriate understanding of how a suffering, loving, forgiving God would choose to bring glory to the divine being. God's insistence on justice would have to be presumed the primary divine attribute. Human salvation, however, is a primary concern of God according to the biblical revelation. This concern suggests a meaningful freedom for humans to choose

---

[69]One key qualification is John Wesley's concern that human responsibility not be undercut by our conception of God. Affirming a place for uncoerced human choice does not necessarily detract from the glory of God. God's grace is resistible. There is genuine human choice and also a truly sovereign God.

[70]So central in the Wesleyan theological tradition, directly influential on the Church of God movement, is the concept of "prevenient" grace. God takes the loving initiative when we sinners are yet incapable of perceiving or responding at all. God's grace is before all things, including our faith in God.

[71]Charles Hodge, "The Decrees of God," in Millard Erickson, ed., vol. 1, *Readings in Christian Theology* (Grand Rapids: Baker Book House, 1973), 433.

for or against the divine offer of reconciliation. In fact, love in search of renewed life in covenant relationship with fallen humanity is seen biblically as a (the?) primary divine attribute.

Nonetheless, drawing attention away from the glory of God can lead to serious error. Much theology appears to be inverted today so that the faith is stated primarily in terms of meeting human needs rather than glorifying and reestablishing right relationship with a truly sovereign God. Ministry too often is understood as satisfying "needs" as individuals perceive them. God becomes a servant of struggling humanity, loved for what can be done for us needy people. The prayer of Samuel (1 Sam. 3:9-10) is switched from "Speak, Lord, for your servant is listening" to "Listen, Lord, for your valuable creation has needs waiting to be met."

The marketplace is now full of books by Christian authors on "how to" everything (have a good marriage, invest money to the best advantage, know all about the future, be healthy, wealthy, and wise). It is not surprising that Millard Erickson finds it "difficult to understand how some people can simultaneously express great concern for the plight of the poor (a clear preoccupation of the sovereign God) and pursue the lifestyle of the rich and famous."[72] Idols often are found right in the church!

The church of today is in danger of being reduced to the utilitarian. The two central virtues of a technological society are utility and efficiency. A demand for achieving desired results governs both the secular and religious life of such modern societies. In these settings "religion is valued mainly for the service it renders to society. The people most highly regarded are producers, not thinkers, and much less pray-ers."[73] This reduction-

---

[72]Millard Erickson, *The Evangelical Mind & Heart* (Baker Book House, 1993), 47.

[73]Donald Bloesch, *The Struggle of Prayer* (Colorado Springs: Helmers & Howard, 1988), 148.

ism is as present in many Christian sanctuaries as it is in the public media and shopping malls. Much as Karl Marx said, religion is used in selfish pursuits.

Worship for many people has become "a quasi-entertaining event providing an 'emotional outlet' and promoting self-esteem and conviviality ('fellowship')."[74] Religion too often is valued because it is found useful in gratifying needs, fulfilling the self, assuring success in the quest for achievement and happiness. Put in economic terms, God is thought of as available "capital" for our careful investing. The interest is said to be good and the yield longterm! Biblically understood, however, God is not to be worshiped because we self-serving "believers" find the process useful. God is God, and God's ways are not our ways. God is not the guaranteed answer to all of our fondest prayers or a heavenly bank account to be drawn on when our own reserves run low. God is *holy,* other, set apart. Believers also are to be holy, not just more reflections of the way the rest of the world lives.

Tiresome and disturbing are some of the mass-media evangelists who seem to have yielded their ministries to the pragmatic questions, Will it work? Will it pay? Will it sell? Will it feel good? Will it protect the status quo that assures traditional values and current comforts? Instead, being loyal to the Creator of heaven and earth will set true and humble believers sharply against the way things presently are. Their existence "must be a sign in the world of the overcoming of these powers of division and domination." Our loyalty "must clearly entail a renunciation of the ways in which we are engaged in 'unmaking' the earth."[75]

What has happened to the call to self-restraint and selflessness? What of the humble awareness of transcendence, the sense

---

[74]C. Allen, R. Hughes, M. Weed, 2nd ed., *The Worldly Church* (Abilene, Tx.: Abilene Christian University Press, 1991), 19.

[75]Theodore Jennings, *Loyalty To God* (Nashville: Abingdon Press, 1992), 57.

that God is great, beyond, other, demanding of change and obedience, even if it means our discomfort? What of the reverence, the awe, the quieting and cleansing of the mystery and majesty of God? What of radical discipleship, even in the face of some "orthodoxies" that have become status-quo and sterile? Biblical answers are absent for the most part in the noisy and busy halls of the typical congregation that is scrambling to be "relevant." Consequently, a contemporary equivalent of the traditional cry of the Church of God movement to "come out" of all church division should be the cry that those called Christian take God seriously again and revolt against *utilitarianism*. The prophetic voice calls for return to a present integrity of faith in God. Believers should abandon the trivial and piously self-serving and dare to *come out* of the business of trying to domesticate the divine.

Loving truth requires remaining open, always searching, always willing to learn and change even that in which one has believed most fondly. Submitting to a truth bigger than ourselves, truly other than ourselves, is to be prepared to have ourselves transformed in whatever ways that truth might direct. The call is for humble believers to "come out" and to fall in love with God and God's truth. The challenge is for Christian believers to find each other as they focus on and are formed by God's presence, so that together they can bring redeeming good news to the world.

For the centennial of the Church of God movement in 1980, the faculty and administration of Anderson University's School of Theology prepared a "WE BELIEVE" booklet that circulated widely in movement circles in the United States and beyond. This concise writing sought to state aspects of the movement's theological idealism that hold crucial implications for the decades yet to come. In part it reads:

> We believe in the principle of openness to all affirmations of the Christian faith which are expressions of the biblical rev-

elation (John 16:13). This is a necessary stance for Christians who would venture on mission to the world with a desire to foster honest and growing relationships with fellow Christians from many cultural and creedal backgrounds.

The intended unity among Christians is not based on the achievement of full agreement on all theological questions. Rather, it is based on a common membership in the church through the grace of God and is anchored by a common commitment to the centrality of Christ and the authority of the Word of God.

As individuals, we seek to remain humble and open to the daily instruction and leadership of the Holy Spirit. As a movement, the Church of God seeks always to allow itself to be reformed so that, by avoiding any development of the stagnation of rigid creed or inflexible structure, it can remain a pliable instrument in the hands of God.

Idolatry ends, disunity is questioned, and mission becomes primary when there is commitment to the whole truth of God as it is in Jesus Christ. Christian truth has a center and should pull all who are committed to this truth toward that center and thus toward each other.[76] So often Christian believers have been divisively parochial in their several perspectives on one or more aspects of this grand truth. This often has done great disservice to the truth, especially to its reconciling mission in the world.

Being truly the church surely means that together we who believe will allow God to do for us and through us a gracious, redeeming, and reuniting work. The fact is that Paul invested in his several New Testament letters as much time telling diverse groups of Christian believers how to live together in unity as he

---

[76]Pilate once asked Jesus, "What is truth?" (Jn. 18:38). Parker Palmer observes that Pilate betrayed the inadequacy of his own perspective by assuming that truth is a "what." Jesus stood there assuming that truth is primarily "who," that those who wish to know truth and be united together by it should enter a living relationship with Jesus, the embodied truth of God (*To Know As We Are Known,* S. F.: Harper & Row, 1983, 48).

did telling them how to preach the gospel. Apparently being a united, reconciled community of reconcilers is itself an essential prerequisite for and a primary method of preaching the gospel.

This vision of the oneness of all Christian believers comes as the faithful rally around the truth, especially around Jesus Christ who is the truth incarnate among us. This vision is "orthodox" in that it is rooted solidly in the revelation of God in Jesus Christ as told by the biblical story. It is "radical" in that it reaches out humbly and in celebration to all who affirm the truth of this grand good news and are prepared to be changed, unified, and sent by it. It focuses on praise to God, in rejection of all idolatries, and in gratitude for the glorious salvation provided in Christ. Christians sing:

> Let all who name Christ's holy name
> give God all praise and glory;
> let all who own his power proclaim
> aloud the wondrous story!
> Cast each false idol from its throne,
> for Christ is Lord, and Christ alone:
> To God all praise and glory.[77]

[77]"Sing Praise to God Who Reigns Above," vs. 4, words by Johann Schutz (1675), in *The United Methodist Hymnal* (Nashville: United Methodist Pub. House, 1989), 126.

CHAPTER THREE

Foundations

Central theological concerns of the Church of God movement have been: back to the Bible; back to the apostolic church;
back to the person of Christ; and back to the joy of the Lord
known within the heart. These reformation emphases have been
intended as reintroductions of the original, the essential, the most
authentic and enduring in Christian life and thought. They have
joined to form the vision of Christian incarnational integrity that
the movement hopes to advance in the reformation of today's
church.[1] This vision rests on the Bible as primary authority, as
illumined by the Spirit.[2] It is nurtured by an apostolic idealism
and "sees" the church as an important outcome of the Spirit's
work. This theological vision is comprehensive and idealistic.

Comprehensive and Idealistic

The commitment of the Church of God movement is not
merely to certain "truths," but to *all truth,* especially as it can be

---

[1]Typically this movement has been known as the "Church of God
Reformation Movement." There is an important tension between restoration and reformation, the former having an essentially backward look to
the "golden age" of the past (Bible and apostolic church) and the latter
focusing more on renewing the *present church* in light of a normative past.
While movement leaders are committed to enduring biblical authority,
they often emphasize the work now to be done. There has been a flavor of
restorationism in the movement's history, but one distinguishable from the
"restorationist" movement originating with Thomas and Alexander Campbell and Barton Stone (the Disciples tradition). For histories of the
Restorationist tradition, see the Select Bibliography at the end of this book
for works by James North, Mark Toulouse, and Henry Webb.

[2]Highlighting the Spirit's present illumination of the biblical revelation
is *not* to disregard disciplined Bible study in light of the best available interpretive tools. It is to highlight the sovereignty of the Spirit over all things.

found in the biblical revelation through the current ministry of the Holy Spirit. This "comprehensive and idealistic objective"[3] was given classic statement by Daniel Warner in 1878. He declared that the Lord had given him "a new commission to join holiness and all truth together." The purpose of this crucial joining was the building up of "the apostolic church of the living God." This faithful joining now has proceeded for many decades. The idealism has persisted, even when achievement has been difficult and only partial.

The years 1929-1930, for instance, were troublesome ones in the movement. Anderson College (University) had just introduced the liberal arts into its curriculum, something very controversial at the time.[4] The editorial staff of the movement's Gospel Trumpet Company (Warner Press) had been receiving criticism for being heavy-handed in theological thought control in the movement. The alumni publication of the Anderson campus, then called the *Broadcaster,* released its January, 1930, issue in an attempt to address the controversy. It featured a doctrinal statement signed by the faculty and a statement of editorial policy made by the editor and associate editor of the publishing company (located across the street).

The doctrinal statement, something uncharacteristic of movement leaders, sought to convey reassurance to "the field." The reassurance was that the movement's academic and national leaders still were committed in every important respect to the Christian faith and "in our present reformation movement as a movement divinely initiated by God as a special medium by

[3]John Smith, *I Will Build My Church* (Anderson, Ind.: Warner Press, 1985), 183.

[4]See Barry Callen, *Guide of Soul and Mind: The Story of Anderson University* (Anderson, Indiana: Warner Press and Anderson University, 1992), chapter four.

which to restore the church to New Testament standards."5 The broadening of the young school's curricular mission was not to be seen as an abandonment of treasured theological foundations.

The editorial statement also sought to bring reassurance to the movement's constituency. By taking a public stance on "doctrine" and "attitude," F. G. Smith and R. L. Berry again reflected the movement's basic theological vision, one that is both orthodox and radical, catholic, and protestant. They wrote:

> As to DOCTRINE, it has been our purpose at least to adhere faithfully to those basic principles of the Word of God that have been generally accepted and taught by us as a people in the past. We have endeavored to stand 100 percent for the reformation, pledged as it has been to the restoration of the New Testament church, and for the truths which have produced it and brought it to its present standard. We are not aware of any fundamental change in us on this point.

> As to our ATTITUDE, it is not our intention to be ultra-conservative. We believe in progress, but at the same time we feel that progress should be consistent with truth already received and should come about naturally, like the growth and development of the human body. There should always be on the part of all of us willingness to walk in the light as God gives us to see the light. We believe we should give recognition to all the working of God wherever the Holy Spirit is clearly seen to be at work; therefore we

---

5 From at least the beginning of the century to the 1940s, the self-understanding of the movement was shaped significantly by a particular reading of the Bible's apocalyptic literature. Many movement interpreters tended to see in these texts (Daniel and Revelation) anticipation of the movement as an instrument of divine activity in the final days before Christ's return. This view called for Christians to "come out" from all sectarian bodies. See Merle Strege, *Tell Me Another Tale* (Anderson, Ind.: Warner Press, 1993), 12-13, and John Stanley, "Unity Amid Diversity: Interpreting the Book of Revelation in the Church of God (Anderson)," *Wesleyan Theological Journal* (Fall, 1990), 74-98. Also see chapter five of this book.

believe in extending Christian fellowship at all times to all true Christians.[6]

Within this theological vision is an approach to Christian unity which presumes the integrity of changed lives and does not rely on creedal compromise or the mere realignments of church organizations. This approach addresses helpfully both of the traditional theological tasks, faithfulness to God's revelation and relevance to the current world. But it goes on to affirm a third task, the necessity of contemporary embodiment, incarnational integrity as essential to complete the full cycle of the theological enterprise. Theologians and all believers are to remember gratefully, translate meaningfully, and live accordingly!

This full-orbed approach to Christian theology is oriented to divine revelation. It is unchanging in its foundations. The biblical revelation is basic. While rooted in a particular past, it is creatively open to the people, places, and needs of today and tomorrow, things always changing. In addition, movement leaders have been most sensitive to their responsibility to *be,* not just to think, write, organize, and maintain. Here is a theological approach based on *spiritual and incarnational integrity* that is foundational to individual and corporate Christian life and mission.

A theology of integrity will evidence in life what is truly biblical and has been put forward in clear and thoughtful language. There should be no separation between belief and life. Orthodoxy, rooted in the original apostolic witness, is to be joined by "orthopraxy," correct teaching combined with a concrete demonstration of Christian community and love that feeds the hungry, frees the oppressed, and otherwise brings to reality the presence of the Kingdom of God in this troubled world.

Beginning about 1880, the new Church of God movement began looking back to the apostolic witness as crucial guidance

---

[6]In the *Broadcaster,* early alumni publication of Anderson College (University), January, 1930, 7.

for a reforming of an establishment Christianity that largely had lost its way. The movement was seeking to embody a flexible theological faithfulness, one like John Morrison ascribed to Charles Brown as Brown was becoming Editor of the movement's Gospel Trumpet Company in 1930. Said Morrison of Brown: "As a thinker and theologian, he is progressive without being dangerous and conservative without being dogmatic."[7]

This is one movement's attempt to model for the whole church a relevant, yet rooted and applied radicalism. This type of radicalism is one always tempered by the mainstream of the believing tradition of Christianity (although not always by its orthodoxies and institutions). It is one seeking not to be paralyzed by centuries of intricate and mandated theological theorizing. It seeks to turn away from any fundamentalistic sterility, creedalistic rigidity, or denominational rivalry. The hope is to retain the freedom, fruitfulness, and true community of the Spirit.

Here are visionary Christians questing for release from any "liberal" ambiguity about theological essentials. This movement is not desirous of any kind of charismatic enthusiasm that enthrones emotion, exalts the human ego, or inordinately devalues the important roles of reason, tradition, and biblical revelation in Christian life. On the other hand, there is little tolerance for a rational faith drained of experiential reality and dedicated discipleship. To be lacking in incarnational integrity is to squeeze the life from the faith, no matter how orthodox it is said to be.

Back to the Bible

"No creed but the Bible" has been a frequent slogan among many renewal bodies. A theological volume very influential in the Church of God movement for decades was F. G. Smith's

[7]In the *Broadcaster* (see previous note), vol. 2, no. 3, July, 1930, 3.

What the Bible Teaches.[8] The book's very title makes clear the presumed center of authority. The point usually intended by a no-creed-but-the-Bible affirmation is not that believers should disrespect and dispense entirely with such classics as the Apostles' Creed or the Westminster Confession. It is that such human constructs should not be elevated to the point that they become an established filter to sort and divide believers (sectism) and thereby tend to end further questing and confessing. The reading of Scripture is never free of the influence of some limiting perspective brought to the reading, whether it is a creed, cultural bias, or personal preference.[9]

The Sadducees once posed for Jesus an absurd theological question so that he might perjure himself regardless of how he responded. Instead, Jesus exposed their awkward theological error (Mark 12:18-27). To avoid such error ourselves, we must evoke the enduring two-fold theological test in regard to any issue: "Do we know the full and in-depth meaning of the Word of God?" and "Do we know from experience the unlimited power of God?"[10] In other words, to inform, control, and give valid substance to spiritual experience, there should be a studied awareness of and obedience to God's revealed Word, both incarnate in Christ and recorded in Scripture.

The real challenge is facing the *hermeneutical* problem. The Bible requires interpretation in order to function as a sure

---

[8]F. G. Smith, *What the Bible Teaches* (Anderson, Ind.: Gospel Trumpet Company, 1913).

[9]My colleague Douglas Welch offers the sobering observation that "truth is most often determined by power." Often someone insists that "the Bible says" when, in fact, "what is read out of biblical texts is there only because it is first read in by the reading strategies of the community." See Douglas Welch, "From Hermeneutics to Reading," unpublished chapel address, Anderson University School of Theology, January 21, 1993, 3-4.

[10]David McKenna, *The Communicator's Commentary: Mark* (Waco, Tx.: Word Books, 1982), 249.

theological guide. It calls for disciplines of interpretation beyond the basics of "knowing the Author" and affirming in principle that the Bible is authoritative. The "free church" is inclined to emphasize the finitude of every scheme of interpretation, seeking rather a constant testing and persistent openness. This implies no lack of sturdy conviction, just a will to avoid any premature closure to the questing. When John Robinson said to the pilgrims leaving Plymouth in the seventeenth century, "The Lord has yet much more light and truth to break forth from His holy Word," he surely meant that new dimensions of biblical understanding were yet possible in a new world and under the guidance of God's Spirit. There is unchanging truth, but human interpretations and understandings of that truth are always limited and changing.

An adequate pattern of religious authority, therefore, will include respect for the central role of authentic Christian experience, a commitment to the normative place of the Bible, and responsible biblical interpretation that can allow the Bible to instruct rather than be overwhelmed by inordinate subjectivity, denominational bias, political expediency, or cultural fashion. Meeting this challenge never will be easy or fully accomplished.

Regarding the exact nature of the Bible as inspired revelation, there is a difference between "simplistic" and "simple." We need to avoid being "too simplistic when we utter slogans like 'what the Bible says, God says,' when a glance at almost any page will show how unsimple such a conviction is in practice. The simple thing we can say about the Bible from the testimony is that it is the text in which the Word of God can be heard and the will of God discerned."[11]

If not expediency, current fashion, or set traditionalism, how does biblical material yield present authority? How do

---

[11]Clark Pinnock, *The Scripture Principle* (S. F.: Harper & Row, 1984), 56.

believers relate conditioned understandings of the Bible's many and even varied teachings to current ways of thinking and claims to truth? A dialogue between Delwin Brown and Clark Pinnock highlights the key issue and suggests elements of an adequate answer.

Brown declares his own liberalism, that is, his commitment to tipping the balance of authority in Christian faith toward the present, resulting in a "reasoned search for truth guided by contemporary criteria of knowledge."[12] For him the Bible remains a crucial Christian resource. It is authoritative in at least one sense. We all are historical persons, products in part of our social past and cultural present. Any body of people lives out of a "canon," a story of reality that shapes perceptions and identity. For Christians, that always will be the Bible. The Bible is an enduring resource, but not the only and not necessarily always the determining one. Concludes Brown, while "the Bible does not 'norm' us, it does form us."[13]

Pinnock responds passionately to Brown's stance: "My heart is moved when you [Brown] speak about its being impossible for liberals simply to return to absolutes that they believe are not there to return to."[14] Pinnock's difference with Brown is that Brown will "not allow the Scriptures to give us information," thus limiting the Bible to "a functional but not a cognitive authority."[15] The challenge is to grant real, revelational, unchanging and unsurpassed quality to the Bible without reducing that quality to a sterile, mechanically cognitive heritage. To be avoided is a prematurely closed intellectual tradition not open to serious interchange with the claimed wisdoms of modern

---

[12]Clark Pinnock and Delwin Brown, *Theological Crossfire* (Grand Rapids: Zondervan, 1990), 27.

[13]Ibid., 29.

[14]Ibid., 36.

[15]Ibid., 249.

times. The balance, judges Pinnock, is to tip the locus of authority toward the norming quality of the Bible, yet without failing
to note that the Bible offers a definitive foundation without a finished theology.

In 1981 the General Assembly of the Church of God movement noted "the secular humanism and doctrinal confusions of
our day." It saw wisdom in reaffirming that the movement gladly
recognizes the Bible as "our only creed" so that "the Bible, supported by the interpretative ministry of the Holy Spirit, has had a
central significance among us." Biblical inspiration was stated as
follows, avoiding the "inerrancy" word being stressed by the
aggressive fundamentalism of the time:

> The Bible truly is the divinely inspired and infallible Word
> of God . . . without error in all that it affirms, in accordance
> with its own purpose, namely that it is "profitable for teach-
> ing, for reproof, for correction, for training in righteous-
> ness, that the man of God may be adequate, equipped for
> every good work" (2 Tim. 3:16-17, NAS), and therefore is
> fully trustworthy and authoritative as the infallible guide
> for understanding the Christian faith and living the Chris-
> tian life.[16]

Added to this affirmation of biblical authority was another
crucial "resolved" of the Assembly. It calls the movement "to a

---

[16]See Barry Callen, *Thinking and Acting Together* (Anderson, Ind.:
Executive [Leadership] Council of the Church of God and Warner Press,
1992), 34. Biblical authority is best defined in direct relation to God's purposes of human salvation and discipleship. A statement similar to that of the
General Assembly comes from the Second Vatican Council of the Roman
Catholic Church. Commenting on 2 Tim. 3:16-17, the Scriptures are said to
teach "firmly, faithfully, and without error that truth which God wanted put
into the sacred writings for the sake of our salvation" (*Dogmatic Constitution on Divine Revelation,* chapter 3). Avoiding being captured by a
mechanical "inerrancy" mentality has been an issue within the Wesleyan
Theological Society, particularly in the 1960s and 1970s (see the historical
essays by William Kostlevy, Leo Cox, Donald Dayton, and Howard Snyder
in *Wesleyan Theological Journal,* 30:1, Spring, 1995), 212-231.

new dedication to faithful biblical scholarship and proclamation, based both upon a commitment to its [the Bible's] authority as described above and upon a fresh quest for studied insight and divine guidance in the crucial tasks of responsible biblical interpretation, teaching and preaching." Proper theological understanding is not automatic just because biblical authority is accepted in principle. The task of responsible biblical interpretation and theological formulation necessarily involves "studied insight and divine guidance."

The theological method of John Wesley is instructive. His is a perspective on authority in Christian faith that is particularly sensitive to central Believers' Church concerns—without being overly vulnerable to typical Believers' Church weaknesses. Wesley was very much a product of both the Reformation and the Enlightenment. From the former he inherited a high view of Scripture which grounds revelation in objective reality. From the latter he gained an appreciation for human reason as an alternative to primitive superstitions and vain imaginations.[17]

Although not a "systematic" theologian in the usual sense, Wesley was interested in providing coherent doctrinal norms that give needed guidance without having to be defined too narrowly or separated from the vibrancy of direct spiritual experience.

---

[17]Randy Maddox notes a fact crucial for the self-understanding of all believers: "Our earliest patterns of preunderstandings are conveyed to us socially long before we begin conscious evaluation of them. As such, few of Wesley's theological convictions were initially 'chosen' in an unbiased conscious manner; they were imbibed with his familial and ecclesial nurture. In other words, 'tradition' (socio-culturally defined) was the initial source of much of Wesley's theology. When experience called some aspect of this assumed theology into question, he then had to decide whether to retain, revise, or reject the conviction at issue. The mature Wesley consciously sought to guide such decisions by Scripture—as enlightened by reason, experience, and 'tradition' " (*Responsible Grace: John Wesley's Practical Theology,* Nashville: Kingswood Books, Abingdon Press, 47).

Wesley's working concepts of doctrinal authority were "dynamically balanced," just what is required to enable the needed gaining of "studied insight and divine guidance."[18]

In Wesley we see a theological method, the so-called Wesleyan "quadrilateral," featuring Scripture as the pre-eminent norm. Scripture, however, necessarily is interfaced with tradition, reason, and Christian experience, three interactive aids in the interpretation of the Word of God in Scripture.[19] Accordingly, God's revelation includes a written witness (the Scriptures), a remembering community (the traditions), a process of existential appropriation (experience), and a way to test for internal consistency (reason).[20]

Wesley was comfortable with some variation in theological formulation if there was consensus at least on essential Christian doctrine (biblically normed and Christ-centered). After all, Christians are called beyond "orthodoxy" to authentic spiritual experience, from the *form* to the *power* of religion, from the *status*-changing before God of our justification to the *character-*

---

[18]Albert Outler, "The Wesleyan Quadrilateral in John Wesley," in T. Oden and L. Longden, eds., *The Wesleyan Theological Heritage* (Grand Rapids: Zondervan, 1991), 24.

[19]This interactive role is explained well in Donald Thorsen, *The Wesleyan Quadrilateral: Scripture, Tradition, Reason and Experience as a Model of Evangelical Theology* (Grand Rapids: Zondervan, 1990). Thorsen sees this quadrilateral as integrating all historic authority claimants. It involves an affirmation of (1) biblical authority as primary, although not exclusive, (2) tradition that extends to classical orthodoxy in Christian antiquity, (3) rational methods of inquiry, viewing theology more as an ongoing process than a completed system, and (4) experience as a genuine source of religious authority (251). He sees in this quadrilateral "invaluable insights for developing a more thoroughly catholic model of evangelical theology" (251). Such is consistent with the vision of the Church of God movement.

[20]Wesley's "quadrilateral" of theological authorities may be described best as "a unilateral *rule* of Scripture within a trilateral *hermeneutic* of reason, tradition, and experience" (Randy Maddox, *Responsible Grace,* 46).

changing of our sanctification by God. The Bible is the *fount* of revelation, while Christian *experience* energizes the heart, empowers truth's fullest discernment, and enables the believer to speak and do the truth in love.[21] In fact, Wesley so valued the fruit of faith that he even measured truth by the moral test of love.[22] As awareness of divine truth emerges from actual participation in the life of God, so the present integrity of that truth can be tested in part by the evidence of the fruit of God's love reflected in the believer's life.

Rather than a mandatory creed or authoritarian institution, on center stage for the Christian should be a heart "strangely warmed" by God and an open, authoritative Bible. The Bible alone, however, rarely has settled a disputed point of doctrine! Prooftexting repeatedly has shown itself able to support a wide range of contradictory points of view on the same subject. So Wesley's dynamically balanced approach includes appeal to "the primitive church" (tradition), critical reason,[23] and Christian

---

[21]Note the disturbing observation of Justo González: "The Bible has traditionally been interpreted in ways that are oppressive to minorities and to powerless groups, and that serve to justify the actions and values of the oppressors" (*Out of Every Tribe & Nation,* Nashville: Abingdon Press, 1992, 38). He sees this fact requiring a broadened understanding of the components of the Wesleyan quadrilateral. For example, "experience" should be more than "religious" experience since the African American community inevitably brings to the interpretative process the experience of slavery, and other groups bring their various backgrounds of oppression (as did the ancient Israelites who worked from their memory of slavery and divine rescue from Egypt). This inclusion of personal and communal stories need not undermine biblical authority. What it does is expose false and self-serving interpretations, thereby enriching the process of interpretation.

[22]David Cubie, "The Theology of Love in Wesley," *Wesleyan Theological Journal* (Spring, 1985), 122-154.

[23]John Wesley did not understand reason to be another source of revelation supplementing the Bible. Rather, it is "the candle of the Lord" given to assist in appropriation of biblical revelation (see Wesley's *Letter to Miss March,* July 5, 1768). Reason's value is helping with *responsible* biblical interpretation and application.

experience. This fourfold authority features the Bible as the norm, supported by these other refining and confirming witnesses to the actual meaning of Scripture. It is a pattern of authority offering wisdom for today's theologizing.[24] It helps the back-to-the-Bible call to stay connected to real life, the whole person, and the whole church while it is being interpreted.

This wisdom is appropriate for the Church of God movement that has championed the "radical" elements of this pattern of authority without always profiting appropriately from other elements. In part the failure has come from an anti-institutional and even anti-intellectual bias prominent especially in the earliest years of the movement. Generally, however, the movement's concerns have focused on human arrogance rather than actually opposing disciplined learning as such. The preference has been to highlight the supernatural.[25]

The Wesleyan pattern of religious authority preserves the primacy of Scripture, profiting from the wisdom of tradition, accepting the disciplines of critical reason, and stressing the Christian experience of grace that enables existential insight and force. Wesley sought to avoid the sterile polarizations of biblicism, empiricism, rationalism, and traditionalism. The envisioned balance is complex and crucial.

---

[24]Donald Bloesch recently offered some critique of this quadrilateral approach (A Theology of Word & Spirit, 208ff). It appears to him that at times reason and experience are portrayed in Wesley's quadrilateral as independent means to knowledge of God apart from faith. Bloesch prefers a "unilateral" authority, divine revelation communicated through various means (received through Scripture and tradition, elucidated by reason and experience), thus safeguarding "the crucial biblical and Reformation principle that it is God alone who saves and it is God alone who makes himself known" (211).

[25]See John Morrison, "Our Pioneers Were Ultra-Supernaturalists," in Barry Callen, Faith, Learning, and Life (Anderson, Ind.: Anderson University and Warner Press, 1991), 5-6.

The biblical revelation of God with us in Israel and in Christ is the authoritative narrative for Christians. Those who believe are to be caught up in Christ so that *His* story becomes *their* story. Baptism by immersion, for instance, dramatizes a retelling of the death and resurrection of Jesus as the precedent and power that now enables the dying and rising to new life in Christ of the new believer (Rom. 6:3-4). The life *of* Christ is translated into life *in* Christ. Believers are to share Christ's sufferings on the way to sharing his glory (Rom. 8:17). Recalling historically and re-presenting personally the life of Christ shapes the believer's understanding of reality and guides life's attitudes, decisions, and actions.

Doctrines are interpretations of the meaning and implications of the biblical revelation in Israel and in Christ. The narrative is primary, while doctrines are judgments about proper ways to read the narrative. For Christians, affirming that "Jesus is the Christ" is the proper way to read the story of Jesus of Nazareth. Read this way, Jesus gives (is!) guidance on what to believe about God, humanity, creation, destiny, etc. Doctrines, while arising from and interpreting the biblical Story, are a secondary language of faith never independent of the biblical revelation itself. Christians, thus, should unite around biblical authority, not divide over differences in doctrinal formulations. For this to be possible, all Bible reading and theological work must proceed under the guidance of the Spirit of God.

A Spirit Reading of Scripture

God, the original Inspirer of the biblical revelation, surely is in the best position to assist with its contemporary understanding. We hear Christ say, "Let anyone who has an ear listen to what the Spirit is saying to the churches" (Rev. 3:22).

The Bible is authoritative for Christians, but wherein does this authority lie? Approaching the answer requires a recognition that many "evangelicals" of recent generations have not evidenced. There is a close link between the reader of a biblical text and that reader's perception of the meaning and authority of that text.[26] Capitalizing on this link without capitulating to its distorting tendencies is the work of the Holy Spirit.

Christians, especially "evangelicals" reacting to classic "liberalism," have tended to be more interested in the *inspiration* than in the *illumination* of the biblical text (authority vested in the received text as opposed to awareness of the text's special significance for life now). Fearing what easily can be the unbridled subjectivism of a reader-driven interpretation, evangelicals tend to focus on historical exegesis, seeking to affirm and even protect the authority of the biblical text as originally inspired. They "attempt to ignore the fact that readers bring interests and presuppositions to the text and settle comfortably into a positivist framework of interpretation, viewing the text as stationary object and the reader as detached examiner."[27] To be "orthodox" is to believe in the reliability of the text itself as a faithful reporter of the biblical revelation of God in Israel and in Christ. To also be "radical," however, is to go beyond historical reliability to present life application.

---

[26]Note: "A Wesleyan hermeneutic, though it gives priority to the Scriptures as the basis of all beliefs, assumes that all truth is existentially perceived and appropriated. One does not simply come to the Scriptures with a blank mind and then rationalistically interpret the Bible. For the Bible is always interpreted through experience, tradition and reason. This is not a subjectivizing of the biblical revelation, but a frank acknowledgement that all truth is mediated in a larger context, rather than merely through a logical and rationalistic framework. This personal-relational dimension is a decisive exegetical and theological presupposition for a Wesleyan hermeneutic. Hence the crucible of life is the laboratory for testing our interpretation of Scripture" (Laurence Wood, "The Wesleyan View" in Donald Alexander, ed., *Christian Spirituality: Five Views of Sanctification* (InterVarsity Press, 1988, 95-96).

[27]Clark Pinnock, "The Role of the Spirit in Interpretation," *Journal of the Evangelical Theological Society* 36:4 (December 1993), 492.

FOUNDATIONS

Many leaders of European Pietism in the seventeenth and eighteenth centuries taught that only the spiritually prepared biblical reader will understand the text properly. In other words, there is an intimate connection between holiness of text, holiness of interpreter, and quality of interpretation. More recently, Mary Ford has rejected the typical Enlightenment ideal of reading Scripture in an "objective" way. Rather, the knowledge that is intended for conveyance by the Bible, spiritual knowledge of God and of the path to restored relationship with God and God's work, comes only through a faith-full reading that is inspired by the Spirit and conducted in the context of the believing community.[28] Stanley Grenz rightly calls for "the reorientation of the doctrine of Scripture under the doctrine of the Holy Spirit."[29]

The model of the ancient Apostles' Creed is wise, establishing the Triune God as the organizing principle for Christian faith affirmation and addressing the content and interpretation of revelation *within* and not *prior to* consideration of the being and work of God. In this way the Bible comes to be seen as a dynamic instrument of the Spirit's work, not a static deposit of propositional truths to be considered in advance of and even separate from a focus on the past and present work of the Spirit. Instead of exclusive attention being given to the past action of the Spirit in inspiring the biblical authors (insuring the adequacy of their writing in relation to divine intent), there also is need to recognize the Spirit's *present* work in speaking through the Scriptures to illumine appropriate interpretation and fresh application. Believers are to listen to the biblical text (historic meaning) and live in front of the text (present significance). Both tasks require the work of the Spirit.

---

[28]Mary Ford, "Seeing, But Not Perceiving: Crisis and Context in Biblical Studies," *St. Vladimir's Theological Quarterly* 35:2-3 (1991), 122.

[29]Stanley Grenz, *Revisioning Evangelical Theology* (InterVarsity Press, 1993), 114. These paragraphs are indebted in part to this work of Grenz, especially his chapter 5.

The canon of biblical materials is itself the result of the Spirit's inspiration of original composition and illumination of the church as it sought ongoing meaning in changing circumstances. Church perception of relevant meaning today rests both on initial divine inspiration, a tradition of divine illumination in the church, and the ongoing illumination work of the Spirit. There is a close relation between Scripture and the believing community. Energized at all stages by the Spirit, the Bible is both a product of the community of faith and a constant resource for that community's fresh belief and application. Consequently, "a closer connection between inspiration and illumination would lead evangelicals to a more profound, Spirit-focused rather than text-focused understanding of the nature of biblical trustworthiness."[30]

The divine dimension of the biblical materials is bound closely to the present illumination provided by the Spirit of God. This was the case when these materials were first written, when later they were edited and then compiled and canonized within the church's life, and still later when they were freshly understood and newly applied. Rather than the truth of God in Scripture being restricted narrowly to fixed concepts and their exact way of statement and precise point of application, there is a more Spirit-oriented dynamism inherent in the process of interpretation. According to 2 Timothy 3:16-17, God "inspires," breathes into the Scripture, thereby keeping it alive, faith producing, and church directing as times and cultures change.[31]

---

[30]Ibid., 124. Also see F. F. Bruce, *The Canon of Scripture* (InterVarsity Press, 1988), 281-282,

[31]The simple and rigid logic of the verbal inspiration (inerrancy) theory of the Bible is inadequate to convey the mutually interactive relationship between Bible and Spirit. If the Spirit only inspired and then fixed forever the very words of Scripture, the exact "facts" of revelation, then we are taken "back to the Jewish scribal position, which assumed that the prophetic Spirit had been withdrawn from Israel" (Norman Kraus, *God Our Savior,* Scottdale, Pa.: Herald Press, 158). Such is not the case with the Pentecost people, the church of Christ's Spirit.

This ongoing illumination of the Spirit need not be an open door to unchecked subjectivism among Christians. Brevard Childs provides one helpful way of avoiding this danger. He approaches biblical understanding by examining the process of the original formation of Scripture as we now have it, particularly the patterns of interpretation and reinterpretation evident over the generations within that very process. Scripture displays examples of its own reinterpretation in ways judged by the faithful community of the time as appropriate to the ongoing and authoritative work of the original inspiring and then later illuminating Spirit. The Spirit enables the interpretation of the Bible as authoritative Scripture through "the canonical context of the church."[32]

The Scriptures play the foundational role of being the "constitution of an ongoing community"[33] because they are the product of the faith's formative stage and because they provide the narrative that reports the pivotal events and enduring meanings that make the church God's church. The *significance* of the biblical texts change, but not their *meaning*. In the Bible is the

---

[32]Brevard Childs, *Biblical Theology in Crisis* (Philadelphia: Westminster Press, 1970), 104. Drawing on Edmund Clowney, *Preaching and Biblical Theology* (1961), and assuming the Protestant principle that the Bible is its own best interpreter, Richard Lints expands helpfully on three "horizons of interpretation," the textual, epochal, and canonical (*The Fabric of Theology*, Eerdmans, 1993, 293-310). These horizons are (1) the immediate context of a biblical passage, (2) the context of the period of revelation in which it falls, and (3) the context of the entirety of biblical revelation. Under the guidance of the Spirit, these horizons help an interpreter discipline the questions asked of a text and determine the current relevance of the points made in a text. Regarding any passage, one asks: Is it in the flow of the biblical Story of salvation, what does it add to the Story, and how is it illumined by looking at it in light of the whole of the Story, especially Jesus Christ? The Spirit's role is crucial in answering all such central questions.

[33]Francis Schussler Fiorenza, "The Crisis of Scriptural Authority," *Interpretation* 44 (October, 1990), 363.

recorded revelation of God's work in the world, the very record that the Spirit is prepared to use to bring new life and to form true Christian community in every time and setting. Through the retelling of this story of primal events,[34] "the Spirit re-creates the past within the present life of the community. And the texts thus provide paradigms and categories by means of which the community under the direction of the Spirit can come to understand and respond to the challenges of life in the present."[35]

While the biblical text is indispensable, at all points it is the work of the Spirit that is primary, breathing authority into the text and illuminating its relevance for the community of its contemporary readers. The biblical canon is closed, and yet in a sense it is open. The openness rests on the sure base that the canon and the challenge of its present significance in the church are both controlled by the power of the Spirit. The Bible is servant to the work of the Spirit. The Spirit's goal is to illumine the Word for the church so that it sheds needed light on her pilgrim way. Good theology is pilgrim theology. Believers should care both about what the Bible says and where it points for life and mission now. Theology that takes the path of discovery requires both the Spirit's historic inspiration and present illumination of the biblical text.

The formative events of Christian faith happened in a very different place and a long time ago. How can they be made understandable now? How can they function relevantly in a technology-driven, post-Christian, secularized world? Paul Tillich, representative of a common kind of Christian theology in recent decades, concentrated his theological work on deciding how the traditional message of the faith can be refocused best for the peo-

---

[34]Of central significance are the exodus, exile, and messianic expectation of the Hebrews, and the life, teachings, death, and resurrection of Jesus.

[35]Stanley Grenz, *Revisioning Evangelical Theology*, 127.

ple of our time. He saw the twentieth century as a time when the world is disintegrating and people are being victimized by the existential anxieties of guilt, meaninglessness, and death. Faith is essential, but an adequate faith, judged Tillich, has to be reconceptualized and culturally conditioned to the times (illuminated).

John Wesley lived in an earlier century when the challenge to "make relevant" the ancient gospel was different only in details. Wesley's way of going about the task differs somewhat from Tillich's. Wesley also faced culture, credibility, and communication gaps. In addition, he recognized the need of facing of *spiritual gap*. Men and women of any age are "dead in trespasses and sins." The only hope of their responding to God's reality and redeeming presence is the gracious work of the Holy Spirit. This is made possible by "prevenient grace," insisted Wesley, divine grace given when sinners are yet "dead," unworthy, unable otherwise to recognize and respond to truth apart from grace. Such gracious enablement provides a way that the gulf of sin, time, and culture can be bridged.

God speaks through the divine Word, Jesus, as witnessed biblically and brought to life by the Spirit. Granted, theological vocabulary must fit the times. Wesley sought to speak plain truth to plain people in plain language.[36] He relied on the ministry of the Spirit to "quicken" the Word and bring "assurance" to the soul. Wesley's chosen option was not to adopt a new God-concept, discarding all those being judged by others as not compatible with the spirit of the age. He relied on the Holy Spirit, the presentness of the God of all times, to contemporize without distorting the gospel message. His way was both "orthodox" and "radical." In the person of the Spirit, the God who always was still is! God can be known only as God assists with the knowing. Such assistance comes when believers are prepared to allow God to be God.

---

[36]Edward Sugden, ed., *Wesley's Standard Sermons* (London: The Epworth Press, 1968), 30.

So far as the theological task is concerned, the Spirit functions in two interrelated ways. One is to preserve the purity of the gospel as witnessed to dependably in the biblical revelation. The other is to make current that gospel in thought, language, and life application appropriate in each new time and place. The church in changing times is tempted either to compromise the gospel to "fit" the times (heavy on context) or to retreat with the gospel in isolation from the times (heavy on text). The Spirit works in either case, making available the promise of illumination that always involves a move toward the right relationship between text and context, the Word lived (Jesus) and written then, and the Word alive and communicating now (Spirit of Jesus).

The integrity of this crucial balance is easily compromised. The rightful authority of inspired Scripture sometimes is narrowed to focus only on the words of the biblical text. John Calvin taught that the Word is the *object* and the *instrument* of the Spirit's witness. This opens the way for "Protestant Orthodoxy to place most of the weight on the former, so that the authority and power of the written Word lay in the inspiration of its writers rather than in that of its hearers."[37]

While leaders of the Church of God movement have been tempted regularly by such unbalanced "orthodoxy," they usually have affirmed with John Wesley the vital role of the inner testimony of the Holy Spirit. Wesley saw such testimony as "the primary basis for the authority of Scripture and the authenticating factor of its inspiredness."[38] In other words, before Scripture can play its revealing role, the same Spirit who originally inspired its

[37]Rob Staples, "Wesleyan Perspectives on the Doctrine of the Holy Spirit," in A. Deasley and R. Shelton, eds., *The Spirit and the New Age,* Vol. 5 of the *Wesleyan Theological Perspectives* series (Warner Press, 1986), 211.

[38]R. Larry Shelton, "John Wesley's Approach to Scripture in Historical Perspective," *Wesleyan Theological Journal* (Spring, 1981), 36.

writers must now inspire its readers. The Word and Spirit fulfill coordinate and interdependent tasks. The written Word cannot work automatically without the Spirit, and seldom does the Spirit work autonomously apart from the written Word.

Here is a "radical" addition to what often passes as adequate orthodoxy. Just as we fallen humans are "dead" in our sins until enabled by God's prevenient grace to respond to the offer of forgiveness, the written Word also lies dormant until enlivened by the Spirit for present readers. In the letters on its sacred pages lie the essential records, the crucial salvation story, and normative interpretations of the meaning of God's pivotal acts in human history. But proper perception, existential power, and contemporary cultural relevance rely on the *present* work of the Spirit. God's Spirit, who first inspired the Word, now chooses to dwell within the searching heart to inspire again, witnessing afresh to the truth in Scripture. Always, the Spirit is God, not the book. The book, clearly essential as an instrument of revelation, does not supplant the Spirit who remains the inspirer, the One revealed and the One revealing.

The integrity of God's ongoing activity in this process should never be compromised. Since the written Word is divinely inspired and normative, the revealing of the Spirit never is contrary to it. Even so, the foundation is theism, not biblicism. The letter of the Word is dead apart from the dynamic of the divine, the Spirit. The Christian tradition, paradoxically, is both a fixed and yet an unfinished journey guided surely by the Spirit. All along the way, "Christian doctrine is revisable but not reversible; it develops along the line of the trajectory that comes from its origins. . . . Underneath this conviction is the trust that the Holy Spirit is present in the church in the ministerial work of the tradition, in the sense of rightness of direction."[39]

---

[39]Gabriel Fackre, *Ecumenical Faith in Evangelical Perspective* (Eerdmans, 1993), 67-68.

Charles Wesley put it well in his hymns that were intended to be sung or prayed before the reading of Scripture. For instance:

> Come, Holy Ghost, for moved by Thee
> The prophets wrote and spoke;
> Unlock the truth, Thyself the key,
> Unseal the sacred book.

Or again, reflecting on the work of the Spirit in bringing light to that first primeval darkness (Gen. 1:3), Charles prays in inspired verse:

> Expand Thy wings, celestial Dove,
> Brood o'er our nature's night;
> On our disordered spirits move,
> And let there now be light![40]

An Apostolic Idealism

The biblical story of God in Israel and in Christ is foundational for Christian faith. But more than foundation is needed. *Orthodox* base is to be accompanied by *radical* relevance. The past is prologue. It is pivotal, but nonetheless preliminary. Believers are to be touched and transformed by a particular past[41] so that they can be positioned to touch the future. The task is to gain true Christian identity, formed by the biblical revela-

---

[40]As quoted by T. Crichton Mitchell, *Charles Wesley: Man with the Dancing Heart* (Kansas City: Beacon Hill Press, 1994), 137-138.

[41]What comes to us from ancient biblical times that can be considered the enduring essence of the Christian faith? Millard Erickson lists five possible answers, each common in church history (*Christian Theology*, vol. 1, Baker Book House, 1983, 108-112). The permanent may be: (1) institutional; (2) a sequence of the historical acts of God, especially the exodus in the Old Testament and the "Christ-Event" in the New; (3) abiding spiritual experiences, such as the universal hope of immortality; (4) a particular way of life; or (5) a set of enduring doctrines, biblically rooted theological propositions that are unchanging and authoritative.

— 113 —

tion as understood in the earliest Christian community, for the sake of Christian life and mission today.

Christian integrity is linked by pioneers of the Church of God movement to a vigorous apostolic idealism. On the cornerstone of a church building in Michigan, used by a congregation of the early movement, was placed an inscription that reads, "The Church of God, Founded A.D. 30." Comments historian John Smith: "The writer was intending to convey a message about the character of the company of people using that building as a meeting place and to identify the point in history which marks the beginning of that kind of fellowship."[42] This particular local body of believers was declaring itself at one with the whole church from the day of its beginning.

For movement leaders, aspirations for the renewal of apostolic integrity in Christian faith, life, and practice have known few bounds. These dedicated disciples have loved God's truth and have wanted to follow wherever they saw it leading. There is no question about their orthodoxy (classic, mainstream Christian stance) in theology. Neither is there doubt about their radical stance in regard to needed changes in approaching Christian experience, church life, and Christian unity. Their approach has centered in (1) the necessity of people experiencing sanctifying power and (2) the results of that power then being applied to altering the typical human structuring and governing of the church. The church is to be a divinely constituted and controlled community, a gifted gathering of the saints, the purified and unified bride of Christ, the church first formed by the resurrected Christ.

Being "apostolic" is crucial. On the other hand, how can contemporary Christians be faithful to historic foundations without blindly romanticizing the past? How can church leaders be

---

[42]John W. V. Smith, *The Quest for Holiness and Unity* (Anderson, Ind.: Warner Press, 1980), ix.

alert to the best of modern or ancient wisdom without idolizing either? God still is active in the searchings and insights of the present, yet God is believed to be known definitively by adherence to apostolic norms declared in the New Testament and formalized by the church "fathers" and ecumenical councils of the church's early centuries. Somehow the issue needs to get beyond being understood as an either-or situation.

The biblical revelation of God with us in particular past times, especially in Jesus Christ, is the believer's special revelation and guide. The past, at least as represented by the biblical narrative about the Christ, remains definitive. Even so, Donald Bloesch warns that we must avoid one of the "pathways to evangelical oblivion," that of becoming "fixated on the past rather than [be] alive to the myriad possibilities that God brings to the church in the here and now."[43] It is no easy task to be both truly apostolic and currently relevant.

Leaders of the Church of God movement have been "liberal" in some ways and "fundamental" in others. They have been on a journey to be apostolic by restoring what they understand to be the true basis of New Testament Christianity. The base of the past, the possibilities of the present, and the freshness of God's future all are affirmed. The apostolic church is judged a priority standard because it reflects the faith at its earliest and purest (though not trouble free) stage. Says historian Charles Brown: "We may safely accept the entire teachings of the Apostles and prophets of the apostolic era, as set forth in the New Testament, as being the standard of gospel doctrine for all time." If such were not the firm standard, Brown argues, "then Christianity is built upon the baseless fabric of subjective imagination and changing human theories."[44]

---

[43]Donald Bloesch, *The Future of Evangelical Christianity* (Doubleday, 1983), 86.

[44]Charles E. Brown, *The Apostolic Church* (Anderson, Ind.: Gospel Trumpet Co., 1947), 29.

The direction of the Church of God movement has been toward a fresh realization of present integrity based on enduring apostolic standards. Being "apostolic pioneers," however, can present a difficult dilemma. Does a restorationist mind-set not lead to a rather mechanical, slavish, and unrealistic imitation of the past, one being remembered only in part and not wholly adequate for what is yet an uncharted future?

Lillie McCutcheon once cautioned: "The difficulty with pioneers is that all too soon they become settlers. . . . Continued change, growth, and development is evidence that we [Church of God] are a movement, not a denomination. Even if it were possible to reproduce the church of the first century, it would obviously be immature and inadequate to serve today's world. . . . God is searching for a body of people who will be fashioned by the Holy Spirit to reveal His design for the church in this age."[45]

The Believers' Church tradition works against the call to any mechanical recovery of an idealized past. To freeze any given set of doctrinal formulations and practices, even those from some stage of the life of the "apostolic church," creates inappropriately a "post-biblical canon."[46] The better, although more ambiguous alternative is a continuing challenge both to affirm historic biblical faithfulness and to engage in present creativity in continuity with the biblical base.

---

[45]As in Barry L. Callen, *The First Century,* vol. 2 (Anderson, Ind.: Warner Press, 1979), 778-779. This observation was made about the Church of God movement as it faced its centennial celebration in 1980.

[46]J. Denny Weaver, *Becoming Anabaptist* (Scottdale, Pa.: Herald Press, 1987), 122, 125. Weaver identifies the regulative principles of Christian faith as (1) Jesus, the norm of truth, (2) the church that follows Jesus as a new social reality, and (3) peace and rejection of violence as the distinctive style of the Jesus way of being the church in the world. See Barry L. Callen, *Thinking and Acting Together* (Anderson, Ind.: Executive [Leadership] Council of the Church of God and Warner Press, 1992), 31-35, for a statement by the movement's General Assembly of the "reformation principles" of the movement (basically a statement of biblical authority).

If not by some mechanical duplication of words, forms, doctrines and practices, just how is the apostolic church to function as the Christian standard for today? Charles Brown employs the analogy of a healthy baby compared to a fully grown adult who is crippled by a disabling disease. That adult hardly needs to recover the ignorance or immaturity of childhood, but rather that childhood's health and normality. Today's church likewise should not imitate the apostolic church in ways not reflective of the massive cultural changes in the intervening centuries. However, "we are under a most heavy responsibility, so far as possible, to reproduce the spiritual life, the truth, the doctrine, the holy equality of the universal priesthood of believers; the warm, rich, deep fellowship; and the burning message of redemption, as well as the overwhelming experiences of the Spirit's complete control of our lives, which were known so well in the apostolic church."[47]

"Primitive" Christianity enjoyed the keen awareness that believers were "living in the presence of the absolute future which has already arrived in the person of Jesus Christ." Therefore, "continuity with the apostles does not mean constructing an irreducible minimum of apostolic doctrines, nor does it mean connecting up with an unbroken chain of apostolic offices of leadership." What then does it mean? It means "to lay hold of the *original eschatological drive of the early Christian apostolate* and to trace its trajectory through the discontinuities of time and history."[48]

This early eschatological drive was rooted solidly in the person and work of Jesus Christ. True primitivism leads back to the Bible, the faithful witness to Jesus Christ. God has spoken in

---

[47]Charles E. Brown, *The Apostolic Church* (Anderson, Ind.: Warner Press, 1947), 31.

[48]Carl E. Braaten, *Principles of Lutheran Theology* (Philadelphia: Fortress Press, 1983), 51.

Jesus Christ who, for the Christian, is the truth. The biblical narrative about Jesus, when enlivened by the Spirit, is the primary avenue to touching and being touched by "apostolic" truth.

Of significance is the fact that the Church of God movement consistently has been "amillennial." With Jesus, the Kingdom has arrived among us (Mark 1:15). In this first advent rests Christian identity and church mission in the world. The church's mission is to be informed and motivated by Christ's first coming, rather than being paralyzed in the present by too heavy a preoccupation with the expectation of Christ's second coming.[49]

Being truly apostolic now is to be about Christ's business of Kingdom building in the enabling wake of the truth and power of the arrival of the Kingdom in Christ's first coming. What, then, is the task of Christian theology? In the words of Jürgen Moltmann, theology "must 'make present' the fundamental historical recollection of Christ, in order to interpret the present in the light of that and to open up the future which is being headed for in that historical past."[50]

Reports Elton Trueblood: "One of the most encouraging ideas which has entered my mind is that we are *early Christians, still alive while the faith is fluid and capable of assuming new forms.*"[51] The faith, ever enduring as the one and only faith once delivered to the saints, is also fresh, definite while yet dynamic, capable of and often needing to assume newly articulated and embodied forms. We contemporary believers indeed are "early

---

[49]See, e.g., Herbert Riggle, *The Kingdom of God and the One Thousand Years Reign* (Moundsville, W.V.: Gospel Trumpet Publishing Co, 1899) and Max Gaulke, *May Thy Kingdom Come—Now!* (Anderson, Ind.: Warner Press, 1959).

[50]Jürgen Moltmann, *Theology Today* (Philadelphia: Trinity Press International, 1988), viii.

[51]D. Elton Trueblood, *While It Is Day* (Harper & Row, 1974), 123-124.

Christians" now living in a secularizing and multi-cultural world.[52] To be early, apostolic, is at once to be close to the origins of the faith and to be facing ahead to a large, unknown, and demanding future of sharing and living out the faith in very new circumstances and probably in some new ways.

Although the New Testament was inspired by the Holy Spirit and therefore is uniquely authoritative for apostolically oriented Christians, the images which appear in the New Testament were "most certainly used because they were needed to elucidate the work of Christ in some particular place and in some special situation."[53] Thus, for believers today to be authentically apostolic includes our being able to distinguish between what is enduring substance and what is dated expression and application. It is to be faithful by seeking to be vitally relevant in needed new expressions and applications. It is being *orthodox* without being rigidly locked into all aspects of a dated past; it is being *radical* without being blindly overwhelmed by all aspects of the shifting present.

An important breakthrough occurred in 1963 at the conference on Faith and Order of the World Council of Churches convened in Montreal, Canada. A crucial distinction was made between church "traditions" and the Christian "Tradition." The delegates came to speak of the goal of ecumenical theology as a recovery of the "Tradition of the Gospel, testified in Scripture, transmitted in and by the Church through the power of the Holy Spirit." The proper task of Christian theology, then, "is not to compare twigs and branches of the Christian tree, but to explore *together* the common trunk. . . . The goal must be to struggle

---

[52]In fact, Justo González sees the situation of today's church as similar to that of its earliest centuries. See his *Christian Thought Revisited* (Nashville: Abingdon Press, 1989), chapter nine.

[53]John Driver, *Understanding the Atonement for the Mission of the Church* (Scottdale, Pa.: Herald Press, 1986), 31.

together to confess the Tradition of the Gospel, not simply to preserve intact our confessional traditions."[54]

Donald Bloesch speaks eloquently of the "confessional theology" he affirms. It is "catholic" and not "reactionary." It advocates "not a return to the past but a critical reappropriation of the wisdom of the past." It espouses "continuity with tradition but is willing to subject even church tradition to the judgment of the Word of God." It, therefore, champions the ancient good news together with the whole community of faith ("evangelical" and "catholic") without being narrowly sectarian or mechanically restorationist.[55] Such confessional theology gladly embraces the message of the biblical revelation, confessing it as the necessary base for an authentic faith today.

Seeing the Church

Given the authority of the Bible, the contemporary illumination of the Spirit, and the important precedent of the apostolic church, the Church of God movement was propelled early by a particular vision of the church. God came to Israel and in Christ to form a people, a community of faith and faithfulness, a united

---

[54]As quoted in Michael Kinnamon in *Baptism & Church,* Merle Strege, ed. (Grand Rapids: Sagamore Books, 1986), 149-150. Kinnamon notes in his *Truth and Community* (Eerdmans, 1988) that biblical scholars Ernst Kasemann and Raymond Brown presented pivotal papers at this 1963 Montreal conference. They stressed the internal variety in the Bible itself, arguing that the Bible "actually canonizes the diversity of Christianity." The Bible, concludes Kinnamon, "frees us from a sterile preoccupation with recovering the shape of the New Testament church and opens us to the possibility of a unity that (following Scripture) is richly diverse and oriented toward the future leading of the Spirit" (1988, 3). Restoration of the apostolic church in our time may vary widely from the specifics of what actually existed in the first and second centuries, all without breaking continuity with that ancient, diverse, itself developing church.

[55]Donald Bloesch, *A Theology of Word & Spirit* (InterVarsity Press), 268. Usually the adjective "confessional" suggests a more fixed and doctrinaire stance than this witness of Bloesch implies.

and rejoicing body of the redeemed that would bring divine light to the nations.

Recalling a story from American church history is helpful. In August, 1801, a communion festival convened in Cane Ridge, Kentucky. This was a revivalistic occasion with a long tradition in Scotch-Irish Presbyterianism and a particular relevance on the American frontier. The host pastor was Barton W. Stone (1772-1844). He rejoiced at the amazing crowd that gathered in this modest rural setting.[56] But more impressive than the number of people was the dramatic evidence of the work of the Holy Spirit that graced this lovely grove.

The extreme emotionalism of some participants in this "revival" brought understandable objections from conservative Presbyterian ministers. Still, as he later reflected on the preaching and the results, Stone was deeply grateful. "All urged faith in the gospel, and obedience to it, as the way of life. The spirit of partyism, and party distinctions, were apparently forgotten. . . . The spirit of love, peace, and union was revived. . . . Happy days! Joyful seasons of refreshment from the presence of the Lord."[57]

The reverberations of this and similar outbursts of spiritual renewal shook the countryside and helped launch the "Christian" movement that later would merge with the work of Thomas and Alexander Campbell, Walter Scott, and others to form the "Disciples" movement. At least for Stone, this movement on behalf of Bible truth and Christian unity stemmed from a vision of the church *beyond division,* made possible by common life in the power of the Spirit of God. "Partyism" was deplored as a cancer

---

[56]Some 10,000—20,000 people participated at a time when Kentucky's largest town, nearby Lexington, had fewer than 2,000 residents.

[57]As quoted by C. Leonard Allen, *Distant Voices: Discovering a Forgotten Past for a Changing Church* (Abilene, Tx.: Abilene Christian University Press, 1993), 11-12.

eating at God's people. Many sects claimed "no creed but the Bible" and still were narrow and exclusive in their attitudes and opinions. Unity, judged Stone, would come only as "Fire Union," when the fire of the Spirit melts hardened attitudes and fills with love even when all of Christ's disciples do not believe exactly alike.[58]

Later in the nineteenth century another reform movement arose with much the same vision as Stone's. This new movement of the Church of God (Anderson, Ind.) spoke often of its vision as "seeing the church."[59] This meant perceiving the identity of the church as the mighty company of all believers redeemed in Christ. These visionary pioneers "saw the Church as a fellowship that transcends all human barriers—race, color, nationality, caste, clan, class, sex, educational level, temperament, or culture. They saw the church, brought together in the 'bond of perfectness,' as the most powerful witness to God's love for all humankind."[60]

John Smith notes six facets of the underlying premise of the early pioneers of this movement, the premise that God was calling them to proclaim and model a visible expression of the one, holy, catholic church. Together these facets were the "light on the church" that these reformers saw. Included were: (1) God had opened to them a vision of the church of God as God intends it to be; (2) the church cannot be identified with any existing sect or denomination; (3) Christians should "come out" of the whole denominational system into an open fellowship of the "saints"; (4) the church is to be holy by its members being holy and

---

[58]Ibid., 19.

[59]For a series of testimonies to having "seen the church," refer to Barry Callen, *The First Century,* I (Warner Press, 1979), 125-240. For a biography of Daniel Warner, most prominent movement pioneer, see Barry Callen, *It's God's Church!* (Anderson, Ind.: Warner Press, 1995).

[60]John W. V. Smith, *I Will Build My Church* (Anderson, Ind.: Warner Press, 1985), 91.

because it is the continuing presence of Christ in the world; (5) since God has a church, not churches, God's ultimate will is a single, united, visible church; and finally, (6) the church should have the quality of openness since the Holy Spirit continues to reveal (always congruent with the biblical revelation), requiring each believer to be open to "light" and to "walk" in the light that she or he currently has.[61]

In 1895 Daniel Warner, pioneer leader of the Church of God movement, wrote a song called "The Bond of Perfectness." It is a poetic celebration of the intimate relationship seen between the life-changing work of the Spirit ("perfectness" or sanctification) and unity among all true Christian believers. What Warner saw, much as Stone had seen earlier, was "how this perfect love unites us all in Jesus."[62] According to this vision, unity is not rooted in common beliefs so much as in common life in the Spirit. In no way is this to suggest that orthodox belief is of no consequence; it is to suggest the more radical view that Christian faith, being inwardly transforming, should enable a precious oneness that is a gift of God—even when understandings of various doctrinal subjects differ.[63]

---

[61]John W. V. Smith, *The Quest for Holiness and Unity* (Anderson, Ind.: Warner Press, 1980), 88-94.

[62]See the full hymn text in *Worship the Lord* (Anderson, Ind.: Warner Press, 1989), 330.

[63]Even unity movements motivated by a hymn like that of Warner in 1895 are subject to subtle party spirits of their own. Historian Merle Strege identifies the 1923 song of Charles Naylor, titled "The Church's Jubilee," as a shift by the Church of God movement toward a unity conceived more on the basis of common beliefs (*Tell Me the Tale,* Anderson, Ind.: Warner Press, 1991, 33). See the text of "The Church's Jubilee" in *Worship the Lord* (Anderson, Ind: Warner Press, 1989), 312. Much in the actual hymn text does not necessarily suggest such a shift. The language "all we are equal in his [God's] sight when we obey His Word" is followed by "no earthly master do we know, to Christ alone we bow" and "we reach our hands in fellowship to every blood-washed one." However, the song has been heard by some as virtually a sectarian marching song of the Church of God movement.

Robert Richardson, friend and biographer of Alexander Campbell, noted a distinctive stance common to the Christian (Disciples) and Church of God movements:

> We differ from all the parties here in one important particular. . . . It is this: That while they suppose this Christian faith to be *doctrinal,* we regard it as *personal.* In other words, they suppose doctrines, or religious tenets, to be the subject-matter of this faith; we, on the contrary, conceive it to terminate on a person—the Lord Jesus Christ Himself. While they, accordingly require an elaborate confession from each convert—a confession mainly of a doctrinal and intellectual character . . . we demand only a simple confession of Christ—a heartfelt acknowledgment that Jesus is the Messiah, the Son of God.[64]

An assumption behind this vision is that, when believers confess with one voice that "Jesus is Lord" and then are linked in the Spirit by divine love, they will see and seek to function as the united church that is God's and not their own. This is an optimistic vision, however, that has to face the pessimistic realism of a Reinhold Niebuhr.

Niebuhr argues convincingly that a sharp distinction should be made between the moral and social behavior of individuals and that of social groups. Human societies are more susceptible to "unrestrained egoism."[65] Presumably even the church, itself a social group, inevitably is a mixture of good and evil, an "impossible possibility" that struggles to avoid embodying within itself the tenacious evil of this fallen world. Niebuhr emphasizes that

---

[64]Robert Richardson, *The Principles and Objects of the Religious Reformation, Urged by A. Campbell and Others* (Bethany, W. Va.: 1853), 26. This emphasis, consistent with the Jesus-as-norm emphasis of the Believers' Church tradition, cautions away from creedalism, churchism, biblicism, etc.

[65]Reinhold Niebuhr, *Moral Man and Immoral Society* (N.Y.: Charles Scribner's Sons, 1932), xi.

the cross of Christ shows the depth of the human predicament and that human perfection is not attainable in human history.[66]

This sobering analysis has justification. Still, if indeed the church is an outgrowth of the power of God's Kingdom already arrived in Jesus, then the church as an "eschatological" community is linked *now* with that which *yet will be*. It is called to be evidence now, by word and deed, of the character and rule of God that already is breaking barriers (like the unrestrained egoism of the usual social groupings of the world). Christian believers are to enter into covenant with God and each other (the church) so that together they can become a "fellowship called into existence in order to pioneer in the present the principles that characterize the reign of God."[67] The church as a social grouping is *intended to be* and therefore, by God's grace, *can be* a sign that the humanly impossible is becoming present reality through the work of the Spirit. As this transition from intention to actuality happens, the true church increasingly comes into being.

Pioneers of the Church of God movement observed how the world of denominational division is sad evidence of the fallenness that plagues even those who seek to represent Christ. But to this pessimism, the hard lesson of the cross, should be added the wonderful news of Christ's resurrection and the Spirit's coming. To Niebuhr's understandable distrust of all social groups should

[66]Reinhold Niebuhr, *Nature and Destiny of Man,* II (N.Y.: Charles Scribner's Sons, 1943), 68.

[67]Stanley Grenz, *Revisioning Evangelical Theology* (Downers Grove, Ill.: InterVarsity Press, 1993), 183. Grenz calls this a "process model" of the church since its life is constituted "by neither its past nor its present, but its future. What the church is, is determined by what the church is destined to become. And the church is directed toward the destiny God intends for humankind: participation in the consummated reign of God" (183). In similar fashion the Roman Catholic Church's Vatican Council II in the 1960s described the church as a "sign and sacrament" of the Kingdom *(Dogmatic Constitution on the Church).*

be added the promise of Christ's presence in the community of faith as it struggles, by the power of the Holy Spirit, to reflect and further Christ's lordship in the church and the world. To the pessimism of sin should be added the optimism of grace (a Wesleyan emphasis). Capitulation to the presumed inevitability of sin, implied in the typical Protestant concept of the "invisible church," should be countered with the optimism of transforming, sanctifying grace. Both individuals and the church itself need to be and can be sanctified. The availability of such transforming grace enables a *visible* church that, in its life of holiness, unity, witness, and service, actually reflects a triumph of Christ in this evil world.[68] The issue is discipleship, a following of Christ that is truly Christian only as it embodies, concretely and visibly, the will and way of Jesus.

A radical discipleship is at the core of the Believers' Church tradition.[69] If Lutheranism is a tradition focused on the search for a merciful God despite the ugly face of human sin (how can we be saved?), Anabaptism "developed around the

----

[68]Note a telling statement by Nietzsche: "They would have to sing better songs to make me believe in their Redeemer: his [Christ's] disciples would have to look more redeemed!" (quoted by Hans Küng, *The Church,* N. Y.: Sheed & Ward, 1967, 150). Being "invisible" undercuts effective mission. Thomas Oden says: "Some have concluded that the nature of the church is something like Plato's vision of an ideal moral community that, though as yet unrealized, is known in our minds as a powerful, moving idea. Classical Christian exegetes repeatedly have disclaimed this understanding of the church, due to its docetic lack of visibility, presentness, and historical palpability" *(Life in the Spirit,* S. F.: Harper, 1992, 329). Wyclif, Hus, and Luther rightly opposed a reduction of the church to a culture-entwined, medieval institution. Their intent, however, was to reform and not abandon the church in its mission to be a very visible presence in human society. Baptism, the Lord's Supper, and the symbolic washing of feet are some of the available means to authentic Christian visibility.

[69]See Harold Bender, "The Anabaptist Vision," *Mennonite Quarterly Review* 18 (1944), 67-88.

central idea of a righteous walk with the Lord after the experience of repentance and rebirth"[70] (how should we then live?). Discipleship also is key to the Wesleyan tradition. John Wesley identified the required conditions for membership in the early Methodist movement this way: " 'Is a man a believer in Jesus Christ, and is his life suitable to his profession?' are not only the *main* but the *sole* inquiries I make in order to his admission into our Society."[71] In this light, faith that is truly Christian will be both orthodox in rootage and radical in application.

For the Church of God movement, this visibility of effectual grace has been affirmed in relation both to individual disciples and to the integrity of the life of the church itself. In 1939 Charles Brown wrote *The Church Beyond Division,* an exposition of the biblical picture of Christ's people united (as intended) in the Spirit. It put in prose the vision of the church that Charles Naylor and Andrew Byers put poetically and musically in one of the loved heritage hymns of the Church of God movement:

> The church of God one body is,
> One Spirit dwells within;
> And all her members are redeemed,
> And triumph over sin.
> O church of God! I love thy courts,
> Thou mother of the free;
> Thou blessed home of all the saved,
> I dwell content in thee.[72]

Believers need the inspiration of such a vision that "sees the church" in a way that fits the grace-filled idealism of the New Testament and leads to a visible expression that encourages the world

---

[70]John Oyer, *Lutheran Reformers Against the Anabaptists* (The Hague: Martinus Nijhoff, 1964), 212.

[71]As quoted in Albert Outler, ed., *John Wesley* (N.Y.: Oxford University Press, 1964), 78.

[72]Hymn "O Church of God" in *Worship the Lord* (Anderson, Ind.: Warner Press, 1989), 289.

to believe. Biblically based, visibility oriented, and styled for our postmodern times, elements of such a vision come helpfully from two theologians, Hans Küng of the Roman Catholic Church and Gilbert Stafford of the Church of God movement. Küng offers four perspectives. The church has a future when it is seen: (1) connected to its origins and the present, not infatuated with the past; (2) free of patriarchy (restricted gender roles usually favoring males) and released to partnership; (3) open ecumenically as opposed to being bound denominationally; and (4) released from its one-sided Eurocentric mentality (nearly exclusive European and American cultural and theological orientation) so that it can be enriched by and be relevant to the universal church.[73]

On what basis can such a vision be realized? On the foundation of Jesus Christ (1 Cor. 3:11) who alone is "the way, and the truth, and the life" (Jn. 14:6). Accordingly, Gilbert Stafford shares a ten-part vision for the church today, also based on key biblical considerations. He sees a church:

1. . . . rejoicing in the grace of God revealed in Christ, a church sitting at the feet of Jesus, a church in community with the church through the centuries and in community with the church throughout the world;

2. . . . discovering the richness of its diverse traditions of the worship of the triune God;

3. . . . praying for each other across the lines of traditions and working with each other for commonly held goals of ministry;

4. . . . committed to biblical scholarship which transcends vested interests, participating in theological discussions which focus on the message(s) of the biblical canon for faith and order, life and work, mission and witness, and a church which facilitates the hearing, reading, study and use of Scrip-

---

[73]Hans Küng, *Reforming the Church Today* (N.Y.: Crossroad, 1990), 155-163.

ture in such a way that each part of the church has a sense of being related to the whole (e.g., the common lectionary);

5. . . . listening to what the Spirit says to the churches (Rev. 2-3). In that the church in all of its variety is ministered to by the Holy Spirit, every historically particularized church (confessional family, denomination, movement, ethnic church, national church) needs to hear what the Spirit is saying to it through all other historically particularized churches;

6. . . . in which never-ending biblical, historical, doctrinal, theological studies and conversations are taking place between and among scholars of all Christian traditions, scholars who are well informed by their own respective traditions and able to contribute to and receive from others of "like precious faith" (2 Pet. 1:1, KJV);

7. . . . in which the aim of our conversations is the eventual convergence of understandings regarding matters of faith, rather than the imposition of legislative decisions;

8. . . . gathered at the one table of the Lord; possessing a common identification; living the holy life; united in mission and witness; committed to the integrative compatibility of services, structures and ministries; and expressing mutual love in diversity;

9. . . . which both works for and looks forward to the universal reign of justice and righteousness and the redemption of the whole created order;

10. . . . which anticipates the eschatological worship of the triune God . . . (Rev. 7:9-12).[74]

Here is a pattern of Christian insights and deep longings that forms a vision of the church as it ought to be, a pilgrim church seeking the better way pictured in the Bible. Eschatological perspective is what enlivens vision in the present. This perspective is exemplified well by Justo González's use of the *mañana* concept

---

[74]Gilbert Stafford, paper for discussion, Ecclesiology Study Group, Faith and Order, National Council of Churches, March 19-20, 1993, Berkeley, California.

in a contemporary Hispanic setting. He notes how the dominant culture in North America has used this word to characterize Hispanics as listless and lazy people (why do today what can be put off until tomorrow?). But the word means more than "tomorrow." It brings into sharp question what is unacceptable today and puts it alongside God's promise that is yet unfulfilled.

There is a *"mañana* vision of Scripture" that sees God doing a new thing, so that the hope of tomorrow already is happening today! *Mañana* may not yet be today, but "today can be lived out of the glory and the promise of *mañana,* thanks to the power of the Spirit."[75] Being the body of Christ requires a deriving of our life from the ruler of the coming order, thus living now in God's community as priests and kings (1 Pet. 2:9; Rev. 1:6; 5:10). The church is a pilgrim people set on a sure way because of the death and resurrection of Jesus Christ, "made present by the Spirit, and made certain by the power and the promise of none other than God Almighty!"[76]

To see this clearly is surely to see the church rightly. To see the church rightly is certainly a timely witness in our kind of world. Michael Kinnamon's words are crucial:

> In a world seemingly bent on self-destruction, in a world where empathy seems so often confined to members of like-minded enclaves, in a world that appears to live more by fear than by hope, the ecumenical vision of Christ's one body, living as sign and foretaste of God's *shalom,* is not an optional commitment, not a luxury that is conveniently demoted on our ecclesiastical lists of priorities, not something best left to experts on the nuances of theological debate. It is an inescapable and indispensable part of what it means to be the church God wills.[77]

---

[75]Justo González, *Mañana: Christian Theology from a Hispanic Perspective* (Nashville: Abingdon Press, 1990), 164.

[76]Ibid., 166-167.

[77]Michael Kinnamon, *Truth and Community: Diversity and Its Limits in the Ecumenical Movement* (Grand Rapids: Eerdmans, 1988), 118.

CHAPTER FOUR

Fruits

The whole point of Christian theology is to assist Christians to be who they are meant to be and do what they are meant to do. Discipleship and mission are central; the fruit of faith is the goal. Adequate theology finally is *incarnational*. The intent is to change the world, not merely analyze and talk about it. The change will come only when believers in Jesus Christ experience new creation and then live before the world the Christ-life in all its individual and corporate integrity. According to an ancient prayer of Jesus: "Your [God's] will be done, *on earth* as in heaven" (Lk. 11:2).

Christianity is an *incarnational* faith. Believers are to be on a journey toward holiness, in quest of oneness, for the purposes of redemption, reconciliation, and peace. All of these are fruits of life in and through the Spirit of God.

Incarnational Integrity

The Church of God movement has had an important focus for its approach to the whole range of Christian believing. Though emerging over time and often not articulated clearly, there has been a distinctive way in which movement leaders have perceived theological issues. To identify this approach, to find this focus, is to enable an appropriate understanding of Christian theology, at least as this particular, visionary body of Christians understands and seeks to embody it.

Randy Maddox observes rightly that, to be "systematic," theology must have an *integrating principle* by which it tends to judge and formulate any particular doctrine. He suggests "responsible grace" as such a principle for understanding the extensive work of John Wesley.[1] I suggest that the principle that in large part has tended to inform theological thinking in the Church of God movement is *incarnational integrity.* The concern is to realize *in the present* the call of Christ for his disciples to be authentic representatives of the coming Kingdom that already has arrived in Jesus. Holiness for the individual means genuine set-apartness so that one's very life becomes a living sacrifice. For the church it means being a visible, united, Spirit-directed presence of the Kingdom of God, an alternative to the patterns and powers of the world. In both cases it means incarnational integrity, a congruence of divine intent and actual occurrence in the world by the power of the Spirit. This is the *radical,* the *responsible* dimension of having received divine grace.

Making visible the *isness* of the *shall be* of God's reign in fallen creation has highlighted for the Church of God movement an eschatological dimension to all of Christian thought and life, just as is the case in the New Testament. For the movement, this dimension typically has taken the form of a transdenominational quest for the realization of Christian holiness and unity.[2] This quest has been a pilgrimage toward actually incarnating through the Spirit the present reign of God in the individual lives of believers and in the corporate life of the church.

The movement's central concern for incarnational integrity tends to follow the burden of the New Testament book of James.

---

[1]Randy Maddox, "Responsible Grace: The Systematic Perspective of Wesleyan Theology," *Wesleyan Theological Journal* 19:2 (Fall, 1984), 7-22. See Maddox, *Responsible Grace: The Practical Theology of John Wesley* (Nashville: Kingswood Books, Abingdon Press, 1994). Note also Thomas Oden, another contemporary Wesleyan scholar, who points to the pervasive role of divine grace (*The Transforming Power of Grace,* Nashville: Abingdon Press, 1993).

[2]The most recent narrative history of the Church of God movement is written by John Smith and titled *The Quest for Holiness and Unity* (Anderson, Ind.: Warner Press, 1980).

James lacked patience with two forms of pseudo-faith, twin infections that often seem to plague the community of Christ. One false form is a faith that is little more than an intellectual assent to some creedal formula. In this case a believer merely mouths the words of sacred tradition and comes to perpetuate only a barren and lifeless orthodoxy. Even demons, says James, can believe like this (2:19)! There is no incarnational integrity here.

The other unacceptable form may be even worse. It is faith that accepts in theory the radical life demands of true Christian discipleship, but still manages to deny them by actual practice (2:16). Pioneers of the Church of God movement have called vigorously for a *practical* holiness and a *united* church. When God's grace yields visible fruit in the believer and in the corporate life of the church, only then do Christians really express incarnational integrity. Such integrity can stop the church from mocking its own mission by the failures of its own life.

Incarnational integrity as a focusing theological vision (1) hopes to be fully faithful to all that is "orthodox" in the Christian tradition, (2) seeks to avoid judging what is "orthodox" by any blind obedience to the accumulation of human traditions, creeds, and church organizations, and (3) determines to put into actual practice in all of life the radical implications of the faith. Orthodoxy should not be equated with any establishment, civil or churchly. The preferred path of judgment has been more through the "radical" approach of (1) returning to the roots of the faith historically and (2) realizing experientially the transforming essence of the faith in opposition to the frequent corruptions of the power arrangements within the church or between church and state.

Movement leaders, for example, have insisted repeatedly that what God intends is hardly an "invisible church." Such a phrase often is used in Protestant circles to distinguish the true church from the maze of churchly organizations and structures

— 133 —

that dot the landscape. Surely, movement leaders have reasoned, God desires genuinely new creations in Christ, redeemed people who gather visibly as Christ's body on earth and act together as agents of the now-come and yet-coming Kingdom of God. While not of this world (i.e., holy), such disciples and the church they comprise are to have wonderful news for this world--and they themselves are to be obvious and credible representatives of this news. The task is to make the true church *very visible indeed* through inspired discipleship, a life obviously different from the world's standards.

Christian incarnational integrity is not to be valued for its own sake. Mission is the primary motive. Unity among believers is God's intention because it is a crucial prerequisite to any credible church mission. Holiness also is God's intention, something providing the only viable way to true Christian unity. Achieving such holiness and unity is viewed as an ongoing quest for God's intended integrity in Christian life. Any success will be a gift of divine grace, the result of the power of transforming and uniting spiritual experience enabled by a gracious God.

Such transforming experience, it is believed, can enable humble and repentant persons to transcend their broken relationships with God (sanctification) and then go on to enable a transcending of their denominational loyalties for the sake of their common Christian mission for Christ (Christian unity). Integrity is required both for the individual, a new creation in Christ, and for the church, the company of the newly created ones shaped by the same biblical revelation, united by the common experience of divine grace, and joined in common mission.

These emphases share much with a recent call for the integrity of God's people as they seek to live out their role as "resident aliens" in this secularized world of the late twentieth century.[3] There must be a renewed confidence in the compelling

---

[3]Stanley Hauerwas and William Willimon, *Resident Aliens* (Nashville: Abingdon Press, 1989).

distinctiveness of central Christian convictions as conveyed by the formative stories of the faith within a committed Christian community. The needed integrity goes beyond the content of what believers remember of divine revelation and what they say they believe theologically based on that revelation. It should reach to a *transformed identity* as believers together, to the realization of a united "colony of heaven" that is responding to and being changed and sent by God's grace.

How do Christians realize true community? What life do they actually model in the world? As answers are sought, what is the problem being faced?

> The biggest problem facing Christian theology is not translation but enactment. . . . No clever theological moves can be substituted for the necessity of the church being a community of people who embody our language about God, where talk about God is used without apology because our life together does not mock our words.[4]

Theology is needed again, urgently, at the very center of church life. Its task is to raise the crucial question of the church's identity in alien surroundings and to answer this question afresh in light of Christ, the only real answer. If this theological process fails to occur, except by a few isolated specialists, the secular society will slowly absorb the church into its own culture and direct it toward secular ends. As David Yeago warns: "To escape this cooption, to have anything distinctive and interesting to contribute to our age, the church must have a mind of its own and a life of its own, and the *thinking* that goes on in that mind and accompanies that life is theology."[5]

In an important way, then, the traditional theological tasks are expanded here from two to three. There is something crucial

---

[4]Ibid., 171.

[5]David Yeago, "A Church with a Mind of Its Own: Theology and the Church Today," *Dialog* (Summer, 1992), 223.

beyond *biblical-apostolic* foundation, the formative revelation, and *contemporary translation* into meaningful concepts and language, the current conceptual challenge. Added is the task of *enactment,* embodiment, visible and viable demonstration of the *fruit* of orthodox, biblically faithful, and cognitively coherent theology. Christian theologians must *be* Christians in the doing of their theology. The Christian church must *be* the church as it remembers, thinks, reformulates, and acts in the world. In 1947, for example, Charles Brown published his significant book, *The Apostolic Church,* helping the Church of God movement gain increased insight into its authoritative base and reforming role.[6] The goal is to *be* the church again, not merely to remember it properly or to speak of it accurately. Incarnational integrity finally lies in *being.*

A glaring church agenda item, one that vigorously grasped pioneers of the Church of God movement like Daniel Warner between 1880 and 1895, was *incarnational integrity.* This central concern tended to focus on two doctrines, both life centered and experience oriented. One was *holiness,* the integrity of the individual Christian's spiritual experience and life; the other was *unity,* the integrity of the resulting life of the church itself. Regarding holiness, the rich insights of the Wesleyan theological tradition came to be valued highly as an appropriate source for understanding biblical teaching.[7] That heritage was accepted as affirming accurately much of the biblical vision of the depths of human sin and the heights of available divine grace that can both forgive and release from such sin.

---

[6]Charles Brown, *The Apostolic Church* (Anderson, Ind.: Warner Press, 1947).

[7]The Wesleyan theological tradition that was so influential was, of course, the form of that tradition popularized in American revivalism. See Melvin Dieter, *The Holiness Revival of the Nineteenth Century* (Metuchen, N.J.: The Scarecrow Press, 1980).

Regarding unity, leaders of the movement went beyond the Wesleyan tradition to many of the theological views and orientations found in the "restorationist" and "radical reformation" or "believers' church" traditions. The integrity of the Christian life should lead to and be nurtured in the context of the church, the gathering of redeemed believers who are seeking "sanctification" so that their life together can be reflective of the fruits of faith. The church, to be its intended self, must be formed by divine grace, governed by the Holy Spirit, and struggle to stand above the control of human desires, institutions, states, and traditions. Only in this way can it exhibit in its own visible life the integrity intended by God as a radical witness to the world. This church integrity is understood to have been modeled well by the "apostolic" church.

Personal spiritual transformation, is central, but only dependable as authoritative for faith when informed, interpreted, and controlled by the inspired biblical record. The earliest "experience" in the Christian community was a recognition of the Kingdom of God that already had arrived in Jesus. The joyous announcement was made that, in Jesus Christ, the final age of human history had been inaugurated. It was "already" present, and it was "not yet" fully consummated. It was the Kingdom of God to be experienced now and expected later. The Kingdom of God has come in Jesus' coming, and the Kingdom will come when Jesus comes. While still future, it is really present. Luke used the phrase "kingdom of God" thirty-two times in his Gospel and another six times in Acts. For him "it means the sovereign will of God in operation. Where God is King, his will is done."[8]

Church of God movement leaders have focused on this present/future paradox and affirmed it gladly. Because of a

---

[8]Leon Morris, *New Testament Theology* (Grand Rapids: Zondervan, Academie Books, 1986), 146.

strong sense of obligation to the *present integrity* of Christian discipleship (living the real presentness of the Kingdom), they have tended, as does the Gospel of John, to stress especially the *nowness* of the future. There will be no Kingdom membership later if there is no Kingdom reality now. The Logos has come to be among us. God is revealed and continues to be powerfully and purposefully present. "Eternal life" is available as a present gift to the faithful believer. It will be received, celebrated, and incarnated now or it will not be a future privilege.

Developments in both biblical and systematic theology have demonstrated that "eschatology is not an addendum to theology but a truth that weaves its way through the warp and woof of the whole system; almost every major doctrine has an eschatological aspect."[9] Therefore, "the soundest biblical scholarship . . . holds to a dualistic view that teaches that the reign of God is both present and future."[10] Accordingly, Thomas Finger proposes that theological reflection in the twentieth century begin, in a sense, at the end. Why? Because in the New Testament "the eschatological atmosphere of the 'already/not-yet' pervades every action and thought. . . . In short the eschatological expectations of the first Christians bestowed a unique vantage point from which to view every dimension of reality and a unique impulsion to act in light of this hope."[11]

Jesus' resurrection was the beginning of the end. It both introduced and anticipates the eschaton and became the very basis for the Christian hope (1 Pet. 1:3). The hope-producing good news is that God remains the source of resurrection through the power of Christ's Spirit (Rom. 8:11; 1 Cor. 6:14, 15:22). For those in Christ, this resurrection life is already at work (Eph. 1:19b-20), forming a Kingdom sphere of existence

---

[9]H. Ray Dunning, Grace, *Faith & Holiness* (Kansas City: Beacon Hill Press, 1988), 13.

[10]Ibid., 390.

as faith and obedience are exercised. A transforming foretaste of what ultimately will be comes from the future into the present, making all things new for faithful believers and the church.

The passage 1 Corinthians 7:29-31 raises problems for contemporary interpreters, unless, that is, Paul's eschatological orientation is considered. Paul's comments on marriage, slavery, and celibacy appear to raise hard questions. Is the reason for marriage merely sexual? Are we to mimic Paul's quietism about slavery and opportunities for freedom? Is the unmarried person really a better servant of Jesus than the married person? The answers lie in Paul's view that the present form of the world is passing away (v. 31). The world's institutions and social arrangements have no longterm future. Current allegiances are lameduck. Believers *are* to be involved in worldly relationships, but in a carefully detached way. The social structures of the world have significance *only in a provisional sense.* Knowing that the world is passing away creates a freedom that avoids the believer being trapped by the world's structures. Christians need not divest themselves of all valuable possessions and relationships, for instance, but there should be no ultimate attachment to them.

The Church of God movement is one group in the holiness tradition that consistently and exclusively has affirmed an "amillennial" position regarding the nature of God's future actions on this earth.[12] In the movement's first years the early return of Christ was expected—not to set up an earthly kingdom, but to

[11]Thomas Finger, *Christian Theology: An Eschatological Approach,* vol. 1 (Scottdale, Pa.: Herald Press, 1985), 102-03.

[12]That is, the Kingdom focus is on the intended reign of Christ-generated spiritual reality now, rather than on a political/military expectation to last a thousand years just before or after Christ's second coming. See, e.g., H. M. Riggle, *The Kingdom of God and The One Thousand Years Reign* (Moundsville, W.V.: Gospel Trumpet Co., 1899), and Russell R. Byrum, *Christian Theology,* rev. ed. (Anderson, Ind.: Warner Press, 1925, 1982), 519ff.

initiate the final judgment and the end of the world. The true church was believed to be the Kingdom made visible in the present. She was being cleansed, gathered into one, made bold for mission, and readied for the return of the bridegroom. The Kingdom of God is spiritual in nature and is to be manifested now in the life of God's church on earth ("spiritual" is not the same as unreal or invisible!). The church is to be pure and one, characterized by holiness and unity, the marks of *present integrity.*

Jesus began His ministry by announcing that "the time is fulfilled, and the kingdom of God is at hand" (Mark 1:15). Jesus accomplished His earthly ministry by exercising kingdom prerogatives (Matt. 12:28) and calling on His disciples to do the same in His name. The kingdom is "the area in which men [and women] are alive in God, motivated by his universal law of love to God and neighbor, and completely captivated by his reign."[13] Thus, the deep prayer of Kingdom citizens, Christians, should be an echo of the prayer of Jesus that the Father's Kingdom come and will be done *"on earth* as it is in heaven" (Matt. 6:10).

Theology has been seen less as a theoretical and systematizing enterprise and more as a *moral* enterprise that cares deeply about who Christian people have been and who they now should be as individuals and together as the church. Merle Strege, for instance, writes his *Tell Me The Tale* in the form of historical vignettes in an attempt "to display to the church some of its deepest moral convictions in a narrative mode and with a self-consciously theological purpose."[14] Such an approach to Christian theology, lying very close to the distinctive vision and special burden of the Church of God movement, fulfills the view of theology held by Johann Arndt (1555-1621), the German

---

[13]Max Gaulke, *May Thy Kingdom Come—Now!* (Anderson, Ind.: Gospel Trumpet Co., 1959), 121.

[14]Merle Strege, *Tell Me The Tale* (Anderson, Ind.: Warner Press, 1991), xiv.

Lutheran who prepared the way for Pietism. As Strege quotes Arndt: "Many think that theology is a mere science, or rhetoric, whereas it is a living experience and practice."[15] It is, in fact, to be the experience and life of *holiness*.

Journey Toward Holiness

The work of the Spirit of God is the creation of new life. The Gospel of John identifies the Spirit as the agent of the second birth of all believers in Christ (Jn. 3:3-8).[16] The Spirit also liberates (2 Cor. 3:17), a continuation of the freeing work of Christ (Gal. 5:1).[17] Such liberation leads not to erratic individualism, but to new and Spirit-disciplined community. The Spirit unites believers to Christ and to each other, launching a new communal existence, the church of God, the Pentecost people.

Salvation understood broadly includes deliverance "(1) immediately from the *penalty* of sin, (2) progressively from the *plague* of sin, (3) and then eschatologically from the very *presence* of sin and its effects."[18] In relation to individual believers, the work of the Spirit involves justification (penalty), sanctification (plague), and vocation (mission).[19] Being delivered from

---

[15]Ibid., xiii.

[16]Jesus told Nicodemus that one sees the Kingdom of God only by being born of "water and the spirit" (Jn. 3:5). He was emphasizing "that the way into life is not by human striving . . . but by a work of the Spirit of God. . . . Jesus did not come simply to tell people to try harder but to bring them new life by the Spirit" (Leon Morris, *New Testament Theology*, Grand Rapids: Academie Books, Zondervan, 1986, 258).

[17]This liberation is a grace-granted freedom from guilt, legalism, and eventually even death. It also is a freedom to act, to risk as a servant, to live in gratitude, hope, and joy rather than in self-seeking and self-justification.

[18]Randy Maddox, *Responsible Grace: John Wesley's Practical Theology* (Nashville: Kingswood Books, Abingdon Press, 1994), 143. See John Wesley's 1765 sermon "The Scripture Way of Salvation."

[19]This three-part approach to viewing the Christian life follows in general the outline of Karl Barth's description (*Church Dogmatics*, IV/1-3).

sin's very presence (glorification) waits the time beyond this life. Together these comprise the human journey toward holiness, being set apart for God, increasingly even becoming like God "in Christ."

The believer's journey toward becoming a redeemed new creation in Christ should not be overly formularized.[20] For the purposes of overview and analysis, however, we review briefly four of its central aspects—justification, sanctification, vocation, fruit and gifts of the Spirit.

Justification. Christian life is grounded in the grace of God. It is based on the completed work of Christ made effective by the continuing work of the Spirit. With the assumption of the open door of prevenient grace and the goal of transformation into the likeness of Christ, justification begins with God's forgiveness that releases the contrite heart from the guilt of committed sin. Regeneration or rebirth is then received through faith alone (Rom. 3:23-28). Believers are justified, restored to right relationship with God by God's initiative of sheer, unmerited grace *(sola gratia)*, and by the response of faith and trust *(sola fide)*.

Salvation is righted relationship. It is being "saved" by true friendship with Jesus. In the Gospel of John a friend is pictured as more than a mere acquaintance. Friendship is full of the deep relatedness of empathy that expresses itself in mutual struggle and support. Jesus refers to His disciples as friends (Jn. 15:15). Friends of Jesus are those who know that they are loved and chosen by their Lord, the One who laid down His life for them (Jn. 15:13). Friends of Jesus are those who, in the fullness of right relationship, love as they are loved and find their own path-

---

[20]Formularizing has been a persistent temptation of revivalism. Spiritual experience becomes standardized, set in clear time sequences. The dynamic working of God and individual differences, however, resist such artificial systematizing.

way brightened by the divine presence (Jn. 14:26). Friends of Jesus are those whose lives have been renewed because they have been captured by the transforming power of the biblical revelation. They have followed the plot from the cross to the empty tomb, and now, in the Spirit's coming, they are finding the light of Friend Jesus, ever present as the Spirit, to guide their way in this world and beyond. It is all by divine grace, made effective by the believer's response of faith and faithfulness.

It is important that the church not misread Scripture and itself assume the place of the sole initiative of God in forgiving sins. Jesus called for his disciples to receive the Holy Spirit and then announced that "if you forgive the sins of any, they are forgiven them; if you retain the sins of any, they are retained" (John 20:23). The observation of Leon Morris is crucial: "the verbs . . . are both in the perfect tense. Jesus is saying that when the Spirit-filled church pronounces that such and such sins are forgiven, it will be found that forgiveness has already taken place. He [Jesus] is not giving the church the power to do it then and there. The Spirit enables the church to declare authoritatively what God has done in the matter of forgiving or withholding forgiveness."[21]

We humans continue to pursue many futile attempts at self-justification. How desperately we need and want lives that are

---

[21]Leon Morris, *New Testament Theology*, 265. Boyce Blackwelder, prominent New Testament scholar of the Church of God movement, agrees with Morris. Fearing "sacerdotalism," the placing in the hands of establishment Christianity the apparent power to forgive sins, Blackwelder also turned to Greek grammar. The "if you retain" then the sins "are retained," he argues, are not simple future tenses. They are "future perfect passive participles" to be translated "whatever you may bind on earth shall have been bound in heaven." See his *Light from the Greek New Testament* (Anderson, Ind.: Warner Press, 1958, 75; reprint Baker Book House, 1976). Whether or not his judgment about the significance of the tense used is grammatically overdrawn, his central point is significant. No earthly institution or its representative can "make pronouncements which heaven is bound to ratify" (76).

meaningful and acceptable. We think and work in ways we hope will win the approval of others. The drive to belong and succeed is strong in our competitive Western societies. We strive to "make it," to acquire or accomplish in order to feel understood, valued, and loved. Paul Tillich addresses this with his fresh statement of the Christian doctrine of justification as taught earlier by Martin Luther and John Calvin. "Just accept the fact that you are accepted," Tillich says, "accepted by a power that is greater than you."[22]

Sanctification. Teachers in the Church of God movement have held, in common with Protestantism in general, this emphasis on justification by grace alone (not by any human works of merit). They have affirmed more, however. The goal of God is the *holiness* of all creation. In fact, the first book authored by a leader of the Church of God movement was *Bible Proofs of the Second Work of Grace*.[23]

John and Charles Wesley certainly were committed to the concern of the Western church for justification. They argue that people cannot be delivered from the *power* of sin (its plague) until first they are delivered from the *guilt* of sin (its penalty). Even so, the burden of the Methodist revival was "Christian perfection." This attempt to unite "pardon" and "participation" may be John Wesley's greatest contribution to the ecumenical dia-

---

[22]Paul Tillich, *The Shaking of the Foundations* (N.Y.: Scribner's, 1948), 162.

[23]Written by Daniel S. Warner (Goshen, Ind.: E. U. Mennonite Publishing Society, 1880). He wrote: "Perfection, as applied to redeemed souls, denotes the complete moral restoration of man from the effects of the fall. Not physical, or mental restoration, for that will not be until the resurrection; but, as David says, *'He restoreth my soul.'* Restore means to bring back to its original condition, [to] its former purity, and Divine likeness. Christian perfection is, therefore, in *kind* and not in degree. In other words, it is the perfection of our moral nature, and not the development or full growth of our powers" (18).

logue.[24] He bridged the Western and Eastern churches, especially by acceptance of the Greek Orthodox stress on "deification," a human participation in the divine life that increasingly transfigures the believer into the image of Christ.[25] Saving grace is both grace as *pardon* and grace as *power.*

Sanctifying grace is the culminating phase of the Christian teaching of salvation. Jesus prayed that those justified persons who already were His disciples might also be sanctified by God's presence and truth (Jn. 17:17). The church's task is to teach and live "so that we may present everyone mature *[teleion]* in Christ" (Col. 1:28).[26] The purpose of the work of the Holy Spirit is to enable believers to become "holy" by loving and serving God as originally intended.

Some historical perspective is helpful. The Church of God movement has used the word "sect" to identify unjustified divisiveness within the church. Ernst Troeltsch, however, defines this word more sociologically. A sect is a voluntary society composed of Christians who have been born anew and are committed to living a distinctive life apart from the world.[27] In this sense the tradition of the Free Church or Believers' Church tradition has been deliberately sectarian, stressing the central place of holiness. Through spiritual rebirth and discipline within their ranks, such Christians have sought to keep the church pure and unblemished from the world.

[24]See Albert Outler, "The Place of Wesley in the Christian Tradition," in K. A. Rowe, ed., *The Place of Wesley in the Christian Tradition* (Metuchen, N.J.: The Scarecrow Press, 1976), 30.

[25]See Randy Maddox, "John Wesley and Eastern Orthodoxy" in *The Asbury Theological Journal* 45:2 (Fall, 1990), 39-40.

[26]The concept of "perfect" is misleading today. John Wesley spoke often of "perfect love" (see Mildred Wynkoop, *A Theology of Love: The Dynamic of Wesleyanism,* Kansas City: Beacon Hill Press, 1972, 294-301).

[27]Ernst Troeltsch, *The Social Teachings of the Christian Churches and Groups* (London: Allen and Unwin, 1931), 2:993.

In America, the Baptists, Methodists, and "Christians" (Stone-Campbell movement) led the way, with the Church of God movement coming along late in the nineteenth century. The age-old paradox has prevailed. How can the church be *in* but not *of* the world, serving the world without sharing its perverted values? How can holiness be a practical reality, a real separation from the world, without leading to social irrelevance? The New Testament, especially the parts written by Paul, argues that the answer lies with the church living in the power of the Spirit, the present power of the messianic age now dawned in Jesus Christ. To be "holy" is to be truly "in Him" and increasingly to become "like him" through the Spirit.

The work of Christ on the cross addresses more than humanity's juridical status before God, justifying past sin by divine grace. It also intends a re-creation of fallen and now forgiven humanity. The already justified can be filled with the Spirit of love (Rom. 5:5) so that they can give thanks always (Eph. 5:18-21) and grow up into the likeness of Christ (Eph. 4:15). Justifying grace "works *for* the sinner; sanctifying grace works *in* the penitent faithful. . . . Justifying grace is juridically a *finished* work of the Son on the cross, while sanctifying grace is actively a *continuing* and current work of the Spirit in our hearts and social processes."[28] The former brings change in a person's relative position before God; the latter effects a real change internally.[29] All believers are called to be *holy.*

---

[28]Thomas Oden, *Life in the Spirit* (S.F.: Harper, 1992), 218.

[29]Real change is regeneration, actual new life. Justification, the forgiveness of sin, is the necessary preface to or first stage of actual rebirth. Regeneration involves reorganization of a believer's motive life by the work of the Spirit so that the prevailing motive becomes love for God and loyalty to Jesus Christ. Such reorganization is sanctification, the larger outworking of justification. John Wesley insisted that God graciously has provided both pardon for sin and an empowering Presence (the Holy Spirit) in the lives of believers and in the church.

To be holy is costly to self-centered egos and middle-class life in a prosperous society. To walk the path of holiness is necessarily to break with the habits of comfortable religion. It is to "renounce the 'cheap grace' that only gives a religious sugarcoating to our worldliness and instead embrace the grace that will cost us our life and give us deliverance not only from the *guilt* but also from the *power* of sin." It entails "a turn toward the despised, the forsaken, the marginalized, the poor, the least of these."[30] It is to follow humbly the God of the Cross into the sordidness of a lost world. To be holy is to engage in costly caring for others in cross-like ways.

To be holy is to move beyond the question "what must I do to be saved?" to "what must I be and do now that I am saved?" To avoid the demands of the second question surely is to reflect negatively on the continuing meaningfulness of the first. In the ministry of John the Baptist people were challenged to turn *from* past sins and receive forgiveness. With the announcement that God's Kingdom had come near in the person of Jesus the Christ (Mk. 1:14-20), Jesus called people to also turn *toward* the new reality of the present reign of God. Beyond forgiveness, faith enables access to the power of the Kingdom for inner healing and active service. To be holy is to be *healed* into a life of *healing*.

One's understanding of the nature of sin controls the understanding of holiness. Thinking of sin as violation of a set of behavioral expectations is to risk a seeking of righteousness by means of human works and to limit holiness to those few (if any!) people who somehow function at a flawless level in relation to these expectations. Thinking of sin only as a pattern of sinful acts committed is to tempt a limiting of the view of salvation to forgiveness of these acts, a commercial transaction

---

[30]Theodore W. Jennings, Jr., "The Meaning of Discipleship in Wesley and the New Testament," *Quarterly Review: A Journal of Theological Resources for Ministry* (Spring, 1993), 18.

whereby human wrong is redeemed by the grace of God's love. Thinking biblically, however, sin is seen more in personal and relational terms. Rather than being a negative "thing" within the person, a scoresheet against an absolute standard, sin is the deliberate turning away from God, introducing a defective or perverted love, and violation of the covenant relationship. Thus, "if sin is the orientation of the whole person away from God, then holiness is the whole person turned in love to God. It is not merely the absence of sin, but the presence of the God-given love for God."[31]

The proper approach to conceiving of Christian holiness is focusing on restored relationship. In this view, believers are free from the dilemmas of perfectionism that have plagued many holiness seekers. The goal is a perfect love characteristic of restored relationship, not perfect performance in spite of human frailty, ignorance, and immaturity. The issue is the set of the will, the focus of one's true affection. John Wesley's phrase "perfect love" should be thought of as mature, life-restoring relationship to God. In this light, Mildred Bangs Wynkoop correctly defines sin as "love locked into a false center, the self." Holiness is "love locked into the True Center, Jesus Christ our Lord."[32]

Justification is the foundation; sanctification continues the reclaiming of the once fallen by the process of set-apartness unto God, the reestablishment of right relationship, "perfect" love. This process of becoming holy should not be thought of as moral flawlessness or a sterile otherworldliness, but as a pattern of maturing into Christ-likeness, a releasing from the compulsive power of self-centeredness so that the believer may genuinely love God and neighbor. Such is the goal, possible only by sancti-

---

[31]Kenneth Jones, *Commitment to Holiness* (Anderson, Ind.: Warner Press, 1985), 73.

[32]Mildred Bangs Wynkoop, *A Theology of Love* (Kansas City: Beacon Hill Press, 1972), 158.

fying grace. The goal is not achieved easily. Wisdom warns that "if we respect the freedom of God's grace and the limitless disguises that sin assumes, we will avoid oversimplification in our portrayals of the process of growth in Christian life."[33]

There is growth when faith and obedience are exercised. As justification is a gift of God's grace, a gift effective only when matched by the human response of accepting faith, so sanctification is a divine gift effective only when enriched by the believer's faithful use of the available means by which grace is made operational. Sanctification, a divine gift, is nonetheless also a human task. When one responds to grace, that believer becomes responsible to the purposes of that grace.

One unfortunate aspect of much preaching on sanctification in many American camp meetings has been the stress on emotionalism and immediacy of result. While there certainly is a point of human decision and commitment, there also is a process of discipline and development. In much of American revivalism, holiness became a very individual experience, often disconnected from the disciplining and nurturing church context. Becoming "holy" was thought to be realized in one crisis experience, sometimes to the near exclusion of its progressive and communal dimensions. Crisis tended to overcome process, altering the better balance held by John Wesley.[34]

---

[33]Daniel Migliore, *Faith Seeking Understanding* (Grand Rapids: Eerdmans, 1991), 178. Migliore lists marks that characterize real growth in sanctifying grace. They are maturing (1) as hearers of the Word of God, (2) in prayer, (3) in freedom, (4) in solidarity, and (5) in thankfulness and joy (178-182).

[34]Wesley's long life appears to have experienced stages of developing thought here, but "his later descriptions . . . lay much more emphasis on the gradual nature of salvation and the interrelationship of its different facets. . . . [These facets], not an ordered series of discrete states, . . . are intertwined facets of an overarching purpose—our gradual recovery of the holiness that God has always intended for us" (Randy Maddox, *Responsible Grace*, 1994, 158).

Holiness, when solidified in a given cultural setting, easily becomes more reflective of the times than of the work of God's Spirit. The Church of God movement, for instance, emerged from the nineteenth century American Holiness Movement and focused heavily on a quest for both the holiness and unity of all Christians by the power of the Spirit. But legalisms of several kinds soon evolved, encouraging in more recent generations a near silencing of this doctrinal emphasis once so central in the movement. Very recently, especially in the movement's international dialogues on doctrine, the urgent need for holiness emphasis has resurfaced, now with greater recognition of the care needed to avoid earlier distortions.[35] The goal is to be captured by God, not by culture! While never easy, this goal of God for human restoration is hardly optional.

Modernity has secularized the concept of sanctification, reducing it to moral improvement or the political gains of upward social mobility. This has resulted in biblical emphases being "cut and squeezed into pop metaphors of psychological growth or stress reduction or creative management."[36] But to sanctify is to set apart for holy use. Today Christians must learn again to resist being shaped by the pervasive and powerful secular culture. Instead, by faith in the Spirit's work, believers are called to become set apart *by* God and *for* God, to be resident aliens in this world,[37] to be shaped by the distinctive reading of reality that is Jesus Christ, to be pilgrims through this life,

---

[35]Recent International Dialogues on Doctrine of the Church of God movement have focused on "Pentecost and the Church" (Nairobi, Kenya, 1983), "Gifts of the Spirit" (Seoul, South Korea, 1987), "Sanctification" (Wiesbaden, Germany, 1991), and "Christian Unity: God's Will and Our Role" (Sydney, Australia, 1995). These dialogues are sponsored and convened by the School of Theology of Anderson University.

[36]Thomas Oden, *Life in the Spirit* (S.F.: Harper, 1992), 212.

[37]See Stanley Hauerwas and William Willimon, *Resident Aliens* (Nashville: Abingdon Press, 1989).

formed by the biblical view of life's fallenness and potential newness in Christ.

Isaiah 6:1-8 serves as a window through which the church today can gain again a vision of the biblical understanding of holiness. This understanding avoids an insistence on experiential formulas like "a second work of grace" that often force the work of the Spirit into overly rigid categories and time frames. This prophetic vision centers rather in the dynamics of an unholy person (people) encountering a holy God. The emphasis is on the life impact of opening oneself humbly to the God who is high, glorious, powerful, pure, and Self-giving love.[38]

To be holy is to allow one's life to be refocused by transforming grace. Newly highlighted is an Isaiah-like vision of a holy God and of one's sinful self that becomes painfully revealed by shocking comparison. It is a grace-granted renewal in the image of God, prompted by a transforming vision of God. Personal and church renewal comes when unholy people are touched by the divine fire so that they become a holy people (humble, righteous, sent, serving). When asked the meaning of Christian perfection or entire sanctification, John Wesley typically responded with "loving God with the whole heart, soul, mind, and strength and our neighbor as ourselves." Holiness is "that dynamic level of maturing within the process of sanctification characteristic of 'adult' Christian life."[39] With love assumed as the essence of Christian life, the intended Christian "perfec-

---

[38]For an exposition of these divine characteristics and their relevance for the renewal of contemporary Christian believers, see Stephen Seamands, *Holiness of Heart and Life* (Nashville: Abingdon Press, 1990). Alan Kreider expands this with three provocative "snapshots" of holiness based on the narratives of Exodus 15, Isaiah 6-7, and Acts 4 (*Journey Towards Holiness*, Scottdale, Pa.: Herald Press, 1987, 19-26). Kreider, representing the Believers' Church tradition, emphasizes well the social dimensions of Christian holiness.

[39]Randy Maddox, *Responsible Grace,* 1994, 187.

tion" is the love of God *ruling* the attitudes, words, and actions of a committed believer. Salvation is to be seen eschatologically, that is, within the context of the coming to human history of the reign of God in Christ, resulting in the potential of a new order of human existence.

Holiness is not a static adoration of the holy (distant) God or a perfect performance in relation to some catalog of right and wrong actions. It is renewed life on the move, transforming and being transformed into the image of the Holy One who is active in the midst of our world. It is a believer whose personal life story has merged with the biblical story of the God who yet journeys among us. As Isaiah learned, experiencing holiness soon sends on mission ("here am I, send me!"). The God who is "majestic in holiness" (Ex. 15:11) invites people both to enter the divine character (sanctification) and take part in God's holy actions (mission). Holiness erodes resistance to God's sovereignty and liberates women and men from all forms of bondage. It is restored relationship, the victory of grace over the power of evil. God calls all believers to holiness!

Vocation. God justifies and sanctifies human life by the power of the Spirit for the immediate purpose of Christian discipleship. To neglect mission and focus only on personal experiences of the Spirit is to pervert the life of grace by yielding to spiritual narcissism. Personal transformation by the grace of God is a calling to service, not an invitation to privilege. Grace received is responsibility assumed. Service is costly; grace is not cheap.[40]

John Wesley's concern clearly was centered more on the *fruit* of the Spirit and less on the *gifts* of the Spirit, especially a

---

[40]See Dietrich Bonhoeffer, *The Cost of Discipleship* (London: SCM Press, 1959). The dramatic life of Bonhoeffer, including his martyrdom at Nazi hands, is a story of grace received and lived out in a costly discipleship.

gift like "tongues" that easily becomes self-serving and not beneficial to the church's mission. Fruit is inevitable if faith is authentic. In fact, the fruit that flows from faith is an essential part of what "salvation" means. Claiming to be "saved" without exhibiting the Christ-life is to profess a lie (1 Jn. 2:9-11). From the "radical" Christian tradition comes the view that salvation is "to walk in the resurrection" (Schleitheim, 1527). Christian conduct, rather than merely emerging as a consequence of salvation, is itself basic to the very meaning of salvation. The "salvific gift of God and its human answer in following Jesus were [are] two sides of one reality."[41]

What God has accomplished in the past, especially in the work of Christ, is intended to send believers on a journey outward to others and forward to the completion of God's redemptive work in the world. Christian life is more than acceptance of the forgiveness of sins and personal transformation. It also is "the vocation to participate in the preparation of all creation for the coming of a new community of justice, freedom, and peace in partnership with the Triune God."[42]

Precedent for such "worldly" vocation is found in the faith tradition which Jesus shared. The ancient Hebrews have been described as "an energetic, robust, and, at times, even turbulent people." For them, "truth was not so much an idea to be contemplated as an experience to be lived, a deed to be done."[43] Israel's religion was a "pup-tent" faith that followed a God on the move, with the followers being God's "movable treasure" (cf. Ex. 19:5).

While, then, it is clear that Christian disciples are to be liberated and dedicated agents of Christ on mission in this world, it

---

[41]James McClendon, *Systematic Theology: Doctrine* (Nashville: Abingdon Press, 1994), 118.

[42]Daniel Migliore, *op. cit.*, 184.

[43]Marvin Wilson, *Our Father Abraham* (Grand Rapids: Eerdmans, 1989), 136.

sometimes is less clear how best to express such sacrificial discipleship. Basic at least are having (1) the mind of Christ as pattern and (2) the enabling Spirit of Christ as power.

John Wesley's teaching of "Christian perfection" closely links doctrine and life, thus closing the inappropriate gap between thought and act, creedal commitment and compassionate application, the "orthodox" and the "radical." Having a "heart strangely warmed" by the Spirit is seen as a social-ethical call to warm a chilled world by the embodied love of God. The manner of love's expression is to be controlled by the way of Jesus Christ in the world. Jesus is the norm of the Christian's life—and His way is radically different from the standard messianic expectations of His time or the typical way the world and even the church functions in our time.

The first Christian disciples had to reorient their understanding of the way God expresses power in the midst of human history so that they could have the mind of Christ in their own living. "If they had been endowed with the gift of the Spirit before that gift had manifested its full range of meaning in Jesus," warns Ray Dunning, "they would have doubtless become raging nationalists, swinging weapons like Samson of old."[44] While life in the Spirit is essential, so is its being understood as one with the historical story of Jesus.

The Spirit of God sends the believing community on mission. The community goes in the Spirit, that is, in the present power of the messianic age already dawned in Jesus Christ. The Spirit "moves us through enemy territory toward God's final victory, along the way offering us a quickening foretaste of the glory to come." But the Spirit's leading is into, not out of this present world. "The Spirit always directs us to the Crucified One

---

[44]H. Ray Dunning, *Grace, Faith & Holiness* (Kansas City: Beacon Hill Press, 1988), 415.

and thus into the way of the cross." So we are put on mission *for* Christ, *by* the Spirit of Christ, and *like* Christ. Like Christ? Yes, "the Spirit implants in our hearts the strength to follow the way of weakness, the power to receive and care for the powerless, the peace to endure and absorb hostility."[45] This is holiness in action in the world.

Fruit and Gifts. God loves the community of Christ, the church, and intends to equip it to fulfill its divinely assigned tasks. A key dimension of this equipping is the giving of divine gifts to enable divine service, thus building up the church for its service in the world. This is the work of the Spirit. So, "do not be foolish, but understand what the will of the Lord is. Do not get drunk with wine, for that is debauchery; but be filled with the Spirit . . ." (Eph 5:17-18).

The relationship between Jesus and the Spirit is theologically crucial. This relationship provides the test by which the "spirits" of teachers can be discerned (1 John 4:2). The test for "prophets" who claim to speak by the Spirit is whether they recognize and affirm the significance of Jesus' humanity. The test for the authenticity of spiritual gifts is their value in the service of the continuing mission of Jesus (1 Cor. 12). Concludes Norman Kraus: "Above all, the test is whether faith produces in us the love of Christ."[46]

In 1985, widely reported abuses of some presumed divine gifts led the General Assembly of the Church of God movement to establish a national study committee on this subject. The resulting 1986 committee report reads in part:

> Which gift or how many gifts a person is given is not a factor in that person's salvation or sanctification. What is a

---

[45]C. Leonard Allen, *The Cruciform Church* (Abilene, Tx.: Abilene Christian University Press, 1990), 163.

[46]C. Norman Kraus, *God Our Savior* (Scottdale, Pa.: Herald Press, 1991), 147-148.

factor is the reception of *the Gift,* that of the Holy Spirit (Acts 1:8 and Romans 8:9). . . . Congregations are urged to teach the central importance of the work of the Holy Spirit in the lives of believers and in the process of genuine Christian worship.[47]

To be holy and in Christ's service is first to receive the greatest gift from God. This gift is the indwelling presence of the Holy Spirit, God actually with us. We are holy only because of God's presence, and because we are privileged to belong to God. We can avoid sin only because we are being sanctified by divine presence and help. We can find our way through dark, difficult places because of divine guidance. We can do whatever God desires only because the Holy Spirit is with us to strengthen and give the abilities we cannot have in our own strength.

The presence of the Holy Spirit and our active life in the Spirit are crucial to the maturing of individual Christians and to the accomplishment of the mission of the church in every age. The quest for such infilling and holy living is encouraged by the New Testament. A lack of the power of Pentecost explains much of the emptiness which the current church renewal and charismatic movements are seeking to fill.

The emergence of the *fruit* of the Spirit (Gal. 5:22-23) should be a goal and is the privilege of all Christian believers, precisely because the fruit are the expected expressions or reflections of the presence of the Spirit.[48] The *gifts* of the Spirit, how-

---

[47]As in Barry Callen, ed., *Thinking and Acting Together* (Anderson, Ind.: Executive Council of the Church of God and Warner Press, 1992), 108-109.

[48]This paragraph is adapted from the report of the Study Committee on Glossolalia made to and accepted by the General Assembly of the Church of God movement, June, 1986. It represents the traditional viewpoint of this movement by seeing spiritual gifts as essential to church life (although caution is expressed, like in the New Testament, about an often misunderstood and abused gift like "speaking in tongues").

FRUITS

ever, are given only as the Spirit chooses (1 Cor. 12:11), not as any person desires or has a right to expect. These gifts are intended primarily for service so that the church may be strengthened and made more effective in its mission. Self-gratification by a gift, or public exhibition of a gift for its own sake, are inappropriate in the church (1 Cor. 14).

A range of divine gifts appear in the New Testament.[49] Those named apparently are representative only, since the Holy Spirit qualifies each believer and congregation to accomplish whatever Kingdom task is at hand. Love is said to be supreme, superceding all forms of spiritual individualism. Gifts are given to the church for the building up of the body of Christ (Eph. 4:11-12). They are present only when God sees need and provides the capacity to meet that need. The fruit of the Spirit (Gal. 5:19-23), however, are characteristics of the Spirit and thus are inherent in the Christian life and *always* should be present.[50]

To summarize, by God's grace and through God's Spirit sinful men and women are enabled to experience restored relationship with God. The restoration involves the forgiveness of sin's guilt (justification), the renewal of existence in the image of Christ (sanctification), and engagement in Christ's service (vocation). All of these are supported by the fruit of the Spirit's presence and the gifts of the Spirit's strengthening and equipping. All are for the upbuilding of the church as it goes about its mission in the world.

Two additional gifts are crucial and require intentional action on the part of believers if they are to be realized as intended. These gifts are *unity* and *peace*. To these we now turn.

---

[49]See Rom. 12:4-6; 1 Cor. 12:8-10; 12:28-30; Eph. 4:11.

[50]See an excellent commentary on the Galatians 5 passage by William Barclay, *Flesh and Spirit* (Nashville: Abingdon Press, 1962).

Movements and the Church's Oneness

One important focus of the praying of Jesus was that His disciples of all times would experience and practice a unity among themselves like exists between God the Father and the Son Jesus (John 17). Such an experience and practice has been a central goal of the Church of God movement.

Many Christian traditions have identified classic "marks" of the church that God intends. These marks are holy, catholic, apostolic, and one. The Church of God movement has affirmed all of these, including the last as a natural outcome of the others. God founded only *one* church (Jn. 10:16; 21:15; Eph. 5:27) and believers are expected to make every effort to maintain its unity in the Spirit (Eph. 4:3-4). The New Testament does speak of churches (plural), meaning only that each is a local extension and expression of the one body united in Jesus Christ, its head, and empowered by the one indwelling Spirit, its life.

This church of God is understood biblically as both the universal church and any local assembly (congregation) of the whole. The church by definition is one (Eph. 2:11-21; 4:1-16). The oneness is to be expressed in each local assembly since each is intended to be a visible appearance of the whole in a given time and place. What an awesome and demanding thought! A congregation belonging to God is to represent the whole church in its particular geographic place. It is the church catholic that is to celebrate, model, and proclaim the good news in its community. All functions of the church and all dimensions of the good news belong in each place. When a congregation baptizes a new believer, for instance, that baptism should be into the *whole church,* not into a cut-off piece of it. The fellowship of the church should evidence an overcoming of human cultural, gender, and racial barriers. Paul says that Jesus brings *shalom* to human hatreds, peace "to you who were far away" (Gentiles) and "to those who were near" (Jews) (Eph. 2:17).

Unity is a crucial mark of the church. Division confuses, weakens, alienates, and thereby hampers mission. Where unity is understood as a dynasty of successor male bishops (apostolic succession), it is oppressive and strangles appropriate diversity and plurality. On the other hand, ecumenism, the quest for the realization of Christian unity, contrasts with the competitive mentality seen commonly in human societies. Accordingly:

> Ecumenism is a way of looking at reality that refuses to absolutize relative perspectives. It is an approach to knowledge which insists that truth is seldom discovered in isolation but rather through dialogue in diverse community. It is a way of living that dares to think globally and live trustfully with differences in community, not as a result of polite tolerance but on the basis of our common commitment to and experience of the creating, redeeming, and sustaining God.[51]

While Christian unity is a gift from God through the Spirit, it is realized only as Christians intentionally open themselves to be in community with other believers.[52] "Unity is given," according to James Earl Massey, "but our experience of it must be gained." The givenness roots in the fact that "the church is the community of those who honor Jesus Christ, sharing his life,

---

[51]Michael Kinnamon, *Truth and Community: Diversity and Its Limits in the Ecumenical Movement* (Grand Rapids: Eerdmans, 1988), 109.

[52]What constitutes true and viable Christian unity? Must there be full agreement on beliefs, or a single organizational network, or is the goal more in the area of attitudes? Early leaders of the Church of God movement envisioned denominational structures collapsing (not merging). For the most part that has not happened. Consideration now should be given to this judgment of Emil Brunner: "Certain as is the fact that a number of competing churches represents a scandal, equally certain is it on the other hand that a variety of forms of Christian fellowship is a necessity. . . . Far more important than organizational reunion of the historical churches is the readiness of individual Christians . . . to cooperate in a spirit of brotherliness" (*The Misunderstanding of the Church,* Philadelphia: Westminster Press, 1953, 112).

teachings, and work. Belonging to him makes every believer belong to all other believers."[53] But what of the persistent dividedness among Christ's people? Believers typically experience the fellowship of God's people in connection with some denominational body. Is this fact division by definition? There appears to exist a perplexing paradox: the multiplicity of Christian traditions is due in part to human sin (Gal. 5:19-21) and in part to the inevitable varieties of human cultures, symbol systems, and historical circumstances that are not sinful in themselves.

We have to face this question: "How may a people who exist as a distinct community within the Church, for the sake of witness unto the unity of the Church, avoid the negation of their witness by their very existence?"[54] To avoid just such a negation, in 1804 there was published *The Last Will and Testament of the Springfield Presbytery* to explain why a reforming Christian group would dissolve its own interim "church" body, would "die the death" organizationally as a witness to Christian unity. "We will," it boldly announced, "that this body die, be dissolved, and sink into union with the Body of Christ at large; for there is but one Body and one Spirit, even as we are called in one hope of our calling."[55]

---

[53]James Massey, *Concerning Christian Unity* (Anderson, Ind.: Warner Press, 1979), 8, 11, 20. Clark Williamson adds that "unity in the church, fragmentarily but really, is where the diverse members of the body of Christ are aware of and appreciate their essential relatedness to each other, where they love one another with the kind of love with which they have been loved" (*A Guest in the House of Israel,* Louisville: Westminster/John Knox Press, 1993, 262). James Evans, Jr., says that "the solidarity of that community (koinonia of the church) . . . is strong enough to render all other stratifications among human beings of only secondary importance. Thus in the holy community 'there is no Greek nor Jew, slave nor free, male nor female' " (*We Have Been Believers: An African-American Systematic Theology,* Minneapolis: Augsburg Fortress, 1992, 136).

[54]Robert Fife, "The Neglected Alternative" in *Celebration of Heritage* (Los Angeles: Westwood Christian Foundation, 1992), 265.

[55]This document, written by Barton W. Stone, is a classic in the "Restorationist" movement.

Can an identifiable Christian body successfully "sink" into the whole of God's people as a unity witness without disappearing and thus forfeiting any real base from which to witness to and help realize Christian unity? Is the divisiveness of our denominationalized Christian community so assumed and entrenched, so sociologically inevitable, that there is no alternative? Because of the hurtfulness of division to the church's mission and because the New Testament witness highlights the goal of Christian unity, even presents it as the personal prayer of Jesus on behalf of all his disciples in all times (John 17), many Christians over the centuries have affirmed that there must be an alternative to rampant division.[56] A movement that serves to upbuild the church, not divide and tear down, may be seen as a gift of the Spirit to the church.

For the Kentucky Christians led by Barton Stone and his colleagues, *The Last Will and Testament* declared an intentional "sinking" by no longer defining Christian fellowship in terms of a particular institution to which all Christians could not belong. These visionary reformers sought to become a microcosm of the whole church, with no other criteria of unity except those which can be the bond of unity for the whole church. There would be no restrictive creed mandated on all members. Evangelizing should be done *as the church* (the whole body of Christ) and for the church. Baptizing would be into the church, not into a given segment of it. The invitation to the Lord's Supper would be issued as representatives of the whole body to any in the body wishing to participate (it is, after all, the Lord's table, not ours).

How, then, should one describe groupings of Christians that seek to represent and serve the whole church in distinctive ways,

---

[56]Theodore Jennings insists that "division is a problem for the identity of the church. Division is a sign of the power of the world and sin. Division is then the antisign (the countersign) to the reign of God" (*Loyalty To God*, Nashville: Abingdon Press, 1992, 188).

without claiming for themselves those characteristics belonging only to the whole body? One helpful distinction is that between the church and "movements" within it. Affirming that the church is one and that such oneness is obscured when denominations divide the church into "churches," Robert Fife defines a "movement" as "a community of understanding and concern which exists and serves within the Church, and for its edification."[57]

Sometimes particular groupings of Christians come into being because their members share certain understandings and concerns about the faith.[58] Such distinctive communities *within* the church (not *as* the church) help facilitate the internal dialogue of the church as the whole body seeks its maturity and unity for the sake of its mission.[59] Movements, therefore, are "characteristic of the church as a living organism." They are actions of the body of Christ rather than separations from or usurpations of the body. While a properly motivated renewal movement is not the church and seeks to keep that very clear, it is a vital part of the church and functions in order to make the church more whole and more effectual.[60]

---

[57]Robert Fife, *op. cit.*, 276.

[58]Even within the New Testament we already see early approaches to understanding a unity in plurality within the church (diversity of spiritual gifts, the Christian conscience and "gray areas," cultural diversity implied in the reality of multiple congregations, their differing settings and range of approaches to problems). In each case, unity left room for some diversity. See Rex Koivisto, *One Lord, One Faith* (Wheaton, Ill.: Victor Books, 1993), 37-42.

[59]Robert Fife, *op. cit.*, 265-271. Fife calls for denominations to cease calling themselves "churches" and assuming for themselves the dignity and prerogatives belonging only to the church (274). In this regard, note C. C. Morrison, early editor of the *Christian Century*, 77:10 (March 9, 1960), 281.

[60]Rex Koivisto attributes such wholesome characteristics to "denominations" (*One Lord, One Faith,* 102ff). Such groupings, he says, are inevitable sociologically. Even people uniting around a non-denominational platform are not thereby kept from potentially being at least part of what they oppose (102). Koivisto quotes Wolfhart Pannenberg: "The mutual relationship of the various regional or denominational traditions

Much like the restorationist movement represented by Robert Fife, the Church of God movement has been sensitive to the damage done to the church and its mission by denominational divisions when such divisions take to themselves the prerogatives belonging only to the whole body. It has thought of itself as a "movement" in Fife's terms, functioning at God's call *within* the body and *for* the body. Too often, however, even this unity movement has managed to facilitate awkward separations, in spite of itself.

A movement can facilitate the internal dialogue of the church only as it engages actively with the church, not when it retreats within its own confines out of self-preoccupation or fear of contamination by the beliefs and practices of other Christian traditions. A "movement" can destroy its own genius by failing to move creatively within the larger body. Lutheranism, for instance, has sought to avoid this trap by thinking of its own confessions of faith as an offer made to the larger church.[61] When, however, an offer moves to ultimatum, lacking apprecia-

---

within the one Christian world should be thought of in terms of that type of multiplicity of concrete forms in which the catholic fullness of the church comes to expression. The multiplicity of such traditions in church order, doctrine, and liturgy does not exclude catholicity as long as each of them holds itself open, beyond its own distinctive features, for the Christian rights of the others and feels a responsibility, not just for its own tradition, but for the whole of Christian history and its heritage" (104). Similarly: "A monolithic denomination is not desirable. In Christian history, revival times have often occasioned a new order in Roman Catholicism or a new denomination in Protestantism—not mergers. . . . The Church can be one and apostolic and catholic right while it exists in denominational forms" (J. Kenneth Grider, *A Wesleyan-Holiness Theology,* Kansas City: Beacon Hill Press, 1994, 484-485).

[61]See E. Gritsch, R. Jenson, *Lutheranism: The Theological Movement and Its Confessional Writings* (Fortress Press, 1976), chapter one. Carl Braaten speaks of Lutheranism much as the Church of God movement always has spoken of itself: "Lutheranism is not essentially a church but a movement. . . . It is a confessional movement that exists for the sake of reforming the whole church of Christ by the canon of the gospel. The . . . structures of Lutheranism are interim measures, ready to go out of business as soon as their provisional aims are realized" (*Principles of Lutheran Theology,* Philadelphia: Fortress Press, 1983, 46).

tion for the valid offers of others, a movement becomes a "sect" in the negative sense.

Denominated bodies can be honorable and effective if they are not honored as ends in themselves, if they function coopera- tively as patterns of partnership in relation to the whole body, and if they function as "movements" seeking to facilitate the health of the whole church. There is nothing inherently divisive in a group of Christians following the natural sociological process of "denominating" itself. In fact,

> no one form should be judged divisive just because it is a form. . . . Diversity is not division when the spirit of relat- ing to those beyond the group is kept alive. . . . Diversity is one thing, while a *spirit* of division is quite another. . . . Every Christian has a legacy in every other Christian. We experience that legacy only as we receive each other and relate, moving eagerly beyond group boundaries.[62]

A helpful analogy was shared at the centennial consultation on the heritage of the Church of God movement.[63] The Gulf Stream is a marvelous movement of water that leaves the Gulf of Mexico and flows as a warming river across the vast expanse of the Atlantic Ocean to the European continent. The general path of the warmer water is obvious. Its influence on the ocean envi- ronment is definite as it moves along. But its boundaries are imprecise. It is open to all the surrounding ocean, influencing and being influenced. T. Franklin Miller judged this an appropri- ate image of what a movement should be like within the larger body of Christ. The opposite, by whatever name, tries delivering

---

[62]James Massey, *Concerning Christian Unity,* 1979, 75, 78, 82.

[63]Convened in February, 1980, at the School of Theology of Ander- son University, Anderson, Indiana. Note also the centennial celebration of the Church of God movement in Germany that occurred in Hamburg, Ger- many, September, 1994. A featured guest speaker was the director of the German Evangelical Alliance, an interdenominational Christian organiza- tion with which the Church of God movement in Germany had recently affiliated. Such affiliation expressed the desire to cooperate with, con- tribute to, and benefit from the larger church.

its water to Europe in a sealed pipeline, neither warming nor being enriched by the much larger body on the way. The opposite of a movement (an isolated "sect") thinks it knows itself to be the true water without need of enrichment and not wishing to risk being chilled by outside contact.

Christian unity is both a gift of God and the achievement of those committed to its fullest realization. Diversity can be a source of freedom and creativity in the church, the opposite of a regimented and premature uniformity. The diamond of Christian truth has many facets. Difference is not bad unless it hardens into an arrogant, anti-catholic exclusiveness, or deviates from the biblical revelation that is to form the church in all of its expressions. Groupings of Christians need not represent an evil just because they exist as distinct groupings. The question is whether they are in conflict or communion, whether they are contributing to or detracting from the whole body of Christ. Bodies that cut themselves off are acting against the church, even if their divisive platforms include the call for Christian unity (an accusation sometimes leveled at the Church of God movement, particularly in its earliest decades).[64]

---

[64]In one sense the church is called to be "sectarian." When it is the eschatological church born of the Pentecostal vision, carrying the distinctive marks, and exercising the distinctive gifts of the Spirit, the church moves toward the "sect" type of ecclesiology described by Troeltsch (*The Social Teaching of the Christian Churches*, 1912). He describes Christianity as having three organizational orientations, church, sect, and mysticism. Books like S. Hauerwas and W. Willimon, *Resident Aliens* (Nashville: Abingdon, 1989) and the whole Believers' Church tradition call for a distinctive, counter-cultural identity as the authentic way of really being the church in our kind of world. In another sense, however, the church should resist sectarianism. "The Disciples of Christ and the Church of God (Anderson, Indiana) have witnessed long and loud about the need to heal the divisions within Christendom, advising that rules and opinions not found in Scripture are injurious to fellowship and the experience of unity. The intent has been to help the rest of the churches become aware of how denominational separatism limits fellowship and hinders having a visible unity" (James Massey, *Concerning Christian Unity*, 90).

FRUITS

The church today is faced with a twin danger. Divisiveness, always tempting, is sinful in its unjustified pride and imperialism. Syncretism, however, often seeks to correct such narrowness by being willing "to do almost anything to gain an external unity" and in the process "is susceptible to mating with any ideological partner around, usually at the cost of loss of centered orthodoxy."[65] The challenge is to be orthodox and radical, belonging to the mainstream of the Christian tradition, but in a distinctive, constructive, and renewing way.

Gabriel Fackre identifies two ideological partners, new "tribes" that sometimes function today like the old sects in a negative, cut-off way. One is an "imperial tribalism" that rallies around the modernist assumption that truth comes by right knowledge and exists to make this world more livable. Since knowledge is thought to root in historical circumstance and vested interest, it is said that one knows true Christian identity only when one acts on behalf of the oppressed. The *doer* is the *knower*. Truth is tribally defined since it is restricted to those involved in the prescribed way.

The other is "confessional tribalism" that knows no final truth, "only illusory claims and interest-laden agendas ripe for deconstruction." In this instance it is assumed that one "can never find 'the truth'; one must be content with what one has, not things truthful but things meaningful." Our tribe is *our* tribe with our distinctive language, lore, and codes. While live-and-let-live is the attitude, there is "border control" that maintains meaningful identity. These two tribal ideologies both threaten a unified church, one by arrogance, the other by apathy.[66]

Organizational variety in the church appears inevitable as Christians of varying backgrounds focus their lives around dif-

[65]Thomas Oden, *Life in the Spirit* (S.F.: Harper, 1992), 313.
[66]Gabriel Fackre, *Ecumenical Faith in Evangelical Perspective* (Grand Rapids: Eerdmans, 1993), 74-76, 85.

fering concerns in order to advance varying understandings of the gospel in multiple cultures. The problem is not the variety as such, but rigid spirits of exclusiveness that act *against* and not *with* and *for* the whole church. The problem of division is its unjustified exclusivism (a sign to the world that is injurious to Christ's mission). Ignoring the necessary mark of catholicity, a divisive body falsely expands some insight, gift, or group tradition into a restricting dominance, failing to hear that "the eye cannot say to the hand, 'I have no need of you.' . . . If the whole body were an eye, where would the hearing be?" (1 Cor. 12:21, 17). True division makes human experience normative, even when insisting on Scriptural authority, since only the official and humanly conditioned reading of the particular "tribe" is judged acceptable by that tribe.

The goal of Christian unity, possible in the midst of diversity by the work of the one Spirit, is commitment to the one Lord who is head of the one church. Such Christ-centered unity is not a matter of creedal uniformity, but consists of communication between Christian groups, the mutual enrichment by varying traditions, with the standard of the faith, Jesus Christ, the exclusive possession of no one group. "The fullness of the gospel proclaimed in the church," concludes Fackre, "will be in direct proportion to the mutual correction and completion of the church's tribal monologues. Let the imperialist who raids and the confessionalist who patrols dismantle their juggernauts and take down their barricades."[67]

The hope is not for a uniformity with all distinctives somehow eliminated. Christians are to be reconciled *in their diversity.* Observing that real differences already existed even in the early

---

[67]Ibid., 86. Down should come all denominational chauvinisms that promote the interests of one Christian body over against and at the expense of others. The concern always should be for the health of the whole.

church, Thomas Oden insists that "genuine unity in the whole body of Christ is not merely a matter of improved organizational management. It is a unity enabled by the Spirit that awakens legitimate diversity without imposing premature uniformity."[68] Being together in Christ by the Spirit is to be "catholic." Being in touch with one's own traditional distinctives within the Christian family, while remaining open to the wisdom resident in the larger reality of the church, is to be "radical" in a divinely-intended sense. The Church of God movement has hoped in this way to be "free-church catholic," a healing and uniting force within the whole body of Christ.

There is to be a careful juxtaposition of unity and diversity, both kept focused and constructive by a divine enablement that incites the wakefulness of Christians and resists efforts at human domestication of others or of God's work. John Frame joins the tradition of the Church of God movement in calling for "ecclesiastical revolutionaries," Christians willing to yield themselves and their status-quo tribal instincts for the sake of the higher calling of God to the church.[69]

The church is God's. The church is one. As the holy, catholic, apostolic body of Christ, it is to be a sign to the world of the already coming Kingdom. How is it to be such a sign? The church, a *holy* community in an unholy world, a *united* community of faith in a divided world of unfaith, is to be an active agent of *reconciliation* and *peace*.

The Kingdom of Peace

The call to the church is to actually be *God's* church, to be holy and united. This is essential for the sake of the church's intended service in the world. The call is not a subtle suggestion that the church withdraw from the world and exist in some stag-

---

[68]Thomas Oden, *op. cit.*, 311.
[69]John Frame, *op. cit.*, 16.

nant pool of self-righteousness. The mission of the church is for it to assume the identity and evolve the resources to stand as a viable witness in the world, a witness that models a kingdom of peace, forgiveness, and reconciliation. The Christian gospel is a "political" gospel in that it is to be engaged by its own life in revealing "the insufficiency of all politics based on coercion and falsehood and finds the true source of power in servanthood rather than dominion."[70]

In the Exodus from Egypt, the Holy One of Israel was revealed in action. God unveiled an involved, historical holiness by liberating an oppressed people. Therefore:

> Never could the Israelites justify amassing material or military power by appealing to the Exodus events. For them, the lesson was the opposite: since Yahweh had freed them *by his grace,* they were called to a life based on truth, not on power.[71]

The ways of divine sovereignty revealed in the Bible refute humanity's usual view of power. The victory that finally overcomes the world is pictured in the Christ who, of all places, reigns even from an old rugged cross. God's weakness is said to be stronger than human strength (1 Cor. 1:25). In light of the biblical narrative, to say that God is omnipotent is to say that, with patience and even suffering, God can and will accomplish all that is promised. Such power "includes the power of self-restraint; it allows a real drama of invitation, rejection and resistance to unfold; yet it also bespeaks a power of persistence that

---

[70]Stanley Hauerwas, *The Peaceable Kingdom* (University of Notre Dame Press, 1983), 102. Hauerwas goes on to note that often the world hates those who call attention to what the world really is. Suffering may result for the church. Christians may even be forced to become political refugees. In fact, Christians are not fully "at home" in any nation, for "our true home is the church itself" (102).

[71]Alan Kreider, *Journey Towards Holiness* (Scottdale, Pa.: Herald Press, 1987), 66.

stubbornly endures until victory is won. . . . It manifests the power of powerlessness."[72]

God works through weakness to confront strength.[73] Abraham, called to be the pioneer of God's new people, moved out as a wandering herdsman, not even sure where he was being called to go. The "suffering servant" songs in Isaiah portray the true servant of God as the one who prevails through selfless suffering (e.g., Isaiah 53). In the terrible experience of Babylonian exile and then the new-exodus return, Israel learned that it could be God's people without functioning as an economic and military power, that God was in control in God's way even when Israel lacked all control of circumstances.

The loving nature of God colors the biblical story with the warm glow of compassion and thereby reveals the character of the divine Kingdom and the conduct appropriate for those who claim to be its citizens. It is the "meek" who will inherit the earth (Matt. 5:5). The biblical story reveals how God chooses, and thus how we should choose to view and do things. John Wesley rightly conceived of God's power . . .

> in terms of *empowerment,* rather than control or *overpowerment.* This is not to weaken God's power but to determine its character! As Wesley was fond of saying, God works "strongly and sweetly." That is, God's *grace* works powerfully, but not irresistibly, in matters of human life and salvation; thereby empowering our *response-ability,* without overriding our *responsibility.*[74]

---

[72]Gabriel Fackre, *Ecumenical Faith in Evangelical Perspective* (Grand Rapids: Eerdmans, 1993), 121.

[73]Weakness, of course, is judged here from a human perspective as the surprising and voluntary avoidance by God of coercion to accomplish the divine will. Jesus on the cross endured those who sneered at him: "He saved others; let him save himself if he is the Christ of God, the Chosen One" (Lk. 23:35).

[74]Randy Maddox, *Responsible Grace: John Wesley's Practical Theology* (Nashville: Kingswood Books, Abingdon Press, 1994), 55.

God always is dependable, although not coercive. God is omnipotent, that is, God is unlimited so far as having the capacity to act decisively in accord with the divine nature and will, regardless of human rebellion. God can and will act as promised, fulfill commitments, is always to be trusted, all because God's nature and intent do not change (Lam. 3:22-23; 1 John 1:9). Divine omnipotence, however, is not characterized biblically as God's instant control of all things at all times. God is *relational*. God is love and chooses to function with a responsive and adapting compassion toward those loved. While not dependent on or defined by the processes of this world (a view of some "process" theologians today), God functions both freely, dependably, and contingently in relation to this shifting and often evil world. The paradox is that God "has the power to be without becoming, yet he has the power to become in his sovereign freedom and grace. God is neither static immutability nor dynamic event when viewed alone. He is the Eternal Being who acts in freedom and is constant through all change."[75]

This understanding of the being and ways of God is central in the Believers' Church tradition, one crucial influence on the theological vision of the Church of God movement. How are Christians to live in this world? They are to be holy as God is holy. In part this means lives of self-less compassion, walking vulnerably along the path of reconciliation and empowerment, not rushing aggressively down the wide road of coercion and violence. There are three *regulating principles* of this "Anabaptist" tradition.[76] They combine to help identify a distinctively Christian social strategy.

First, Jesus is the *norm* of truth. Behind and beneath the doctrines that have developed about His nature, work, and rela-

---

[75]Dale Moody, *The Word of Truth* (Grand Rapids: Eerdmans, 1981), 99.

[76]See J. Denny Weaver, *Becoming Anabaptist* (Scottdale, Pa.: Herald Press, 1987), 120.

tion to God is the New Testament narrative of the historical life and teachings of Jesus. This pre-doctrinal witness is crucial as a model for Christian living in this world. Second, the church is the *community* of those changed and guided by the truth of Jesus. Following Jesus leads to new and redeemed relationships. Faith finds fulfillment in the new social reality of those now belonging together in Christ. Third, *peace* is a distinctive Christian way of being together in Christ and being in the world with Christ.[77] Quakerism, for example, has been called a way of life, "not just a set of beliefs or a statement of faith; it is a practical, ethical, and functional religious approach to life. . . . The inward journey of faith can never be separated from the outward journey of practice. . . . Quakers believe that the way of the cross of Jesus is entirely inconsistent with war or preparation for it."[78] God triumphs by a cross, not by coercion.

The gift of peace is central both to a Christian's inward life with Jesus and outward calling to Jesus-like discipleship. Inwardly, the shalom of God includes all that makes for one's highest good. It should be no surprise that our shalom is the goal of God. The Greek word *eirene* (peace) appears in every New Testament book, focusing on right relationships in the home (1 Cor. 7:15), between Jew and Gentile (Eph. 2:14-17), within the church (Eph. 4:3), and between the believer and God (Rom. 5:1; Col. 1:20). God is the God of peace (Rom. 15:33; 1 Thess. 5:23; Heb. 13:20-21). Paul prayed that God might fill the Christians in Rome "with all joy and peace in believing" (Rom. 15:13). This peace of God passes all understanding (Phil. 4:7) and was the

---

[77]For a brief historical overview of the "peace witness" in church history, see Donald Durnbaugh, *The Believers' Church* (Scottdale, Pa.: Herald Press, 1968, 1985), 254-259.

[78]Wilmer Cooper, *A Living Faith* (Richmond, Ind.: Friends United Press, 1990), 99, 108. Reference often is made to Jesus' statements that "if my kingdom were of this world then would my servants fight," "love your enemies," and "blessed are the peacemakers."

departing legacy of the risen Christ (John 14:27). Such marvelous well-being is a divine gift that believers are privileged to receive and are expected to let rule in their hearts (Col. 3:15).[79]

Outwardly, the Believers' Church witness to the church catholic focuses on rejection of church-state unions that in the past and present confuse national citizenship and Christian identity.[80] Jesus avoided the Zealot approach of resorting to violence to solve problems, choosing instead to be the Prince of Peace, the "suffering servant."[81] According to the prophecy of Isaiah 49:1-7, God's true servant will be a light to the nations, causing rulers to be surprised by the great reversal, God choosing "weakness" as a channel for power. Christians are called to be people of God's Kingdom who live by serving. The Kingdom is one of peace and righteousness, not one of anger and bullets. Believers are to be in this world in a special, cross-like way.

How can one determine the proper relation between the option of violence, the will of God, and a believer's duty to the nation-state? Ultimate loyalty, of course, is to be to the will of God. Nevertheless, equally conscientious Christians disagree about how God works through civil authorities to accomplish the

---

[79]One of the loved hymns of the Church of God movement is Barney Warren's "The Kingdom of Peace" (in *Worship the Lord*, Anderson, Ind.: Warner Press, 1989, 481). Given the fact that "the kingdom of God is not a matter of eating and drinking, but of righteousness, peace and joy in the Holy Spirit" (Rom. 14:17), the refrain affirms: " 'Tis a kingdom of peace, it is reigning within, It shall ever increase in my soul; We possess it right here when He saves from all sin, And 'twill last while the ages shall roll."

[80]Current examples of such unions of religion and nationalism include Israel-Judaism and Iran-Islam. Christianity too often has functioned in a similar way. "Holy war" concepts arise in such settings, with frightening military results that threaten to destroy the essential nature of the faith involved and justify the most violent of actions in the name of God.

[81]Alan Kreider (*Journey Towards Holiness*, 1987, chaps. 9-10) surveys the several Jewish approaches to the oppressive Roman occupation of Palestine in the time of Jesus. He notes the distinctive way taught by Jesus, a "social holiness" of a very different sort, one that set aside all "holy wars."

divine will. While all war is highly undesirable, some Christians are more prone than others to see God working through "just" wars[82] to enable one party to defend itself or others against aggression and injustice.

Participation in organized violence often is justified by Christians because they assume that a citizen is obligated in principle (Rom. 13)[83] since the nation is seen as the instrument of divine justice. Other Christians assume a more "pacifist" position. They are not blind to injustice. They recognize the possibility that God may be active in a given conflict and that they may be responsible to be involved as representatives of God. What they see primarily, however, is the divine call to address problems by nonviolent means, to take a suffering-servant stance, pursuing the potential of love rather than the destructiveness of war as God's distinctive way of engaging evil.[84] All Christians hear Jesus saying, "love your enemies and pray for those who persecute you" (Matt. 5:44); but some believers can love, pray, and fight when necessary, while others consider any fighting as direct disobedience to the call of God.[85]

---

[82]See Paul Bock, *In Search of a Responsible World Society: The Social Teachings of the World Council of Churches* (Philadelphia: Westminster Press, 1974), 92-93.

[83]Note that the "state" spoken of positively in Romans 13 is the same state spoken of very negatively in Revelation 13.

[84]For a good case study from the historical narrative of biblical materials (1 and 2 Samuel), see Walter Brueggemann, "The Seduction of Violence: Bloodguilt Avoided and Denied," chap. 3 of *Power, Providence & Personality* (Louisville: Westminster/John Knox, 1990), 49-85.

[85]A classic example of the two options appeared soon after Japan's invasion of Manchuria in 1932. Such aggressive violence by Japan brought fear that a much wider conflict might follow. What should be the church's response to such a tragic world event? The Niebuhr brothers wrote articles stating the dilemma for Christians. One argued a "pacifist" position (H. Richard). The other (Reinhold) called for limited military response to prevent violence on an even wider scale. See H. Richard Niebuhr, "The Grace of Doing Nothing," *Christian Century* 49 (March 23, 1932), 378-80, and the responding Reinhold Niebuhr, "Must We Do Nothing?" *Christian Century* 49 (March 30, 1932), 415-17.

One group of Christians faces the dilemma of how to keep loving while in the process of killing; the other group struggles with how to act constructively and effectively when tyranny reigns and the majority opt for military action as the necessary alternative. In both cases the unprecedented weapons of mass destruction developed in recent decades have lifted the stakes to truly frightening levels, raising anew the question about whether a "just war" is even conceivable in this new circumstance where the very survival of human life on the planet could quickly be on the line.

In 1948, soon after World War II and actual use of the atom bomb against Japan, the initial meeting of the World Council of Churches insisted that "war as a means of settling disputes is incompatible with the teaching and example of our Lord Jesus Christ." How are Christians who know the peace of God in their hearts supposed to spread that peace into the outer world of unjust and deeply entrenched institutions where the weapons of mass destruction are in the hands of greedy tyrants? While governments certainly should not be permitted to capture what ought to be the believer's prime loyalty to Christ, does not that very loyalty to Christ call disciples to active social responsibility? Did not Jesus himself actively engage in protesting obvious evil, even with a whip on at least one occasion? Rather than the mere absence of overt violence, does not real peace require active initiatives toward reconciliation and justice? What is the best way to go about being socially responsible in a fallen world like ours?

The conflicting issues related to Christian obligation for social justice were framed well by John Winebrenner, who in turn influenced the earliest thinking of the Church of God movement. In the 1830s Winebrenner added a peace witness to his outspoken opposition to human slavery, saying that "all civil wars are unholy and sinful, and in which the saints of the Most

High ought never to participate."[86] In the midst of his country's war with Mexico (1846-48) he wrote with passion:

We are surprised at some of the good people of Harrisburg [Pa.] who profess to be Christians, to send their sons to military schools, and have them trained for carnage and bloodshed. Between the spirit of war and the spirit of Christianity there is an utter incompatibility.[87]

Merle Strege points out the irony inherent in the identification of two buildings on the Anderson University campus, one named for the revered college dean of many years, Russell Olt, who was a staunch Christian pacifist, and the other named for Charles Wilson, Secretary of Defense in the first administration of President Dwight Eisenhower. Here is an institutionalized reflection of the Church of God movement's ambiguous "peace" witness.[88] During World War I people associated with the movement from both the United States and Germany were active combatants, possibly facing each other violently at some unrecorded moment of battle!

Clearly the Church of God movement has been opposed to war[89] and has assumed that Christians are to love their enemies and can manage to do so constructively by the sanctifying grace

---

[86]As quoted by Richard Kern, *John Winebrenner: 19th Century Reformer* (Harrisburg, Pa.: Central Publishing House, 1974), 144.

[87]John Winebrenner, "Fourth of July," *Advocate* (July 15, 1847).

[88]Merle Strege, "Demise (?) of a Peace Church," *Mennonite Quarterly Review* (April, 1991), 128. Anderson University, Anderson, Indiana, is the largest institution of higher education associated with the Church of God movement. Dean Olt, beloved campus academic leader from 1925-1958, was an outspoken pacifist, as were others like sociologist Dr. Valorous Clear (longtime professor at Anderson University). For detail see Barry Callen, *Guide of Soul and Mind: The Story of Anderson University* (Warner Press, 1992).

[89]The movement's national periodical, *Gospel Trumpet* (August 20, 1914, 1), responded judgmentally when war broke out in Europe in 1914, calling the conflict "a form of legalized murder."

of God. Why, then, has this movement (and many others) been so outspoken against war and yet contributed so many people to its military ranks? Maybe, in part, it is because the movement's anti-organizational bias makes uniformity of thought undesirable and group discipline an uncertain affair. The primary reason likely is that patriotism has been a cherished value that at times has managed to dilute a Christian witness in the sordidness of the social arena.

Judges movement historian Merle Strege: "To grant the state sufficient authority to require or even expect Christians to kill undermines the church's position against war. Sooner or later, Caesar will insist on his pinch of incense."[90] Since an apparent majority in the movement have assumed that there is God-given authority granted to civil governments, it has been possible to oppose war in principle and at the same time insist that no Christian who chooses to participate in war should thereby be "un-Christianized."[91]

This ambiguous stance must face the unsettling witness of the biblical revelation. The church has been entrusted with the message of reconciliation (2 Cor. 5:19). With the crucified and resurrected Jesus as the basis and pattern for current mission, the goal is for the church to be engaged in peacemaking, seeking the peace of Christ (Col. 3:15) and maintaining the "bond of peace" (Eph. 4:3). Life in the Spirit without question is to be one of

---

[90]Merle Strege, *Tell Me Another Tale* (Anderson, Ind.: Warner Press, 1993), 59.

[91]See in Barry Callen, *Thinking and Acting Together* (Anderson, Ind.: Executive Council of the Church of God and Warner Press, 1992) the several formal resolutions of the General Assembly of the Church of God on this subject. While a 1932 resolution calls war "unchristian, futile and suicidal," a 1971 one reads: "We believe that the cause of Christ is best served when the Christian of draft age responds freely to his own conscience. Because we believe this, we support those who take the position of the conscientious objector. At the same time we insist that the conscientious military person has similar privileges and responsibilities before God."

peace. The question is whether the Christian commitment to peace should be limited to spiritual reconciliation with God (holiness), resulting in a faith community bound together by grace (unity), or extend also to a wider reconciliation and quest for justice (social holiness).

The full reach of the biblical revelation, especially as centered in Jesus Christ, clearly calls the church to a social witness beyond itself. Recent church history in the West, however, has introduced an inappropriate and costly restriction. Elements of the Protestant tradition have helped spread an individualistic concept of peace, focusing on the individual's experience of forgiveness, assurance, and personal holiness. Today Protestant evangelicalism commonly perpetuates this privatistic understanding of the intended peace with God. The concept "peace of mind" now has become "so identified with the biblical message that the rich, multifaceted dimensions of the biblical meaning of peace have been largely overlooked."[92] A self-serving psychological orientation has replaced a world-serving biblical orientation. The means of the world have wound themselves around and limited the message of the Saviour.

Spiritual experience surely has been of central concern in the history of the Church of God movement; but so have the radical implications of inward renewal for social relationships in the church and beyond. The African-American presence in the North American movement,[93] and increasingly the Hispanic also, has (1) heightened the focus on Christian experience as opposed to sterile theological abstractions, (2) nurtured a musical tradition that encourages self-expression in worship and the narrative (tes-

---

[92]C. Norman Kraus, *The Community of the Spirit,* rev. ed. (Scottdale, Pa.: Herald Press, 1993), 133.

[93]Of the 199,786 constituents reported for the Church of God movement in the United States and Canada in 1989, 37,435 were African Americans.

timony) sharing of pivotal life experiences, (3) forced a multi-
cultural caution about premature rigidities in truth formulations
and institutional structures, and (4) pointed to the necessity of
social as well as individual implications of being Christian. In a
sense, this prophetic presence in the movement has helped to
counter what Delwin Brown calls "the terribly individualistic
orientation of conservative doctrines of salvation and . . . [the]
conservative addiction to the rhetoric of guilt and eternal punish-
ment [that have] weakened a redemptive concern for this life and
this world."[94]

Testimonies of God's faithfulness in personal and corporate
struggles in the present should fill church life with stories and
songs of pain and prayer, with victory made possible by God's
power and grace. There should be a narrative trail of evidence
that the resurrected Jesus is truly alive in this world. The resulting sense of apostolic authenticity should always reflect anew
the pioneering atmosphere of the book of Acts. The new Pentecost people, the church, is to know itself to be a community of
the Spirit that is alive and at work. God is with us on our journey
together through life.

There has been fostered in the life of the Church of God
movement a questing for "orthodox" belief in a "radical" context.[95] On the one hand, salvation and social justice are not the

---

[94]Delwin Brown, in Clark Pinnock and Brown, *Theological Crossfire*
(Grand Rapids: Zondervan, 1990), 178. Wolfhart Pannenberg also
expresses concern about the negative results for Christian credibility and
church mission emerging from what he judges an almost pathological
emphasis on guilt (*Christian Spirituality*, Philadelphia: Westminster Press,
1983, chapter one).

[95]See James Earl Massey, "A Positive Force" in Wilfred Jordan and
Richard Willowby, eds., *Diamond Jubilee: National Association of the
Church of God* (Anderson, Ind.: Warner Press, 1991), 3-5. Says Massey:
"Unlike other church groups whose doctrinal positions accented nonrela-
tional themes and teachings, the central theme of the Church of God was a
relational one, namely the unity of believers."

same thing. On the other hand, as Martin Luther King, Jr., puts it: "A religion that professes a concern for the souls of men and is not equally concerned about the slums that damn them, the economic conditions that strangle them, and the social conditions that cripple them, is a spiritually moribund religion."[96] The God who chose incarnation as the clearest way of being among us surely chooses incarnation as the way the church is to be on God's mission in the world. It is to be an incarnation of the Kingdom of Peace.

[96]Martin Luther King, Jr., *Strength To Love* (N. Y.: Harper & Row, 1963), 138.

CHAPTER FIVE

Frontiers

The Church of God movement has evolved across the twentieth century as an experimental, maturing, growing, and now greatly internationalized body of believers.[1] Generally, and ironically, the movement often has stood apart from the larger ecumenical dialogues about Christian faith, life, and mission. Such separation stems in part from the movement's isolationist tendencies rooted in its early "come-outism" stance. This movement, nonetheless, has been impacted by the theological struggles of the "evangelical" community,[2] and in its modest way has sought a distinctive and constructive role.

Today the movement seeks a fresh sighting of the vision that should carry it forward into the twenty-first century. What "cause" should now be compelling? What about biblical prophecy, evangelicalism, the hope of Christ's second coming? What frontiers yet beckon God's faithful people? What hope sustains? What responsibility burdens and sends?

A Compelling Cause

In various ways, the Church of God movement has shared Carl Henry's critiques of both fundamentalism and neo-orthodoxy, two of the major theological forces of the twentieth cen-

---

[1]In 1983, the Church of God movement became larger outside than inside the United States and Canada. The 1992 *Yearbook of the Church of God* lists congregations of the movement in 78 countries other than the U.S. and Canada, with a total non-North American constituency of 303,000.

[2]See the discussion later in this chapter for the meaning of "evangelical" and its complex relation to the theological vision of the Church of God movement.

tury, each reacting to "liberalism" in the church's life.[3] Of particular concern has been fundamentalism's rigid theological creedalism, accompanied often by loveless attitudes toward any who disagree. Typical also of fundamentalism has been a denominational separatism that readily justifies and prolongs the deep dividedness among God's children and exhibits relative disconnectedness from the urgent social, economic, and political needs of the world. Such negative tendencies have been resisted by the Church of God movement, a movement confident that it is not necessary to be *dogmatic* in order to be *conservative,* and that the church should not be *socially irrelevant* in the process of being *orthodox.*

Neo-orthodoxy, on the other hand, has been a theological emphasis reacting to classic liberalism in a somewhat different way. It has reasserted emphasis on the transcendence of God, seeking to deal a deathblow to many modern and sometimes idolatrous diversions from the historic mainstream of Christian believing. However, neo-orthodox leaders like European Karl Barth (1886-1968) and American Reinhold Niebuhr (1892-1971) joined fundamentalism in drinking deeply from certain Enlightenment wells. In this case, the real authority of the Bible as a normative guide for all Christian theology was subtly brought into question (more "neo" than "orthodox"). Church of God leaders have rejoiced readily in the severe critique leveled at various liberalisms, but have struggled against any loss of real integrity accorded the biblical revelation in the process.

Christian people who have come to this movement of the Church of God over the generations have known that they did not have all the answers. What they have been confident about is that, for the church, human authority structures and theological thinking are limited at best and destructive at worst. They have

---

[3]See Bob Patterson, *Carl F. H. Henry* (Peabody, Mass.: Hendrickson Publishers, 1983), 38-50.

sought to be humble about their own perceptions and even apologetic about the appropriateness of their own evolving traditions and structures. At least these believers have been sure that they have encountered the real presence of God, have found new life through divine grace, have thereby "seen the church," and have tried to model the visible integrity of that church by allowing God to really be its Lord. The result has been an inspired, dynamic, sometimes awkwardly experimental approach to the many questions of Christian belief and practice.

Today we live in an age of technology where consumerism devours ever more "things" and super computers store and manipulate more and more "data." Information is everywhere and wisdom seems rarer than ever. The scientist is revered and the stock broker handles what commonly is sought above all else—money. Christian theologians who seek to identify and communicate relevant truth in this sick setting could benefit from the same advice Walter Brueggemann once gave preachers. Bring on the poets!

After the engineers, inventors, managers, and empire-builders have done their best, finally there should come the power of poetry. Poetry is "shattering, evocative speech that breaks fixed conclusions and presses us always toward new, dangerous, imaginative possibilities."[4] On occasion there arises a prophetic voice that disrupts the religious status quo. Sometimes there emerge Christian leaders who envision and experience, not merely standardize and enforce. Sometimes prophetic voices are heard in the church, voices that money can't buy and human agendas have not yet consumed.

The Church of God movement intends to be more than merely a collection of friendly, community congregations of

---

[4]Walter Brueggemann, *Finally Comes the Poet* (Minneapolis: Fortress Press, 1989), 6.

Christian people.[5] It has been and should continue to be a *compelling cause*, a prophetic voice speaking boldly, not rashly, but radically to the whole church. It has been, and hopes yet to be, a renewal movement of the Spirit that furthers holiness and encourages unity among all of God's people. A key movement frontier is finding effective ways to accomplish this goal in the current circumstances of the church.

An early example of such bold speaking, driven by a concern for the integrity of God's people, is that of Daniel Warner in 1881. With more wisdom than tact, Warner wrote about the sharply divided world of Christianity:

> In what a disgraceful light sectism presents the church! Does that look like a divine and heaven-born family that is composed of numerous, rival, jealous, independent, and conflicting organisms? Oh, I beseech you for Christ's sake, do not dishonor God by confounding his church with Babylon confusion.

Another example emerged in the movement's national camp meeting convened in Anderson, Indiana, in June, 1913. Herbert Riggle preached a sermon titled "The True Standard." This standard he identified as the written Word of God, God's inspired witness to the truth centered in Christ. "The Methodists," he insisted, "say that John Wesley set the standard. We go beyond Wesley; we go back to Christ and the apostles, to the days of pure, primitive Christianity, to the inspired Word of Truth." Adherents of the movement have great respect for the

---

[5]Recent years have seen a leveling tendency that, unfortunately, has reduced many congregations of the Church of God movement to generic community churches. A lack of apparent theological concern and clarity, complicated by television "theologians," has encouraged confusion and lack of prophetic distinctiveness. There now is a tendency to remove the name "Church of God" from public congregational identifications to better relate with the geographic community being served and avoid being misidentified with some other groups that use the same name.

teachings of John Wesley, but he is not accepted as the final standard of truth (nor would he have wished to be). For that matter, neither were the pioneers of the movement itself.[6]

With the movement only about thirty-five years old at the time, Riggle acknowledged that "so many folks talk about going back to the 'old paths,' meaning the teachings and practices of the church [the movement] thirty years ago. They say that must be the standard. But to go only thirty years back would be to follow in the rut of the sects about us." The theological challenge is more radical, more dynamic, daring, and apostolic than that.

How might the body of believers avoid division and remain focused on its true mission? Riggle concluded his sermon by calling for a rebuking of "every spirit of division and strife" and for all believers to "stand for the truth, the whole truth, and nothing but the truth." That "truth" was understood to be a Christ-centered cause. "Let us close in our ranks, and press forward, side by side, heart in heart, against the combined powers of sin and hell. . . . Mounted on our holiness steeds, let us rush forward in the battle, each one a giant for God, zealous in one common cause, carrying in every direction the message of full salvation from sin till the kingdoms of this world shall become the kingdoms of our Lord." Here indeed were the elements of a compelling cause. Christians can and should find a genuine oneness in Christ that, in turn, will enable a unified, credible advance into a sinful world with a life-changing, church-changing, and world-changing message of "full salvation."

Without question the first generations of participants in the Church of God movement saw themselves as the privileged heralds of God's will for the church. All their beliefs were tinted with the bright colors of this sense of divine destiny. The sense of urgency came in part from the assumption that the end of time was near and that their own reformation work was one of the

---

[6]See Barry Callen, *It's God's Church! Life and Legacy of Daniel Warner* (Anderson, Ind.: Warner Press, 1995), chap. 9.

signs of the last days.[7] Increasingly they drew upon the Bible's apocalyptic literature to characterize the times. Often preachers would rely on the church-historical way of interpreting the prophetic books of the Hebrew Scriptures and New Testament to explain the apparent role of the movement itself in the divine work being accomplished during those last days.[8]

More than a century now has passed. The "last days" have lengthened unexpectedly and the movement of the Church of God, in some tension with its own renewal emphases, has acquired certain establishment characteristics of its own. At first the movement perceived no need to formulate theology or build institutions for the long haul. Any subsequently acquired preoccupation with maintaining churchly institutions, a mixture of sociological maturation and cultural accommodation, tends to distract from the movement's "radical" reason for being. So there is need for reassessment. The movement has no desire to settle into a standard denominational pattern. Only a compelling cause will satisfy this fellowship's traditional sense of group identity under God for the sake of the whole church and its mission in the world.

A community of faith requires a "story" that informs, binds together, and motivates its members. Walter Brueggemann identi-

---

[7]Such urgency, excitement, and expectation of early and dramatic results were not unusual. One precedent is the Cane Ridge Revival (Kentucky, August, 1801) that launched the "Stoneite" movement (joining the Campbellite movement in 1832 to create the "Disciples" or "Christian" tradition). As quoted by C. Leonard Allen ("The Stone That the Builders Rejected" in A. Dunnavant, ed., *Cane Ridge in Context,* Nashville: Disciples of Christ Historical Society, 1992, 50), revival participants Robert Marshall and John Thompson wrote: "We confidently thought that the Millennium was just at hand, and that a glorious church would soon be formed." Those thousands caught up in the spiritual euphoria of this marvelous event, says Allen, believed that "the old order, dominated by creeds, traditions, and the clergy, was passing away . . . and a whole new order of Spirit-formed holiness and unity was fast approaching" (*op. cit.,* 50).

[8]John Smith, *The Quest for Holiness and Unity* (Anderson, Ind.: Warner Press, 1980), 96-100.

fies three constituencies upon whom biblical faith should concentrate its evangelistic efforts. Using Nehemiah 8 as a biblical model, one of these constituencies is the "jaded insiders."[9] These are members of the faith community who, despite their membership, no longer know or are moved by the community's "core memory" of faith. They have "become hollow and uncaring, honoring empty forms of faith and practice, but [are] completely cut off from the gifts, demands, and joys that belong to this relationship."[10]

In recent years thousands of Christians have associated with the Church of God movement (and with Christian fellowships generally) for reasons other than sharing a motivating vision for the role of the movement within the whole of today's Christian community. To many observers, this is viewed as having led the Church of God movement, as one example, to be increasingly narrative-less, a community without a common story. Warns Arlo Newell: "There is no more perilous time in the life of any movement than when the vision is being carried out by people who have never seen it."[11] The result of vision-less people is self-preoccupation, the meeting of only immediate needs, accommodation to current models of "success," loss of distinctive group identity, and/or reversion to an earlier model of the movement's vision in the absence of an apparent alternative.[12]

---

[9]The other constituencies identified are outsiders (Joshua 24) and the children of believers.

[10]Walter Brueggemann, *Biblical Perspectives on Evangelism* (Nashville: Abingdon Press, 1993), 71-72.

[11]Arlo Newell, "Campmeetings . . . In Trouble?" *Vital Christianity* (August, 1992), 13.

[12]A recent expression of attempts to revive an earlier model of the vision of the Church of God movement is the Pastors' Fellowship. This "conservative" fellowship is a series of voluntary annual gatherings of movement leaders by geographic region. They seek to inform, inspire, and encourage movement leaders, especially by "old-time" preaching, teaching, and singing that reminds one of the movement in much earlier decades. The fellowship was begun by Pastor Lillie S. McCutcheon following strained relations within the movement very evident in the 1972 General Assembly in Anderson, Indiana. See Barry Callen, *She Came Preaching* (Anderson, Ind.: Warner Press, 1992), 288ff.

Seeing the vision that traditionally has inspired the Church of God movement requires dealing forthrightly with at least two important relationships. The first is how the movement often has seen itself in relation to "prophetic" biblical literature. This centers in the movement's self-understanding, where it fits in the perceived pattern of God's present actions. The second is how the movement *is* and is *not* reflective of contemporary "evangelicalism." We turn first to a review of the movement's changing perception of the apocalyptic context.

The Apocalyptic Context

A significant development emerged in the self-understanding of key leaders of the young Church of God movement around the time that the publishing work moved to Grand Junction, Michigan, in 1886. In part it was the acquiring of a new way of establishing the movement's emerging identity, a way being drawn increasingly from biblical prophecy. Seventh-day Adventism was strong in this part of Michigan and soon Daniel Warner, movement pioneer, was well acquainted with the work of a leading Adventist editor and writer, Uriah Smith.[13] Smith had developed a complex interpretive system that coordinated a reading of biblical prophecy with the emergence and historical role of Adventism.[14] Warner initially was repelled by this system and its presumed justification of Adventism; but then he became attracted to much of it—with key refinements.[15]

---

[13]R. W. Schwarz, *Light Bearers to the Remnant* (Boise, Id.: Pacific Press Publishing Assoc., 1979), 81, 185, 192.

[14]Uriah Smith, *Thoughts, Critical and Practical on the Books of Daniel and Revelation* (Battle Creek, Mich.: Review and Herald Press, 1882).

[15]Daniel Warner's personal copy of Uriah Smith's 1882 book (more than 800 pages long) now is in the archives of Anderson University. It includes handwritten marginal notes by Warner, clear evidence of his extensive interaction with this material.

Warner, a skilled debater, studied Smith's writing with care and came to oppose his application of these biblical texts to Adventism. The basic disagreement between Smith and Warner involved the identity of the lamblike beast of Revelation 13:11-19. Warner was especially concerned that Adventist theology applied the "cleansing of the sanctuary" concept to a cleansing in heaven to begin in 1844.[16] He saw the cleansing related instead to the holiness reform of his own day. For persons in Indiana, Ohio, and Michigan who were intrigued at the time by such eschatological issues, Adventists and Church of God movement pioneers clearly became competitors on the scene of prophetic interpretation. There was agreement, however, that these biblical materials in the book of Revelation portray a map of the church's history from the first to the second coming of Christ.

Warner became absorbed in Uriah Smith's general system of interpretation. Soon, having altered key details, Warner was himself presenting this general plan of biblical prophecy, now as a prophetic framework and a dramatic rationale to be applied to the young Church of God movement! This plan began appearing with the October 15, 1883 issue of the *Gospel Trumpet* when Warner identified the first "beast" of Revelation 13 as Roman Catholicism and the second as the Protestant "churches" that sprang from it. The one was a harlot, the other the harlot's daughters.

Shortly Warner would be working on a major manuscript, *The Cleansing of the Sanctuary,* a work completed by his friend Herbert Riggle in 1903. A *Gospel Trumpet* article by this title appeared under Warner's name in the June 1, 1887, issue. This was the first time Warner developed from biblical prophecy a chronological timetable for the reformation of the church, now being seen was "an exact parallel" between the description in

[16]Daniel Warner and Herbert Riggle, *The Cleansing of the Sanctuary* (Moundsville, W.V.: Gospel Trumpet Pub. Co., 1903), 38.

Nehemiah 2-6 and "the present work of cleansing the sanctuary, or restoring the complete walls of salvation." In the April 7, 1892, *Gospel Trumpet* is a large chart detailing the key dates of church history, with their prophetic references, all culminating in the "fall of sectism, A.D. 1880."

A key biblical verse was Zechariah 14:7, which says that "it shall come to pass that at evening time it shall be light." Was it not now the "evening time," with God's full and final light coming fast to those who would receive? Were not the walls of salvation being restored fully? Martin Luther had recovered justification by faith from Roman darkness (sixteenth century). John Wesley had reintroduced true Christian holiness (eighteenth century). Now Warner and his colleagues (nineteenth century) were catching it all up and bringing it to maturity by seeing the final gathering into one of all the saved and sanctified saints of God.

This vision was exhilarating and, as usual, was captured in lyrics written by Warner that still are sung by Church of God people:

> Brighter days are sweetly dawning,
> O the glory looms in sight!
> For the cloudy day is waning,
> And the evening shall be light.
>
> Lo! the ransomed are returning,
> Robed in shining crystal white;
> Leaping, shouting home to Zion,
> Happy in the evening light.

It may be that there was "a moment, heavy with destiny, when Warner felt in his heart that God, in the year 1880, was breaking again into history, that it was foretold by the prophets, and that Warner was a central figure, being used of God to usher in the last phase of history before the end of the age."[17] The scat-

---

[17]Robert Reardon, *The Early Morning Light* (Anderson, Ind: Warner Press, 1979), 22. See also Barry Callen, *It's God's Church! Life and Legacy of Daniel Warner* (Warner Press, 1995), chapter 8.

tered "saints," the courageous come-outers, were no longer an isolated and insignificant phenomenon in the larger Holiness Movement. They understood themselves to have the role of heralding the initiation of the final fulfillment of God's ultimate will for the church. They represented the leading edge of the "last reformation."[18]

Convictions long held about church divisions and heart holiness now were combined by Daniel Warner to create a sense of group destiny. This focusing of identity greatly accelerated a "movement" consciousness. While not expecting an earthly millennium before or after the return of Christ,[19] Warner came to see the work of restoring the pure and united church as a sign of the rapidly approaching reappearing of Christ. There was the urgency of a God-ordained mission in the "last days," an urgency generating a self-conscious "movement" now being driven by a prophetically fired biblical vision. The themes of unity, holiness, and biblical prophecy blended and were conveyed powerfully by the preaching skill of Daniel Warner and an increasing number of others.

In Warner's early ministry, the primary theme (beyond salvation itself) was Christian unity. Then it was holiness and unity, and finally it became unity and holiness in light of biblical prophecy. Warner thus was involved in "two different interpretations of the movement's reason for being."[20] One is represented well by his song "The Bond of Perfectness" that highlights the unity of Christians enabled by the sanctifying power of God. Here is a classic expression of the clear relationship seen by Warner between the sanctifying experience (perfectness) and the intended unity of God's people. States the chorus:

---

[18]See Melvin Dieter, "Primitivism in the American Holiness Tradition," *Wesleyan Theological Journal* 30:1 (Spring 1995), 78-91.

[19]Church of God theologians consistently have maintained an "amillennial" position.

[20]Merle Strege, *Tell Me Another Tale* (Anderson, Ind: Warner Press, 1993), 12.

Beloved how this perfect love,
Unites us all in Jesus!
One heart, and soul, and mind we prove,
The union heaven gave us.[21]

The other interpretation of the movement's reason for being, seen in Warner's later writings, is represented well by the work of William Schell. In 1893 Schell published *Biblical Trace of the Church,* the first major work to define the movement's evolving identity by a "church-historical" interpretation of the Bible's prophetic material. There also is Schell's song "Biblical Trace of the Church." Here the movement's identity is pictured as a prophetically foretold instrument of God. In the last days the movement of the Church of God was to help regather from divided Romanism and Protestantism the one church comprised of all God's children.

This view became widely influential in the Church of God movement for decades, largely through the ministry of the third editor of the *Gospel Trumpet,* F. G. Smith. It finally began to be questioned widely as adequate biblical interpretation.[22] By the late 1920s various nationally prominent persons in the Church of God movement were rethinking the nature and role of this reformation movement, in part because of an ingrown narrowness that by then had evolved. Some, like Russell R. Byrum and E. A. Reardon, were questioning whether the movement, dedicated to a vision of Christian unity, had begun to violate its own vision

---

[21]See "The Bond of Perfectness," in *Worship the Lord* (Anderson, Ind.: Warner Press, 1989), 330.

[22]See especially Otto F. Linn (*Studies in the New Testament,* vol. 3, 1942), Marie Strong (*Basic Teachings From Patmos,* 1980), and Kenneth Jones, "Babylon and the New Jerusalem: Interpreting Revelation," in Barry Callen, ed., *Listening to the Word of God* (Anderson, Ind: Warner Press, 1990), 133-150. While these books all were published by Warner Press, the Linn volume does not carry the Warner Press name because of its handling of the Book of Revelation. Also see John Stanley, "Unity Amid Diversity: Interpreting the Book of Revelation in the Church of God (Anderson)," *Wesleyan Theological Journal* 25:2 (Fall 1990), 74-98.

by itself growing too narrow and isolated. "We must beware," warned Byrum, "lest we lose our vision of real Christian unity and degenerate into mere Church of God sectarians. . . . Not a few persons among us in the past have supposed that all true Christians would soon leave their denominations and come to us." By 1928 Byrum judged that such come-to-us thinking had lessened considerably within the movement and he hoped that "we may further promote unity by refraining from sectishness in our attitude."[23]

Rev. E. A. Reardon agreed and wondered "why it is that we are so far away from others of God's people who have so large an amount of grace and truth, and why we have so little to do with them. . . . Many [in the Church of God movement] seem to have imbibed the spirit of exclusiveness to the extent that they are seriously prejudiced against even that which is good in others, simply because it does not have our stamp upon it. They have shut themselves up in the reformation and bolted the door." He admitted that "there is such a thing as stressing the reformation to such an extent that we cause our people to be reformation centered, reformation sectarians."[24]

The task for the future is to seek fresh perceptions of what God *now is doing*, in light of disciplined biblical study, and how that fits into "the big picture" of God-with-us for the world's salvation. Such perceptions will arise in part from what is thought about biblical prophecy and what should follow the current decay of "modernity" and "evangelicalism."

Post-Modern, Post-Evangelical

The tasks of Christian theology, we have said, are three: (1) faithful *maintenance* of a normative past (primarily biblical

---

[23]Russell Byrum, as in Barry Callen, ed., *The First Century,* vol. 2 (Anderson, Ind.: Warner Press, 1979), 632-34.

[24]E. A. Reardon, as in Barry Callen, ed., *The First Century*, vol. 2 (Anderson, Ind.: Warner Press, 1979), 637.

revelation); (2) skilled *communication* of that past in the language and culture of today (including preaching, Christian education, and evangelism); and (3) committed *living out* of that past as individual believers and as the church community (radical discipleship in private and public life). In addressing these tasks, there are three general *types* of Christian theology. They tend to be distinguished by which of these three tasks is given highest priority.

Justo González has reviewed the thought of the earliest Christian centuries and identified three theological types.[25] The first focuses on morality, law, and the proper way of Christian thinking and living. The theologian Tertullian (c160-220) defined Christianity with care, holding it up with pride in the face of the surrounding culture with all its ineffective idolatries. The second type focuses on philosophy and metaphysics. It is represented by Origen (185-254) who was more of an apologist seeking to demonstrate to the intellectually respectable of his time that Christianity is compatible with the best of Greek philosophy.

The third type focuses more on pastoral concern for Christian people trying to be faithful in unsympathetic surroundings. The theologian Irenaeus (c130-200) concentrated on the needs of persecuted Christians, showing them the nature of faith and obedience in the midst of a world lacking either moral goodness or philosophic wisdom. González sees in the first type the distant ancestor of modern fundamentalisms and in the second a pattern for recent liberalisms. Both, he observes, cared in different ways about showing the world the superiority of Christianity. In the process both became shaped and used by that world to an unfortunate degree.

In the third type, however, lies promise for the present. It is an approach to Christian theology especially appropriate for the

---

[25]Justo González, *Christian Thought Revisited* (Nashville: Abingdon Press, 1989), 19-33.

late twentieth century and beyond. Types one and two carry the motive of making the faith understandable and even acceptable to the established order or, vice versa, making the current culture acceptable to the faith. Type three, however, tends to disavow any preoccupation with such a motive. Respectability in the eyes of the world and compatibility with the thinking of that world are not central issues. The right issue is more the *integrity* of the faith in the face of the world. Faith centers in God's own Kingdom with its distinctive promise of liberation and renewal. The church is to understand itself as a colony of resident aliens whose first priority is to be itself, not to be congenial with, respected by, or the agent of helpful improvements for the surrounding society.[26]

A similar view of theological types is presented by Carl Braaten. The first type, he says, is concerned primarily with the issue of Christian *identity.* The focus is on the inspiration and authority of Scripture and establishing the truthfulness of the classic creeds. The second is more concerned with a rational *intelligibility* "which reassesses the claims of religion or Christianity on the basis of a commitment to contemporary modes of experience and understanding." The third centers chiefly in the faith's social *applicability* and now features a wide range of "liberationist" theological models set forth by some African Americans, feminists, political activists, and others. Americans have been attracted especially to this third type because, judges Braaten, "it is equated with the idealistic vision of a transformed society abounding with peace and justice—a kind of utopian dream of the kingdom brought down to earth."[27]

---

[26]For an extended elaboration of this perspective, see Stanley Hauerwas and William Willimon, *Resident Aliens* (Nashville: Abingdon Press, 1989). Such an approach is characteristic of the Believers' Church tradition, a tradition vital to the theological vision of the Church of God movement. It highlights the issue of holiness, the real and visible integrity of the faith.

[27]Carl Braaten, *No Other Gospel!* (Minneapolis: Fortress Press, 1992), 18-23.

The Church of God movement has emphasized *identity,* stressing biblical authority as central and essential. Usually it has focused on the task of reasserting the spiritual dynamic of the apostolic past more than striving for rational *intelligibility* in contemporary categories (a preoccupation of much modern theology). The movement certainly has had strong commitment to a *real-life applicability* of the faith (resisting dogma and championing discipleship). God's Kingdom has arrived in Christ. Christians are to concentrate on understanding the true nature of this Kingdom and its present relevance. Only secondarily should there be focus on an intellectual reassessment of the faith in light of modern experiences and understandings. A central motive should not be the gaining of respectability in an alien culture. First, the church should concentrate on *being the church,* evidence of the Kingdom now come.

In summary, the Church of God movement has been thoroughly *catholic* in the breadth of its whole-church vision. It has been clearly *protestant* in its insistence on proper Christian identity by faith alone through Christ alone. Finally, it has been genuinely *radical* in its insistence on real change in believers (holiness) and in the church (unity) as a result of God's grace and as evidence of the Kingdom's presence now. The phrase "free-church catholic" is applicable, especially when the experience and power of Pentecost are presumed foundational.

The dominant intellectual tradition of the West roots in a Hellenistic (Greek) philosophy that prepared the way for the reasonableness of modern science. This has been a tradition of *order.* It "seeks to discern, understand, decipher, know, and, if possible, master and control."[28] The biblical tradition, however, is more a vision of *hope* that lives dynamically, forwardly, and usually critiques the status quo of this world in light of the cur-

---

[28]Walter Brueggemann, *Hope Within History* (Atlanta: John Knox, 1987), 72.

rent presence and still-to-come fullness of the Kingdom of God. Thus the perpetual paradox of order and hope.

Any viable community, including the church, needs both order and hope, structure and spirit, the foothold of tradition and the dynamic of expectation. The church of the West in recent centuries has faulted on the side of excessive order. Denominational and creedal structures have dotted the broad landscape of Protestants and a settled hierarchy has dominated Roman Catholics.[29] Too much humanness has been apparent. There have been too many claims to theological certainty, too much institutionalized control. At the same time that orthodoxy often has been reduced to a sterile scholasticism, reactions have tended to produce too much undisciplined emotionalism and unchecked individualism. Balance is a virtue not easily maintained.

The Church of God movement has been especially resistant to the tendency to any overemphasis on order. It has opposed vigorously all forms of false order, the heavy laying of human hands on the life of God's church. In fact, the movement's own principle of proper order has centered in placing priority on the liberating, empowering, and commissioning presence and power of God (assumed to be orderly indeed). Always insisting that God is sovereign over the church, the movement has championed a Spirit-directed freedom, a divinely-controlled governance of the church's life. Christian leaders are not authorized to organize as a way to master, protect, and control. Their role is to obey God so that the result can be uniting, enabling, healing, and serving.

---

[29]Frederick Norris discusses helpfully the significant dilemmas of Protestant fundamentalism's doctrine of biblical "inerrancy" and similar authoritarian dilemmas in Roman Catholicism. Many "evangelical" leaders among Protestants and the impact of Vatican II on Catholicism have begun bridging a previously wide ecumenical gap. See Norris, *The Apostolic Faith: Protestants and Roman Catholics* (Collegeville, Minn.: The Liturgical Press, 1992), 35ff.

The movement has sought a distinct alternative to the maze of twentieth century Christian theologies. While *radical,* the movement is solidly rooted in the historic Christian tradition. While *orthodox,* meaning in the mainstream of Christian believing, it nonetheless is more flexible, less rationalistic and propositional than the usual scholastic and sectarian expressions of orthodoxy. To use the categories of Clark Pinnock, the Church of God movement is a theological "moderate," viewing "progressives" as apostate reductionists and "conservatives" as divisive denominationalists.[30]

One helpful way to approach identifying a viable "post-modern" Christian theology is to see how the Church of God movement is and is not "evangelical." Evangelicalism has become the general term designating one of the more prominent and influential Christian movements in the twentieth century. It now is (or always was) such a diverse movement that defining "evangelicalism" has emerged as a major issue for American religious historiography. A special issue of *Christian Scholar's Review*, e.g., recently was dedicated to this issue.[31]

Donald Dayton and Robert Johnston have sought to provide a map of this complex territory, with at least Dayton concluding that the "evangelical" category has lost its descriptive usefulness and should be discarded. The term's traditional use is "derived from the fundamentalist/modernist controversy [and] has conditioned us to understand the label primarily in terms of a conservative/liberal spectrum, in which an 'evangelical' is more 'con-

---

[30]Clark Pinnock, *Tracking the Maze* (S.F.: Harper & Row, 1990), chapter 1.

[31]Special issue: *Christian Scholar's Review,* "What Is Evangelicalism?" 23:1 (September, 1993).

servative' than a 'liberal,' but not so 'conservative' as a 'fundamentalist.' "[32]

In their excellent review of twentieth century Christian theology, Stanley Grenz and Roger Olson work with the traditional use of the term "evangelical." They see fundamentalism as a reactionary response to nineteenth and early twentieth century liberalism. Fundamentalism is pictured as a movement of Bible-believing Christians who tend to abandon the larger intellectual and cultural arena that had become so critical of much of traditional Christian orthodoxy. Those, then, who by mid-century chose to re-enter the dialogue in the broad theological arena, and to do so in a less separatistic and combative spirit, came to be known as "evangelicals."[33]

Bernard Ramm separates the two theological traditions by saying that fundamentalism "attempts to shield itself from the Enlightenment" whereas evangelicalism "believes that the Enlightenment cannot be undone."[34] He sought to demonstrate in his own numerous writings that Christians still can be intellectually responsible "without either making the concessions char-

---

[32]Donald Dayton, "Some Doubts About the Usefulness of the Category 'Evangelical'," in Dayton and Robert Johnston, eds., *The Variety of American Evangelicalism* (Univ. of Tenn. Press, 1991, InterVarsity paper ed.), 246. Dayton suggests that the label "evangelical" arose largely from "the power politics of the neo-evangelicals after World War II. The leaders wanted to claim as large a power base as possible for the ecclesiastical struggles in which they were engaged. This led to the forging of certain alliances that had varying degrees of historical and theological justification" (250-51).

[33]Stanley Grenz and Roger Olson, *20th Century Theology* (InterVarsity Press, 1992), 288. For excellent reviews of these developments from the "evangelical" point of view, see Bob Patterson, *Carl F. H. Henry* (Peabody, Mass: Hendrickson, 1983), 13-57, and Carl. Henry's autobiography, *Confessions of a Theologian* (Waco, Texas: Word Books, 1986).

[34]Bernard Ramm, *The Evangelical Heritage* (Waco, Texas: Word Books, 1973), 70.

acteristic of modern theology or resorting to the blind faith or hyper-rationalism of fundamentalism."[35] Progress along this path is a promising frontier.

Seeking points of unity in the midst of this wide diversity in contemporary evangelicalism, Donald Bloesch argues that "the key to evangelical unity lies in a common commitment to Jesus Christ as the divine Savior from sin, a common purpose to fulfill the great commission, and a common acknowledgement of the absolute normativeness of Holy Scripture."[36] Similarly, Stanley Grenz views an "evangelical" as one participating "in a community characterized by a shared narrative concerning a personal encounter with God told in terms of shared theological categories derived from the Bible."[37]

The Church of God movement is part of the diversity and the unity of this evangelicalism. It has affirmed gladly the points of evangelical unity set forth by Bloesch, especially when the "absolute normativeness of Holy Scripture" is understood in the narrative style of Grenz. Even so, Merle Strege judges it improper either historically or theologically to identify the movement in the present evangelicalism stream. His point is not that there is disagreement about biblical authority, the redemptive role of Christ, or the necessity of sharing the gospel with all the world. There is a disagreement, however, that tends to affect all of these.[38]

Strege's concern is about theological genealogy and focus. Prior to the more recent fundamentalism/liberalism conflict was

---

[35]Grenz and Olson, *op. cit.,* 300.

[36]Donald Bloesch, *The Future of Evangelical Christianity* (Doubleday, 1983), 5.

[37]Stanley Grenz, *Revisioning Evangelical Theology* (InterVarsity Press, 1993), 17.

[38]Merle Strege, *Tell Me Another Tale* (Anderson, Ind: Warner Press, 1993), 17-18.

the seventeenth century clash between the Pietists, whose assurance lay in the witness of the Spirit, and the "Protestant scholastic dogmatists" whose trademark was "the intellect's assent to sound doctrine." The lineage of the Church of God movement lay more in Pietism, as mediated (1) through the Wesleys by way of American revivalism and (2) through John Winebrenner, and less in Protestant scholasticism and propositional fundamentalism (even as moderated somewhat by Carl Henry, Bernard Ramm, Donald Bloesch, and other neo-evangelicals).[39]

A significant epistemological assumption is at stake, according to Strege. What label is most appropriate for the Church of God movement? To begin, the movement is not comfortable with the limitations and divisive tendencies of labels in general. So, if there must be a label, the movement probably would prefer something as inclusive as "Christian." Especially uncomfortable would be a rationalistically derived creed that encourages conformity, fosters exclusivism, and breeds division

---

[39]Stanley Grenz, himself highlighting the narrative and experiential characteristics of a sound evangelicalism, differs with Bloesch. Bloesch is said to posit for evangelicalism a tension between Reformation theology and Pietism, one he finally resolves by giving priority to the Reformers and doctrine, over the Pietists and spiritual experience. Grenz, leaning more toward the Pietists, as would the Church of God movement, says that "any revisioning of evangelical theology must begin with a rethinking of the typical 'card-carrying' evangelical understanding of the essence of the [evangelical] movement as a whole with its focus on certain theological commitments. . . . Evangelicals are pietists," insists Grenz, "in that they . . . focus on the dynamism of the presence of Christ in the life of the believer" (*Revisioning Evangelical Theology*, 29, 40). An insightful review of the complex relationship between Pentecostalism and Fundamentalism, one helpful in understanding the theological tradition of the Church of God movement, is D. William Faupel, "Whither Pentecostalism?" *Pneuma* 15:1 (Spring 1993), 9-27.

(the classic Calvinistic model typical of evangelicalism).[40] Thought more Christian in the view of this movement is a focus on divine grace received, human lives changed, true community fostered, and church mission engaged.

Stanley Grenz sees proper evangelicalism as less a rigid body of beliefs and more a *distinctive spirituality*. His vision, like the vision of the Church of God movement, centers in faith's present integrity—not primarily in precise doctrinal formulation, but in the radical emphasis on "our shared desire to make the Bible come alive in personal and community life." He speaks of the evangelical vision focusing on "shared stories," testimonial narratives about life-changing transformations. The biblical revelation and traditional theology are, of course, crucial in norming and understanding all spiritual experiences; but at the heart of the "evangelical" vision of the faith is "this experience of being encountered by the living God understood by appeal to categories derived from the biblical drama of salvation."[41]

---

[40]The epistemological question is explored by Douglas Jacobsen through reviewing "The Calvinist-Arminian Dialectic in Evangelical Hermeneutics" (*Christian Scholar's Review* 23:1, September, 1993). He identifies the Calvinistic model illustrated by Francis Turretin (1623-1687) via the later Princeton theology of Hodge and Warfield. Here "hermeneutics and theology in general become largely a matter of maintaining boundaries. Established truths are to be repeated for the instruction of the faithful, and those who differ in theology from the 'orthodox' position are to be cut off from fellowship" (73-77). The Arminian model based on Jacobus Arminius (1559-1609) is much less doctrinaire and more dialogical, less rationalistic and more experientialist. "The hermeneutic of Arminianism recognizes diversity and stresses tolerance; the hermeneutic of Calvinism affirms the singularity of meaning in the text and seeks uniformity" (81). While twentieth century evangelical hermeneutics has seen the rising dominance of Arminianism, "evangelicalism" maintains a tension between the two. It is still typed in public view more by the Calvinistic model, the one least compatible with the Pietistic-Wesleyan tradition informing the Church of God movement.

[41]Stanley Grenz, *op. cit.*, 31-35.

People on the Way

The "saints" of the Church of God movement often sing vigorously, couching their theology in original verse and rousing melody, relying as much on poetry as on prose. One learns as much about this movement's theology in its songs as in its sermons and theology books. No song captures better the vision, the excitement, the sense of divine call and resulting human commitment of the early movement than the one titled "The Church's Jubilee."[42] By the time of its composition in 1923, the self-understanding of the movement had come to be expressed commonly in the apocalyptic and restorationist images of the biblical books of Daniel and Revelation. God was on the world's center stage and was thought to be moving toward a glorious climax. The movement humbly rejoiced, thinking it had found itself in the divine script with a mission to fulfill.

"The light of even-tide now shines," begins this corporate testimony, this musical clarion call to church reform. The purpose of the shining of this divine light is "the darkness to dispel." No wonder God's children were so excited, "for out of Babel God doth call his scattered saints in one, together all one church compose, the body of his Son." There is believed to have been centuries of deep darkness, of severe dividedness that had burdened, in fact, nearly had buried the church. But now God is on the move, moving the redemptive plan forward toward a climax, stimulating a fresh movement among people willing to be shaped by the power of the Spirit. It is a dramatic move of God's in which God is understood to be calling together the true church. Those who "see the church" thus begin moving toward Christ and toward each other. It is nothing less than "the day of jubilee." The church of God is called to "rejoice, be glad!" Why?

---

[42]Charles Naylor and Andrew Byers, in *Worship the Lord* (Anderson, Ind.: Warner Press, 1989), 312.

Because "thy Shepherd has begun, his long divided flock again to gather into one."

While the adequacy of the biblical and historical interpretations underlying this view now have been questioned widely, the dramatic sense of God's reality and present calling has not disappeared, nor has its validity been undermined.[43] A keynoting and enduring characteristic of this reformation movement is its consciousness of God and its radical commitment to God, and to God alone. False churchly and creedalistic allegiances of the past are seen as often having been so hurtful, so human, so divisive. No more! Verse two of this visionary song begins, "The Bible is our rule of faith and Christ alone is Lord." So, "no earthly master do we know, to Christ alone we bow." There was for this composer a great sense of renewed freedom because, in the fullness of God's time, "the day of sects and creeds for us forevermore is past." To God's blessed will there would be total submission, and "from the yokes of Babel's lords from henceforth we are free."

The radical commitment of this movement, then, is the same one that is basic to the biblical revelation in general. The Christian's allegiance is to be to God and God alone. This commitment, always enlightened by Christ, the norm of truth, guided by the Bible, the narrative medium of truth, and enabled by the Spirit, the presence and power of truth, is fully orthodox (in the mainstream of Christian belief). There is to be nothing new, nothing strange, no novel theological twists, just a return to what always has been basic and biblical. The goal envisioned by this

---

[43]For reviews of the changing history of the interpretation of the Bible's apocalyptic literature and the relation of interpretation to the Church of God movement's understanding of its own role in God's plan, see: John Stanley, "Unity Amid Diversity: Interpreting the Book of Revelation in the Church of God (Anderson)," *Wesleyan Theological Journal* (Fall, 1990), 74-98; and Merle Strege, *Tell Me Another Tale* (Anderson, Ind.: Warner Press, 1993), 10-14.

movement is a return to being truly submissive to the truly sovereign God known in Christ and as recorded in the biblical narrative. Such a stance, orthodox as it is, certainly has "radical" implications.

Here is a body of Christian believers freshly experiencing central relationships and making affirmations much as they are found in the Hebrew Scriptures.[44] The origin of their believing is not the well-crafted, God-proving bottom line of some abstract philosophic argument about the existence of the divine. Like the Bible itself, God's existence is assumed and celebrated. At issue instead is the *who,* the identity of the Creator God, the *what* of God's intent for all that has been created, and the question of *whether* God's people are prepared to rejoice in the divine being and yield to the divine will for today.

This movement of the Church of God has understood itself to be only an *interim* body. It has sought to be one significant expression of the "protesting" reformation of the whole church that made its major appearance beginning in the sixteenth century. The cause it affirms is to be a movement on behalf of the whole church, a continuing and hopefully heightened (radicalized) phase of the much larger protesting and reforming movement of Luther, Calvin, Zwingli, Wesley, Campbell, and many others.

As with all reforming movements, the Church of God struggles not to become smug and institutionalized itself, to the point of thinking and acting like it is self-sufficient, self-perpetuating, and self-justifying. That would subtly convert the interim status of a movement into a permanent church establishment, in effect

---

[44]In this work the phrase "Hebrew Scriptures" is used on occasion instead of "Old Testament." Since the Christian faith rests so significantly on the foundation of the Old Testament, there is good reason to avoid the "old" word since, for many Christians, this word conveys inappropriately the negative meaning of something now outdated and theologically meaningless for Christians, the people of the "New Testament." See Marvin Wilson, *Our Father Abraham: Jewish Roots of the Christian Faith* (Eerdmans, 1989).

leaving the pilgrimage of the protesting visionaries and joining the often sterile settledness of the divided denominational world. Instead, this movement hopes to walk a dynamic path along which all church structures are seen as intended only for the service of gospel truth. None have establishment rights in and of themselves. Each phase of church life is to be directed to (1) advancing the reforming of the whole church of Christ by the canon of Christ's gospel and (2) evangelizing the whole world by the power of that gospel.

The continuing challenge is to envision and then enflesh an authentic middle way. How can Christian people be new "protestants" who, as Clark Pinnock puts it, "rail equally against undue accommodation to modern culture . . . and stubborn rigidity,"[45] and who at the same time maintain integrity both with yesterday's Christian foundations and today's Christian mission? While this challenge is daunting, it is primary and unavoidable. It is the question of whether the church can and will emerge as a beacon of hope when, all around it, the foundations of our Enlightenment culture and our denominationalized church traditions seem to be crumbling.

Into such a demanding circumstance, one that seemed as real in many ways near the close of the nineteenth century as it does at the close of the twentieth, there emerged and yet remains a special movement of God's people. This Church of God movement is comprised of protesting believers in the tradition of the Protestant Reformation. But it has envisioned more than protesting criticism. This movement has felt called to a particular divine destiny. The urgency of a "cause" has been felt. Especially in the first decades following 1880, little time was thought to be available before Christ's return to bring final judgment and an end to this world. So a "flying" ministry had no words to mince and no time to lose.

---

[45]Clark Pinnock, *Tracking The Maze* (S.F.: Harper & Row, 1990), 54.

Since this cause was believed to be God-ordained, those who committed themselves to it were willing to accept hardship and face persecution if necessary. Neglected truths needed lifting up. The abuses of distorting ecclesiastical systems were ripe for challenging. The shallowness of Christian living called out for a deepening by the cleansing fire of true holiness. God's truth again awaited the Spirit's illumination and the Church's implementation. To such a cause this movement determined to be true.

The Church of God movement is not envisioned as a rigid and closed operation. When at its best, it treasures the questing dynamic of a true movement. It is committed to the truth as a basic principle of faith, whatever that truth turns out to be (see chapter two). It seeks to be one with all of God's people, espousing only that original and universal faith "once delivered to the saints." Arriving at such an ideal place has not proven easy, but this movement still seeks to be on the way. That is the core of the cause—truth envisioned, experienced, and yet pursued. The foundation is yet a frontier!

Being a pilgrim people, a visionary people, has been enabled in large part because movement members know themselves to be voluntary actors in a divine drama. The biblical revelation of God's creating and reclaiming is still unfolding. God remains active and has the script of human and church history fully under control, despite the real freedom and frequent apostasy of so many of the human participants. Timely Christian believing, it is judged, should be caught up in and formed by this divinely directed salvation drama. Discipleship should be shaped by its gracious flow and should join gladly in its current scenes. Theology should have a timeliness about it, based on the eternal plan and in touch with the present status of that plan. The context of truth and mission is a narrative, the biblical story of God for us, in us, and through us.

In its earliest decades the Church of God movement was nurtured in the womb of a compelling cause. Passing time,

maturing insight, institutional development, and a changed setting have altered in some ways the perception of the cause.
Surely the movement has reached a different stage of its own
existence. Whatever the case, a viable theology for the closing of
the twentieth century and certainly for the twenty-first must be
enlightened by a vision of what God now wishes to do for and
through a faithful people. This vision, constantly updated, will
provide *fresh contours* for an *enduring cause.*

These contours, however fresh and timely, necessarily will
be rooted in biblical basics and should still reflect central concerns of the historic vision of the Church of God movement.
Theologian Jürgen Moltmann suggests five, all worthy of careful
note:

> 1. Christian theology today should champion the gospel's
> potential for impacting our *present* time. Rather than being
> shackled by the past or immobilized in anticipation of the
> second coming of Christ, it should be a theology of the
> future that has historic roots and focuses on present realiza-
> tion. The incarnational God cares about concrete existence
> now, placing "political" responsibility on Christians. Theol-
> ogy should address the big public issues of our time, offer-
> ing hope and change;
>
> 2. Christian theology today, not presenting itself as a rigid
> authoritarianism, should make clear to "liberated" modern
> people that faith in the transcendent God made known in
> Christ is the *basis of genuine human freedom.* The true God
> is the biblical God of exodus and resurrection, the One who
> frees from slavery and even death;
>
> 3. Christian theology today should reflect a *radical
> restorationism* that reforms the church, theology, and Chris-
> tian existence "in the truth of its origin, in order to arrive at
> authentic testimony in the present." As theology
> approaches the truth of its origin, as dogmatic theology is
> grounded in biblical theology, it finds a relative freedom
> from subsequent cultural orientations and bondages and
> thus becomes a unifying force;

4. Christian theology should always place *Jesus at the center*. Jesus is not only the origin but also the principle of all Christian theology. His cross in particular is central. Here we see who God is and who we are. Here the pressing questions of today's suffering humanity finally find answers;

5. Christian theology should emphasize that *Christian unity is necessary and possible*. The missionary and ecumenical movements of the twentieth century have "freed the churches from European provincialism and confessional particularism and put them on the way to being a universal church of the nations." Now, in a post-denominational environment, there is a forced reflection on essentials, an earnest looking for the true church in the many forms of the church.[46]

As always, the vision of the Church of God movement (if not always its practice) has insisted that God's people must be *together* if they are to accomplish God's mission for the church. Togetherness requires intentional action. The 1984 Consultation on Mission and Ministry of the Church of God (convened in Indianapolis) stated plainly this goal for the movement: "To expand ministries through voluntary relationships with church groups outside the Church of God Reformation Movement. Our quest for Christian unity brings us into relationships with all members of the Body of Christ. Through voluntary relationships we can often achieve our mission more effectively and expand our ministries."

This goal was developed further in 1985 when the General Assembly of the Church of God (in North America) received a crucial document from the Long Range Planning Committee and Executive (Leadership) Council of the Church of God. It encourages the movement "to seek intentional inter-church relationships

---

[46]Jürgen Moltmann, *Theology Today* (Philadelphia: Trinity Press International, 1988), 88-94.

through which its own ministries are strengthened and enriched and which provide opportunity for the Church of God to live out its message of Christian unity through enriching the entire Body of Christ." Then in 1988 the General Assembly affirmed a set of guidelines for inter-church relationships. Cautions were urged when other bodies fail to believe basic and essential Christian teaching such as the divinity of Jesus Christ. But the cautions were not meant to impede the original 1984 call to cooperative action on behalf of Christian mission.[47] Finding effective strategies for such cooperation poses a significant frontier for the movement, a people still on the way rather than having arrived.

In the Wilderness with God

Intentional actions toward a yet unexplored future set a people on pilgrimage. Pilgrims often mix with their gratitude and celebration times of questioning and murmuring. Exodus 17:1-7 is the classic model of God's very own people wondering whether the Lord is still with them as their journey wears on in the difficult wilderness. Yes, the Lord had freed the slaves from Egypt and had sent them on their way to the land of promise. That way, however, proved to be troubled terrain that left them a people still at risk. Lacking Egyptian support, they had to rely on divine favor to survive. When water supplies got low and there was no clear map to the future, when previous certainties were shaken and a new identity was still being formed, the question was natural: "Did we go up from Egypt simply to die?" Is there really a continuing cause and the divine resources to accomplish it? Frontiers are hard to locate when one is wandering in a vast wilderness.

The movement of the Church of God, and the Christian community in general, have suffered from the wilderness of

---

[47]For detail on the 1984 Consultation and the 1985 guidelines, see Barry Callen, *Thinking and Acting Together* (Anderson, Ind.: Executive Council of the Church of God and Warner Press, 1992, 103-07, 28-30).

accommodations with secular culture. A new way now is needed. Are there acceptable substitutes for God? No. Is God still faithful to those in a divine-human covenant relationship? Yes. Moses learned that living water in abundance was available! It is a matter of faith expressed by the people who choose to remain on the way to God's future.

Today Christians must allow themselves to be formed and nourished anew by the ancient narrative of God's mighty acts among us and for us. The center of the salvation script is Exodus 14, the pivotal text even for the Christian's Easter vigil.[48] In the Hebrew Bible it is this exodus event that is the beginning of a recounting of the history of salvation. From this redeeming experience the faithful could look backward and see God's hand in creation, and forward to what eventually would become the highlight of the whole biblical revelation, the birth, death, and resurrection of Jesus Christ.

Journeying with God through the wilderness of our time is our privilege and faith challenge as believers. On the journey we who are faithful travelers come to know God, ourselves, our mission, our brothers and sisters, and our mission destiny together. It is life on the road. The road is lighted by a theological vision similar in many ways to the one that has motivated the Church of God movement from its earliest years. In the words of Daniel Warner, words still sung often in the movement today:

> Beloved, how this perfect love,
> Unites us all in Jesus!
> One heart, and soul, and mind we prove,
> The union heaven gave us.[49]

---

[48]See Thomas Dozeman, Kendall McCabe, Marion Soards, *Preaching the Revised Common Lectionary,* Year A, Lent/Easter (Nashville: Abingdon Press, 1992), 106.

[49]"The Bond of Perfectness" by D. S. Warner and B. E. Warren, as in *Worship the Lord* (Anderson, Ind.: Warner Press, 1989), 330.

Based on Colossians 3:14, this vision is of Christian unity in the sanctifying Spirit of the God who desires to renew the repentant and unify the faithful, all for the sake of the divine mission in the world. Holiness is God's will for all believers; unity is made possible by holiness; discipleship and mission are the immediate implications.

Vision is an image, a paradigm or stance very helpful in interpreting the Christian faith in a time like ours. It is apt "not only because it suggests a deep modern sensibility, but because it is a refrain within the Christian tradition itself."[50] Ours is a time of visual media. Television shapes public perception. The oppressed around the world have visions of liberation. All are looking, many for an entertaining way of escape, and many for a glimpse of hope.

The Christian vision is seen in the image of Martin Luther King, Jr., standing before that massive outdoor crowd in Washington, D. C. and announcing the vision he had. In electric fashion, he said, "I have a dream!" The old world of class divisions and racial discriminations, all rooted in human sin, one day will be gone. The biblical revelation tells about the God who still has a redeeming dream for all creation—and the forgiving grace and restoring power to make it true![51]

The biblical narrative is filled with dreams, visions, and prophecies reaching beyond the compromised present to the promised future. God comes to us from our future and pulls us toward what ought to be and yet can be. The God of Exodus, Easter, and Pentecost still opens the eyes of faith so that they can

---

[50]Gabriel Fackre, *The Christian Story,* 2nd ed. (Grand Rapids: Eerdmans, 1978, 1984), 31.

[51]As one example of courageous ministry in the face of persecution by a resistant social establishment and sometimes even a reluctant church, sec Charles Ludwig, *A Dangerous Obedience: The Life and Ministry of J. Horace Germany* (Anderson, Ind.: Warner Press, 1994).

really see and freshly hope. A vision is "an imaginative leap into the Not Yet. . . . Thus the yearnings of the culture and the hopes of biblical faith can be expressed in the language of vision."[52]

The people of the Church of God movement have tended to be visionary people. Whatever its historical and theological shortcomings, the movement has caught at least a glimpse of what God intends for the chosen people. It has "seen the church." Motivated by this visionary glimpse, the movement still calls for "the emergence of Christian persons who are deeply committed to Christ, who have been genuinely changed by the Spirit, who are hungering daily for a further maturing of their spiritual experience and understanding, who have been seized by a vision of all of God's people as one united and loving family, and who are humble and tolerant enough to keep growing and learning without restricting the freedom of others to do the same."[53] Here is an enduring cause that is distinctly Christian and also very contemporary.

Altered cultural patterns certainly have brought reassessment of how holiness and unity, central theological concerns of the Church of God movement, should be understood and achieved. The year 1995 certainly is not 1880. The ecumenical movement of the twentieth century has helped to revise significantly the patterns of denominational loyalties that originally brought sharp anti-sectarian criticisms from Church of God movement leaders. While pioneers of this movement are respected by today's movement leaders, it is respect, not reverence. Pioneer thought is appreciated as formative of a distinctive and enduring tradition; it is not to be mimicked uncritically. Being faithful now to this particular reforming tradition calls for applications of the authenticity/integrity principle in ways appro-

[52]Fackre, op. cit., 32.
[53]Barry Callen, A Time To Remember: Teachings (Anderson, Ind.: Warner Press, 1978), 9.

priate to today's setting, regardless of whether such applications duplicate what was appropriate in circumstances of a past time. A "movement" is to remain faithful to its own reforming vision, in part by remaining dynamic and flexible, by continuing *to move* toward the will of God for this time.

The detail of what lies ahead is not yet ours to know. We live in the dim light of the already—not yet, the dawning rather than the high noon of the Kingdom. But we know the Christ who is key to both past and future, and we know that the powers of darkness do not control the future. So we travel confidently on, making the tents of God our daily home.

Beloved church leader Louis (Pete) Meyer died of cancer in December, 1993. On Easter Sunday morning, 1993, he stood weakly in the pulpit of Park Place Church of God in Anderson, Indiana (his home congregation), to share his testimony of Christian hope, even as his body was dying of a humanly incurable disease. He shared with a quiet assurance:

> . . . the real test is to leave the future in God's hands without demanding a detailed road map. That requires much more trust than many of us have. Therein is the lesson of Easter—the power of the resurrection. . . . There is hope. God can be trusted. There are no conditions, not even death, that can rob us or have the power to divert us from the path to abundant life. May God make it so in your life.[54]

There is a God, a goal, the possibility for salvation, a right way to go, hope! Along life's roadways, believers, as God's loving agents, are privileged to leave signs pointing toward the New Jerusalem. All the while, whatever the pain or doubt, the Spirit enables the glad song of the saints of God:

> The future lies unseen ahead, It holds I know not what;
> But still I know I need not dread, For Jesus fails me not.

---

[54]"Pete Meyer's Testimony," in *Vital Christianity* (April, 1994), 21.

The glory of eternal dawn, Shines from His smiling face;
So trusting Him, I follow on, With heart made strong by grace.

I'll follow Him with rejoicing, With rejoicing, rejoicing;
I know He safely will lead me, To my eternal home.[55]

On the way to that home, always avoiding eschatological escapism and millennial diversions from present Kingdom responsibility, Christians should join with joy in affirming:

Let us labor for the Master from the dawn till setting sun,
Let us talk of all His wondrous love and care;
Then when all of life is over and our work on earth is done,
And the roll is called up yonder, I'll be there![56]

As we labor and talk for the Master here below, it always should be recalled that the wisdom and power that sustains the church comes from God, not from ourselves. Thus, as Martin Luther said long ago:

It is not we who can sustain the church, nor was it those who came before us, nor will it be those who come after us. It was, and is, and will be the one who says, "I am with you always, even to the end of time." As it says in Hebrews 13: "Jesus Christ, the same *yesterday, today,* and *forever.*" And in Revelation 1: "Who *was,* and *is,* and *is to come.*" Truly, he is that one, and no one else is, or ever can be.[57]

The "Consultation on Doctrine" of the Church of God concluded this way its published report to the movement's General Assembly in June, 1974:

---

[55]"I'll Follow with Rejoicing," in *Worship the Lord* (Anderson, Ind: Warner Press, 1989), 436, verses 1, 4, and chorus.

[56]"When the Roll is Called Up Yonder," in *Worship the Lord* (Anderson, Ind: Warner Press, 1989), 725, verse 3.

[57]Martin Luther, as quoted by Alister McGrath, *Spirituality in an Age of Change: Rediscovering the Spirit of the Reformers* (Grand Rapids: Zondervan, 1994), 196.

God's Spirit is moving in the midst of the church today. Fires of revival and renewal are being kindled where sparks in years past have been difficult to find. . . . The breath of God is stirring among the once dying members of old and established denominations. The Holy Spirit is moving ecumenically, purging and refining the traditions and practices of Catholics and Protestants alike. . . . He [God] is moving worldwide, establishing an international brotherhood in Christ as Lord and Savior which transcends all barriers and is hurdling all obstacles. Walls of division among Christians are crumbling, and many who have been separated by sectarian fences and traditional loyalties are finding new depths of relationship with each other and new experiences of "fellowship in the Spirit of Jesus Christ." . . . This is the church at its glorious best. Now is the time for the ideal to become the actual, in order that there may be "glory in the church by Christ Jesus throughout all ages, world without end. Amen" (Eph. 3:21).

The enduring concerns of this Church of God movement are holiness and unity, integrity and reconciliation,[58] righted relationship with God (holiness) and other believers (unity), all for the sake of the Christian mission in this world. Gloria Gaither may be right: "If the Church of God will continue to take seriously the message of unity, if it can remain true to the central theme of the fellowship of all believers across denominational lines, . . . then there is no group in a better position to help bring joyous reconciliation among God's people and to spread that joy to all the precious human beings God created."[59] This is the vision. By God's grace, may it become real.

---

[58]The April 1995 issue of *Vital Christianity* featured on its cover a photo of Samuel George Hines (1929-1995), honored leader of the Church of God Movement, recently deceased. He was recognized and loved as a minister of *reconciliation*. He was a symbol of the ongoing work of God.

[59]Gloria Gaither, in Holly Miller, "The Church With a Mind of Its Own," in *The Saturday Evening Post* (Nov. 1985), 101.

We conclude as Paul concluded his letter to Rome, the most theological of all his writings. The final lines are a doxology. Following a long and complex argument through sixteen chapters, Paul comes to a final outburst of affirmation, joy, and blessing. All good theology finally comes to expression in worship.[60] So:

> Now to God who is able to strengthen you according to my gospel and the proclamation of Jesus Christ, according to the revelation of the mystery that was kept secret for long ages but now is disclosed, and through the prophetic writings is made known to all the Gentiles, according to the command of the eternal God, to bring about the obedience of faith—to the only wise God, through Jesus Christ, to whom be the glory forever! Amen (Rom. 16:25-27).

---

[60]Geoffrey Wainwright entitles his whole systematic theology *Doxology: The Praise of God in Worship, Doctrine and Life* (London: Epworth Press, 1980).

The Vision in Stained Glass

The magnificent stained glass window in the Adam W. Miller Chapel of Anderson University School of Theology (pictured below) is a result of the joining of the theological concepts of the faculty of Anderson School of Theology (representing the Church of God movement)with the artistic and engineering skills of the Willett Company of Philadelphia, Pennsylvania. The window was designed and built in 1974 and dedicated in June, 1976, in memory of Edward E. and Norma J. Willhardt of Toledo, Ohio, whose interest and generosity made it possible.

The window seeks to portray a *universal* expression of the Christian faith, with its theological assumptions and symbols being particularly sensitive to the Christian faith as that faith has been experienced and proclaimed by the Church of God movement (Anderson, Indiana).

The message of the window begins at its highest point. Here is symbolized, by the downward flight of the heavenly dove, the initial and primary facts of our faith—that God exists and our knowledge of Him begins only as He chooses to come to us. God has come to us and, by the continuing ministry of His Holy Spirit, we come to know God's very character and purpose among us.

Moving from this point of beginning to the extreme left and downward, the window symbolizes the three great truths about God which we have come to know through the divine Self-revelation. God is the *Creator* and continues to hold the creation firmly in His hands. Even though that creation has chosen to corrupt itself with evil, God has demonstrated Himself to be a *Redeemer.* Like a sacrificial lamb, He constantly comes to us, fully prepared to absorb the penalty and forgive the wrong. However, it is crucial to realize that the creating and redeeming love of God is not mere sentimentalism. We also know Him to be *Judge,* a just God whose word is law and whose judgments are definite and final.

When a person becomes aware of the gracious presence of the creating, redeeming, and judging God, that person has the opportunity of responding appropriately. Accordingly, the window proceeds to depict the normal sequence of events which are characteristic of a person's appropriate response.

Moving from the uppermost point of the right side of the window and downward, there is symbolized the daily possibility of our knowing the creating, redeeming and judging God through the open pages of the *Bible.* When we have studied these pages and have been convicted by their truth, we have the opportunity to enter into a life-changing experience of *Conversion,* which is capable of making of us new creatures in Christ. It is like an ever-burning bush which sanctifies our lives and empowers us to do the will of God. And that will is a unique life of *Service,* a basin-and-towel experience which becomes our privilege as we come to have the mind of Christ.

When God is known and responded to appropriately, there comes into reality a new fellowship of persons known as the Church. The lower portion of the window seeks to express, through the use of human hands, two very distinct emphases in the heritage of the Church of God movement—the themes of *Healing* and *Fellowship.* To the left is a solitary human hand reaching confidently toward the hem of the Saviour's garment, and to the right are two hands clasped together in the bond of unity which should characterize God's people.

Central to the entire window is the *Person of Jesus Christ.* Although we know many truths about God, and our response to God as these are represented around the borders of the window, the primary truth is not contained in doctrines or traditions or books or practices, but in the person of God's Self-revelation in Jesus Christ. Immediately behind the life-size portrayal of Christ is the *Cross,* encouraging us to remember the sacrifice of our

Lord and the critical relationship between what He has done for us and what is now possible for us. This cross is crucial, but it is fading into the background because it is not our primary focus of attention.

Of principal concern is the person of Christ, who no longer is nailed to the cross—but obviously is freed from its grip through the power of His resurrection. He wears royal robes and is identified to the right and left of His head by the ancient symbols of Alpha and Omega, the beginning and the end. From His body there emerges a green vine, which moves outward and encircles the several basic truths we have come to know about God and humankind. These others are important words of truth, but Jesus Christ is *the Word*, the eternal vantagepoint from which comes the fullest understanding of the significance of all other words. He lives. He inspires. He interprets. He fulfills.

Christ stands with His arms outstretched *toward you*. He speaks that you might be awakened to new life in Him. As the *Triumphant Christ,* He is saying to you, "I am the resurrection and the life. He that believes in me, though he were dead, yet shall he live" (John 11:25). As the *Inviting Christ,* He calls to you, saying, "Come unto me all you who labor and are heavy laden and I will give you rest" (Matt. 11:28).

As the *Nurturing Christ,* He says, "I am the Vine, you are the branches. He who abides in me, and I in him, he it is who bears much fruit, for without me you can do nothing" (John 15:5). As the *Commissioning Christ,* He commands, "Go therefore and make disciples of all nations" (Matt. 28:19). As the *Ascending Christ,* He promises, "I go to prepare a place for you. And if I go . . . I will come again and receive you unto myself, that where I am, there you may be also" (John 14:2b-3).

This description of the theological intent of this window was written by Barry L. Callen, Dean of Anderson School of Theology, 1974-1983.

The theological significance of the symbolism of this Miller Chapel window is representative of central convictions of the Church of God movement. These are described on the preceding pages.

Select Bibliography

Published Sources Related to the Theological Tradition
of the Church of God Movement (Anderson, Ind.)

Adams, Robert. 1980. "The Hymnody of the Church of God (1885-1980) as a Reflection of That Church's Theological and Cultural Changes." Doctoral dissertation. Fort Worth, Texas: Southwestern Baptist Theological Seminary.

Alford, Charles. 1953. *"A Comparison of the Doctrine of Christian Unity in the Church of God and in the Disciples of Christ."* B.D. thesis, Anderson School of Theology.

Allen, C. Leonard and Richard Hughes. 1988. *Discovering Our Roots: The Ancestry of Churches of Christ.* Abilene, Texas: Abilene Christian University Press.

_____. and Richard Hughes. 1988. *Illusions of Innocence.* University of Chicago Press.

_____. 1990. *The Cruciform Church.* Abilene, Texas: Abilene Christian University Press.

_____. 1993. *Distant Voices: Discovering a Forgotten Past for a Changing Church.* Abilene, Texas: Abilene Christian University Press.

Bassett, Paul. 1983. "The Holiness Movement and the Protestant Principle." *Wesleyan Theological Journal* 18:1 (Spring), 7-29.

Bender, Harold. 1944. "The Anabaptist Vision" in *Mennonite Quarterly Review,* vol. 18, 67-88.

Berry, Robert L. 1931. *Golden Jubilee Book.* Anderson, Ind.: Gospel Trumpet Co.

Blackwelder, Boyce W. 1958. *Light from the Greek New Testament.* Anderson, Ind.: Warner Press. Reprint, 1976, Baker Book House.

_____. 1963 (Aug.). "The Gifts of the Spirit." Three parts. *Vital Christianity.*

_____. 1965 (May). "The Nature of True Holiness." Two parts. *Vital Christianity.*

_____. 1966. "Christian Unity in the Prayer of Jesus," in *Vital Christianity* (April 10).

Bolitho, Axchie A. 1942. *To the Chief Singer.* Anderson, Ind.: Gospel Trumpet Co. Biography of Barney Warren.

Boyer, Harold W. 1960. *The Apostolic Church and the Apostasy.* Anderson, Ind.: Gospel Trumpet Co.

Brooks, John. 1891. *The Divine Church: A Treatise on the Origin, Constitution, Order, and Ordinances of the Church: Being a Vindication of the New Testament Ecclesia, and an Exposure of the Anti-Scriptural Character of the Modern Church or Sect.* Columbia, Mo.: Herald Pub. House.

Brown, Charles E. 1927. *The Hope of His Coming.* Anderson, Ind.: Gospel Trumpet Co.

_____. 1931. *A New Approach to Christian Unity.* Anderson, Ind.: Gospel Trumpet Co. (Warner Press).

_____. 1939. *The Church Beyond Division.* Anderson, Ind.: Gospel Trumpet Co.

_____. 1940. *The Way of Prayer.* Anderson, Ind.: Warner Press.

_____. 1944. *The Meaning of Salvation.* Anderson, Ind.: Warner Press.

_____. 1945. *The Meaning of Sanctification.* Anderson, Ind.: Warner Press.

_____. 1947. *The Apostolic Church.* Anderson, Ind.: Warner Press.

_____. 1948. *The Reign of Christ.* Anderson, Ind.: Warner Press.

_____. 1951. *When the Trumpet Sounded.* Anderson, Ind.: Gospel Trumpet Co.

_____. 1954. *When Souls Awaken: An Interpretation of Radical Christianity.* Anderson, Ind.: Gospel Trumpet Co.

_____. 1954 (Nov. 6). "A New Approach to Sanctification." Anderson, Ind.: *Gospel Trumpet.*

_____. 1957. *We Preach Christ.* Anderson, Ind.: Warner Press.

Brueggemann, Walter. 1987. *Hope Within History.* Atlanta: John Knox Press.

_____. 1992. *Old Testament Theology.* Minneapolis: Fortress Press.

_____. 1993. *Biblical Perspectives on Evangelism.* Nashville: Abingdon Press.

Buehler, Kathleen. 1993. *Heavenly Song: Stories of Church of God Song Writers and Their Songs.* Anderson, Ind.: Warner Press.

Burgess, Joseph A. 1991. Editor, *In Search of Christian Unity.* Minneapolis: Fortress Press.

BIBLIOGRAPHY

Byers, Andrew L. 1907. *The Gospel Trumpet Publishing Work Described and Illustrated*. Anderson, Ind.: Gospel Trumpet Pub. Co.

_____. 1920. "Pioneers of the Present Reformation, D. S. Warner," in *Gospel Trumpet*, February 5.

_____. 1921. *Birth of a Reformation: Life and Labors of D. S. Warner*. Anderson, Ind.: Gospel Trumpet Co. Contains large sections of Warner's surviving personal journal. Republished 1966, Guthrie, Okla.: Faith Publishing House.

Byrum, Enoch E. 1904. *Ordinances of the Bible*. Anderson, Ind.: Gospel Trumpet Co.

_____. 1919. *Miracles and Healing*. Anderson, Ind.: Gospel Trumpet Co.

_____. 1928. *Life Experiences*. Anderson, Ind.: Gospel Trumpet Company.

Byrum, Noah. 1902. *Familiar Names and Faces*. Moundsville, W. Va.: Gospel Trumpet Co.

_____. 1931-32. "Memories of Bygone Days," *Young People's Friend* (Dec. 1931—Aug. 1932).

Byrum, Russell R. 1925. *Christian Theology*. Anderson, Ind.: Gospel Trumpet Co. Revised, 1982.

_____. 1928. "Reviewing the Goal of Christian Unity," in Barry Callen, *The First Century*, vol. 1. Anderson, Ind.: Warner Press, 1979. Pages 632-634.

Callen, Barry L. 1962. "The Urbanization of a Holiness Body," in Robert Lee, *Cities and Churches*. Philadelphia: Westminster Press.

_____. 1969. "Church of God Reformation Movement (Anderson, Ind.): A Study in Ecumenical Idealism" (masters thesis, Asbury Theological Seminary).

_____. 1973. *Where Life Begins*. Anderson, Ind.: Warner Press.

_____. 1978. *A Time to Remember: Teachings*. Anderson, Ind.: Warner Press.

_____. 1979. *The First Century*. Vols. I and II. Anderson, Ind.: Warner Press.

_____. 1983. "The Church: Tomorrow's People for Today's World," in Lane Scott and Leon Hynson, eds., *Christian Ethics*. Anderson, Ind.: Warner Press.

_____. 1983. *Faculty Academic Freedom in Member Institutions of the Christian College Coalition*. Ed.D. dissertation, Indiana University.

_____. 1985. *The Assembly Speaks*. Anderson, Ind.: Warner Press.

_____. 1988. *Preparing for Service: A History of Higher Education in the Church of God*. Anderson, Ind.: Warner Press.

_____. 1990. *Listening to the Word of God*. Anderson, Ind.: Anderson University and Warner Press. In honor of Boyce W. Blackwelder.

_____. 1991. Editor, *Faith, Learning, and Life: Views from the President's Office of Anderson University*. Anderson University and Warner Press.

_____. 1992. *She Came Preaching*. Anderson, Ind.: Warner Press. Biography of Lillie S. McCutcheon.

_____. 1992. *Thinking and Acting Together*. Anderson, Ind.: Executive Council and Warner Press.

_____. 1992. *Guide of Soul and Mind: The Story of Anderson University*. Anderson, Ind.: Anderson University and Warner Press.

_____. 1993, with North, James. "Open Forum: A Meeting of Two Movements," *Vital Christianity* (Feb.), 46-47.

_____. 1995. *It's God's Church! Life and Legacy of Daniel S. Warner*. Anderson, Ind.: Warner Press.

_____. 1995. "Daniel Warner: Joining Holiness and All Truth," *Wesleyan Theological Journal* 30:1 (Spring).

_____. 1995. *Contours of a Cause: The Theological Vision of the Church of God Movement* (Anderson). Anderson, Ind.: School of Theology, Anderson University.

_____. 1995. Editor, *Sharing Heaven's Music*. Essays on preaching in honor of James Earl Massey. Nashville: Abingdon Press.

Campmeeting Sermons. 1913. Preached at the annual camp meeting held in Anderson, Ind., June, 1913. Anderson, Ind.: Gospel Trumpet Publishing Co.

Carver, Everett. n.d. *When Jesus Comes Again*. Phillipsburg, N.J.: Presbyterian and Reformed Publishing.

Clear, Valorous B. 1977. *Where the Saints Have Trod*. Chesterfield, Ind: Midwest Publications. Revision of Clear's Ph.D. diss., University of Chicago, 1953.

_____. 1963 (Jan. 16). "Reflections of a Postsectarian," *The Christian Century*.

BIBLIOGRAPHY

Cole, Mary. 1914. *Trials and Triumphs of Faith.* Anderson, Ind.: Gospel Trumpet Company. Autobiographical.

Confer, Robert L. 1992. *Remembering, Reflecting, Renewing: A Look at the Historical Developments of the Church of God In and Around Grand Junction, Michigan.* Grand Junction: Warner Camp (for its centennial).

Cooper, Wilmer A. 1990. *A Living Faith: An Historical Study of Quaker Beliefs.* Richmond, Ind.: Friends United Press.

Crews, Mickey. 1990. *The Church of God [Cleveland, Tenn.]: A Social History.* Knoxville: University of Tennessee Press.

Crose, Lester. 1981. *Passport for a Reformation.* Anderson, Ind.: Warner Press. History of the Missionary Board.

Dayton, Donald. 1987, 1991. Rev. ed. *Theological Roots of Pentecostalism.* Peabody, Mass.: Hendrickson Publishers.

_____. 1991, with Robert Johnston. *The Variety of American Evangelicalism.* Downers Grove, Ill.: InterVarsity Press.

Dieter, Melvin E. 1980. *The Holiness Revival of the Nineteenth Century.* Metuchen, N.J.: The Scarecrow Press.

_____. 1995. "Primitivism in the American Holiness Tradition," *Wesleyan Theological Journal* 30:1(Spring).

Doctrines and Discipline of the Evangelical United Mennonites. 1880. Goshen, Ind.: E. U. Mennonite Publishing Society.

Dunning, H. Ray. 1988. *Grace, Faith & Holiness.* Kansas City: Beacon Hill Press.

Durnbaugh, Donald. 1968, 1985. *The Believers' Church: The History and Character of Radical Protestantism.* Scottdale, Pa.: Herald Press.

Dye, Dwight. 1963. *"Asceticism in the Church of God Reformation Movement from 1880 to 1913."* Unpublished masters thesis, University of Tulsa.

Evans, James H., Jr. 1992. *We Have Been Believers: An African-American Systematic Theology.* Minneapolis: Fortress Press.

Fackre, Gabriel. 1984. Rev. ed. *The Christian Story: A Narrative Interpretation of Basic Christian Doctrine.* Grand Rapids: Eerdmans.

Ferrel, Lowell. 1988 (Spring/Fall). "John Wesley and the Enthusiasts," in *Wesleyan Theological Journal.*

Fife, Robert O. 1992. *Celebration of Heritage.* Selected writings of Fife. Los Angeles: Westwood Christian Foundation.

Forney, C. H. 1914. *History of the Churches of God*. Harrisburg, Pa.: Pub. House of the Churches of God—Winebrennerian.

Forrest, Aubrey. 1948. "A Study of the Development of the Basic Doctrines and Institutional Patterns in the Church of God (Anderson, Ind.)." Unpublished doctoral dissertation, University of Southern California Graduate School of Religion.

Frame, John M. 1991. *Evangelical Reunion: Denominations and the Body of Christ*. Grand Rapids: Baker Book House.

Froese, Walter. 1982. *Sounding Forth the Gospel on the Prairies: A History of the Church of God Reformation Movement in Western Canada*. Camrose, Alberta: Gospel Contact Press.

Garrett, Clarke. 1987. *Spirit Possession and Popular Religion*. Baltimore: Johns Hopkins University Press.

Gaulke, Max R. 1959. *May Thy Kingdom Come—Now!* Anderson, Ind.: Gospel Trumpet Publishing Company.

González, Justo L. 1987, rev. ed., *A History of Christian Thought: From the Protestant Reformation to the Twentieth Century*, vol. 3. Nashville: Abingdon Press.

_____. 1989. *Christian Thought Revisited: Three Types of Theology*. Nashville: Abingdon Press.

_____. 1990. *Mañana: Christian Theology from a Hispanic Perspective*. Nashville: Abingdon Press.

_____. 1992. *Out of Every Tribe & Nation: Christian Theology at the Ethnic Roundtable*. Nashville: Abingdon Press.

Gospel Trumpet. Jan., 1881 to present (now *Vital Christianity*). Indexed at Anderson University School of Theology.

Gossard, J. Harvey. 1986. "John Winebrenner: Founder, Reformer, and Businessman" in *Pennsylvania Religious Leaders* (History Study No. 16), The Pennsylvania Historical Association.

Gray, Albert F. 1922. "Distinctive Features of the Present Movement," *Gospel Trumpet* (Feb. 23).

_____. 1944-46. *Christian Theology*. 2 vols. Anderson, Ind.: Gospel Trumpet Co. (Warner Press).

_____. 1960. *The Nature of the Church*. Anderson, Ind.: Warner Press.

_____. 1966. *Time and Tides on the Western Shore* (autobiography). Published privately.

Grenz, Stanley, with Roger Olson. 1992. *20th-Century Theology: God & the World in a Transitional Age*. Downers Grove, Ill.: InterVarsity Press.

_____. 1993. *Revisioning Evangelical Theology*. Downers Grove, Ill.: InterVarsity Press.

Grubbs, Dwight. 1994. *Beginnings: Spiritual Formation for Leaders*. Lima, Ohio: Fairway Press.

Hall, Kenneth. 1977 (Jan. 2). "Just Who Are We?" In *Vital Christianity*, as quoted in Barry Callen, ed., *The First Century* (vol. 1, 1979). Anderson, Ind.: Warner Press.

Harman, Daniel. 1990. *What the Church of God Means to Me*. Anderson, Ind.: Warner Press.

Hartman, Marvin. 1958. *"The Origin and Development of the General Ministerial Assembly of the Church of God, 1917-1950."* B.D. thesis, Butler University.

Hatch, Nathan. 1989. *The Democratization of American Christianity*. Yale University Press.

Hauerwas, Stanley. 1983. *The Peaceable Kingdom*. University of Notre Dame Press.

_____. 1989. With William Willimon. *Resident Aliens*. Nashville: Abingdon Press.

Hetrick, Gale. 1980. *Laughter Among the Trumpets: A History of the Church of God in Michigan*. Centennial Edition. Lansing: The Church of God in Michigan.

Hines, Samuel G. 1993. *Experience the Power*. Anderson, Ind.: Warner Press.

History of Berrien and VanBuren Counties, Michigan. 1880. Philadelphia: D. W. Ensign & Co. Area of Grand Junction, Mich., significant to life of Daniel Warner.

Hughes, Richard T. 1988. (See C. Leonard Allen above for two joint volumes, 1988).

_____. 1988. Editor, *The American Quest for the Primitive Church*. Urbana: University of Illinois Press.

_____. 1992. "The Apocalyptic Origins of Churches of Christ and the Triumph of Modernism," *Religion and American Culture* 2:2 (Summer).

Jones, Charles Edwin. 1974. *Perfectionist Persuasion: The Holiness Movement and American Methodism* (chap. six, "The Come-Outers"). Metuchen, N.J.: The Scarecrow Press.

Jones, Kenneth E. 1980. *The Word of God*. Anderson, Ind.: Warner Press.

_____. 1985. *Commitment to Holiness*. Anderson, Ind.: Warner Press.

_____. 1990. "Babylon and the New Jerusalem: Interpreting Revelation," in Barry Callen, *Listening to the Word of God*. Anderson, Ind.: Anderson University and Warner Press.

Jordan, Wilfred, and Willowby, Richard. 1991. *Diamond Jubilee: National Association of the Church of God*. Anderson, Ind.: Warner Press.

Kern, Richard. 1974. *John Winebrenner: Nineteenth Century Reformer*. Harrisburg, Pa.: Central Publishing House.

_____. 1984. *Findlay College: The First Hundred Years*. Nappanee, Ind.: Evangel Press.

Kinnamon, Michael. 1988. *Truth and Community: Diversity and Its Limits in the Ecumenical Movement*. Grand Rapids: Eerdmans.

Kraus, C. Norman. 1991. *God Our Savior*. Scottdale, Pa.: Herald Press.

_____. 1993. Rev. ed. *The Community of the Spirit*. Scottdale, Pa.: Herald Press.

Kreider, Alan. 1987. *Journey Towards Holiness*. Scottdale, Pa.: Herald Press.

Krenz, Willi, Editor. 1987. *Church of God, Europe and the Near East, Including the German Churches of North America*. Printed in Germany.

Kühn, Hans. 1990. *Reforming the Church Today*. N.Y.: Crossroad.

Leonard, Juanita Evans, ed. 1989. *Called To Minister, Empowered To Serve: Women In Ministry*. Anderson, Ind.: Warner Press.

Linn, Otto. 1941-42. *Studies in the New Testament*. 3 vols. Anderson, Ind.: Gospel Trumpet Pub. Co. (vol. 3 by "Commercial Service" of Warner Press).

Littell, Franklin. 1961 (April). "The Discipline of Discipleship in the Free Church Tradition." *Mennonite Quarterly Review*.

Lodahl, Michael. 1994. *The Story of God: Wesleyan Theology & Biblical Narrative*. Kansas City: Beacon Hill Press.

Long, L. Leon. 1976 (Feb.). "To What Extent Was Warner a Winebrennarian?" *Church Advocate*.

Ludwig, Charles. 1994. *A Dangerous Obedience: The Life and Ministry of J. Horace Germany*. Anderson, Ind: Warner Press.

— 229 —

BIBLIOGRAPHY

McCutcheon, Lillie. 1964. *The Symbols Speak: An Exposition of the Revelation*. Published privately.

_____. 1995. *If I Be Lifted Up*. Anderson, Ind.: Warner Press.

Maddox, Randy. 1994. *Responsible Grace: John Wesley's Practical Theology*. Nashville: Kingswood Books, Abingdon Press.

Martin, Earl. 1942. *Toward Understanding God*. Anderson, Ind.: Gospel Trumpet Pub. Company.

_____. 1952. *This We Believe, This We Proclaim*. Anderson, Ind.: Gospel Trumpet Pub. Company.

Massey, James Earl. 1957. *An Introduction to the Negro Churches in the Church of God Reformation Movement*. N.Y.: Shining Light Survey Press.

_____. 1967. *Raymond S. Jackson: A Portrait*. Anderson, Ind.: Church Service Printing/Warner Press.

_____. 1970. *The Soul Under Siege: A Fresh Look at Christian Experience*. Anderson, Ind.: Warner Press. Second edition, Francis Asbury Press/Zondervan, 1987.

_____. 1975. "Semantics and Holiness: A Study in Holiness Text Functions." *Wesleyan Theological Journal*. 10 (Spring).

_____. 1979. *Concerning Christian Unity*. Anderson, Ind.: Warner Press.

_____. 1995. Biographical interview in Barry Callen, ed., *Sharing Heaven's Music: The Heart of Christian Preaching*. Nashville: Abingdon Press.

Mead, Sidney. 1963. *The Lively Experiment: The Shaping of Christianity in America*. Harper & Row.

Meyer, Louis P. 1992. *Pioneering New Frontiers in North America* (historical overview of the Board of Church Extension and Home Missions of the Church of God, 1921-1991). Anderson, Ind: Bd. of Ch. Ext. and Warner Press.

Miller, Adam. 1950. *We Hold These Truths*. Booklet. Anderson, Ind.: Mid-Century Evangelistic Advance (Church of God).

Miller, Gene, editor. 1972. *Dynamics of the Faith: Evangelical Christian Foundations*. Houston, Texas: Gulf-Coast Bible College.

Miller, Holly G. 1985. "The Church with a Mind of Its Own" [Church of God]. *The Saturday Evening Post* (Nov.).

Mitchell, T. Chrichton. 1994. *Charles Wesley: Man With the Dancing Heart*. Kansas City: Beacon Hill Press.

Moltmann, Jürgen. 1988. *Theology Today*. Philadelphia: Trinity Press International.
_____. 1992. *The Spirit of Life*. Minneapolis: Fortress Press.
Morrison, John. 1962. *As The River Flows* (an autobiography). Anderson College Press.
_____. 1974 (June 9 through August 25). Biographical article series on Daniel Warner in *Vital Christianity*.
Myers, Linfield, edited by Larry Osnes. 1973. Anderson, Ind.: Anderson College Press.
Naylor, Charles. n.d. (1948?). *The Teachings of D. S. Warner and His Associates*. Published privately.
_____. 1919. *Winning a Crown*. Anderson, Ind.: Gospel Trumpet Publishing Co.
Neal, Hazel, and Bolitho, Axchie. 1951. *Madam President*. Anderson, Ind: Gospel Trumpet Co. Biography of Nora S. Hunter.
Newberry, Gene W. 1955. *Primer for Young Christians*. Anderson, Ind.: Warner Press.
_____. 1972. *Soundings*. Anderson, Ind.: Warner Press.
Newell, Arlo F. 1972. *The Church of God as Revealed in Scripture*. Anderson, Ind.: Warner Press.
_____. 1978. *Receive the Holy Spirit*. Anderson, Ind.: Warner Press.
_____. 1995. *A Servant in God's Kingdom: The Story of Max R. Gaulke*. Anderson, Ind.: Warner Press.
Norris, Frederick W. 1992. *The Apostolic Faith: Protestants and Roman Catholics*. Collegeville, Minn.: The Liturgical Press.
North, James. 1993 (Feb.), with Barry Callen. "Open Forum: A Meeting of Two Movements," in *Vital Christianity*. Also appeared in *Christian Standard*.
_____. 1994. *Union In Truth: An Interpretive History of the Restoration Movement*. Cincinnati: Standard Publishing.
Oden, Thomas C. 1993. *The Transforming Power of Grace*. Nashville: Abingdon Press.
_____. 1992. *Life in the Spirit*. S.F.: Harper.
_____. 1994. *John Wesley's Scriptural Christianity*. Grand Rapids: Zondervan.
Oldham, Dale. 1973. *Giants Along My Path* (autobiography). Anderson, Ind.: Warner Press.

Osborne, Ronald. 1989 (July). "The Irony of the Twentieth-Century Christian Church (Disciples of Christ): Making It To the Mainline Just At the Time of Its Disestablishment," *Mid-Stream.*

Packer, J. I. 1992. *Rediscovering Holiness.* Ann Arbor, Mich.: Servant Publications.

Phillips, Harold L. 1968. *Knowing the Living God.* Anderson, Ind.: Warner Press.

_____. 1974 (June 9 through October 20). Editorials in *Vital Christianity* on the life of Daniel Warner.

_____. 1979. *Miracle of Survival.* Anderson, Ind.: Warner Press. History of the Gospel Trumpet Co. (Warner Press).

Pinnock, Clark. 1984. *The Scripture Principle.* S.F.: Harper & Row.

_____. 1990. *Tracking the Maze: Finding Our Way Through Modern Theology from an Evangelical Perspective.* S.F.: Harper & Row.

Preston, Lee Dean. 1969. *"Charles E. Brown: His Life and Influence as Editor-in-Chief of the Gospel Trumpet Company on the Organization of the Life and Work of the Church of God."* S.T.M. thesis, Iliff School of Theology.

Proceedings of the Western Union Holiness Convention. 1881. Bloomington, Ill.: Western Holiness Association. Available in archives of Anderson University.

Pruitt, Fred. 1978 (7th ed., original 1933). *God's Gracious Dealings.* Guthrie, Okla: Faith Publishing House.

Pudel, Kurt. 1991. *When the German Trumpet Sounded.* Edmonton, Alberta, Canada.

Ratzlaff, Leslie. 1965. *The Implementation of Christian Goals in Christian Liberal Arts Colleges.* Ed.D. dissertation: Columbia University.

Reardon, E. A. 1929. "Taking an Honest Look at Ourselves," in Barry Callen, *The First Century,* vol. 1. Anderson, Ind.: Warner Press. Pages 635-638. Previously unpublished sermon.

Reardon, Robert H. 1943. "The Doctrine of the Church and the Christian Life in the Church of God Reformation Movement," unpublished masters thesis, Oberlin School of Theology.

_____. 1979. *The Early Morning Light.* Anderson, Ind.: Warner Press.

_____. 1979. "A Glossary of Church of God Terms," in Barry Callen, ed., *The First Century*, vol. 2, 615-616.

_____. 1991. *This Is The Way It Was: Growing Up in the Church of God*. Anderson, Ind.: Warner Press.

Rees, Seth. 1897. *The Ideal Pentecostal Church*. Cincinnati: The Revivalist Office.

Reid, Daniel, et. al., eds. 1990. *Dictionary of Christianity in America*. InterVarsity Press.

Riggle, Herbert. 1899. *The Kingdom of God and the One Thousand Years' Reign*. Moundsville, W.V.: Gospel Trumpet Publishing Co.

_____. 1903 (with Daniel Warner). *The Cleansing of the Sanctuary or The Church of God in Type and Antitype, and in Prophecy and Revelation*. Moundsville, W.V.: Gospel Trumpet Pub. Co.

_____. 1909. *Christian Baptism, The Lord's Supper, and Feet Washing*. Anderson, Ind.: Gospel Trumpet Publishing Company.

_____. 1912. *The Christian Church: Its Rise and Progress*. Anderson, Ind.: Gospel Trumpet Co.

_____. 1918. *Christ's Kingdom and Reign*. Anderson, Ind.: Gospel Trumpet Co.

_____. 1919. *Christ's Second Coming and What Will Follow*. Anderson, Ind.: Gospel Trumpet Co.

_____. 1924. *Pioneer Evangelism*. Anderson, Ind.: Gospel Trumpet Co.

Royster, James. 1958. "Historical and Analytical Survey of Anderson, Indiana, Camp Meeting Preaching in the Church of God, 1907-1957." B.D. thesis, Anderson School of Theology.

_____. 1967. "A History of the Church of God in South India, 1897-1960." Masters thesis, Hartford Seminary Foundation.

Schell, William. 1893. *Biblical Trace of the Church*. Grand Junction, Mich.: Gospel Trumpet Co.

Schwarz, R. W. 1979. *Light Bearers to the Remnant* (denominational textbook for Seventh-day Adventism). Boise, Idaho: Pacific Press Publishing Association.

Seamands, Stephen. 1990. *Holiness of Heart and Life*. Nashville: Abingdon Press.

Select Camp Meeting Sermons. 1928. Preached at the international camp meeting, Anderson, Ind., June, 1928. Anderson, Ind.: Gospel Trumpet Publishing Co.

Smith, Frederick G. 1908. *The Revelation Explained.* Anderson, Ind: Gospel Trumpet Publishing Co. Eleventh edition, 1943.

_____. 1911. *The Evolution of Christianity: Origin, Nature and Development of the Religion of the Bible.* Anderson, Ind: Gospel Trumpet Co.

_____. 1913. *What the Bible Teaches.* Anderson, Ind: Gospel Trumpet Co.

_____. 1919. *The Last Reformation.* Anderson, Ind: Gospel Trumpet Co.

_____. 1920. *Look on the Fields: A Brief Description of the Missionary Work of the Church of God.* Anderson, Ind.: Missionary Board of the Church of God.

_____. 1926. "Fundamentals for Which We Stand," *Gospel Trumpet* (Nov. 18).

_____. 1927. *Brief Sketch of the Origin, Growth and Distinctive Doctrines of the Church of God Reformation Movement.* Anderson, Ind.: Gospel Trumpet Company.

Smith, John W. V. 1954. "The Approach of the Church of God (Anderson, Ind.) and Comparable Groups to the Problem of Christian Unity." Unpublished doctoral dissertation, University of Southern California Graduate School of Religion.

_____. 1955. *Heralds of a Brighter Day.* Anderson, Ind.: Gospel Trumpet Co., chapter two, "D. S. Warner."

_____. 1956. *Truth Marches On.* Anderson, Ind.: Gospel Trumpet Co.

_____. 1965 (July 11, 18, 25). "D. S. Warner: Pioneer Leader," *Vital Christianity.*

_____. 1967. "The Church of God at Eighty-Six," *The School of Theology Bulletin,* Anderson College (University), Spring.

_____. 1975. "Holiness and Unity." *Wesleyan Theological Journal* 10 (Spring).

_____. 1980. *The Quest for Holiness and Unity.* Anderson, Ind: Warner Press.

_____. 1981. "The Bible in the Church of God Reformation Movement: A Historical Perspective," in *Centering On Ministry* (Center for Pastoral Studies, Anderson University School of Theology). 6:3 (Spring), 4-6.

_____. 1985. *I Will Build My Church: Biblical Insights on Distinguishing Doctrines of the Church of God.* Anderson, Ind.: Warner Press.

Smith, Sarah. n.d. *Life Sketches of Sarah Smith: A Mother in Israel.* Guthrie, Okla.: Faith Pub. House.

Smith, Uriah. 1882. *Thoughts, Critical and Practical, on the Books of Daniel and the Revelation.* Battle Creek, Mich.: Review and Herald Press.

Snyder, Howard. 1980. *The Radical Wesley.* Downers Grove, Ill.: Inter-Varsity Press.

So This Is the Church of God. 1969. Booklet. Anderson, Ind.: Executive Council of the Church of God.

Stafford, Gilbert. 1973. "Experiential Salvation and Christian Unity in the Thought of Seven Theologians of the Church of God (Anderson, Ind.)." Unpublished doctoral dissertation, Boston University School of Theology.

_____. 1977. *Beliefs That Guide Us.* Anderson, Ind.: Center for Pastoral Studies, Anderson University.

_____. 1977. *The Person and Work of the Holy Spirit.* Anderson, Ind.: Center for Pastoral Studies, Anderson University.

_____. 1979. *Life of Salvation.* Anderson, Ind.: Warner Press.

_____. 1983. "Frontiers in Contemporary Theology," in Charles Carter, ed., *A Contemporary Wesleyan Theology,* vol. 1. Grand Rapids: Francis Asbury Press/Zondervan.

Stall, Stephen. 1980. "The Inspiration and Authority of Scripture: The Views of Eight Historical and Twenty-one Current Doctrinal Teachers in the Church of God, Anderson, Indiana." Unpublished masters thesis, Anderson University School of Theology.

Stanley, John. 1990. "Unity Amid Diversity: Interpreting the Book of Revelation in the Church of God (Anderson)." *Wesleyan Theological Journal* (Fall).

Stanley, Susie. 1993. *Feminist Pillar of Fire: The Life of Alma White.* Cleveland: The Pilgrim Press.

Starr, William H. 1857. *Discourses on the Nature of Faith and Kindred Subjects.* Chicago: D. B. Cook and Company.

Sterner, R. Eugene. 1960. *We Reach Our Hands in Fellowship: An Introduction to the Church of God.* Anderson, Ind.: Warner Press.

BIBLIOGRAPHY

_____. 1972 (June 11). "This We Believe." Anderson, Ind.: *Vital Christianity.*

_____. 1978. *Healing & Wholeness.* Anderson, Ind.: Warner Press.

Strege, Merle D. 1986. Editor, *Baptism and Church: A Believers' Church Vision.* Grand Rapids: Sagamore Books.

_____. 1986. "Lovers of Truth" in *Vital Christianity* (Aug. 24).

_____. 1987. *A Look at the Church of God: The Story of the Church for Children.* 2 vols. Anderson, Ind.: Warner Press.

_____. 1987. "A Dialogical Church," in *Vital Christianity* (Aug. 2).

_____. 1991. *Tell Me The Tale: Historical Reflections on the Church of God.* Anderson, Ind.: Warner Press.

_____. 1991 (April). "Demise (?) of a Peace Church: The Church of God (Anderson), Pacifism, and Civil Religion," *Mennonite Quarterly Review*, 128-140.

_____. 1993. *Tell Me Another Tale: Further Reflections on the Church of God.* Anderson, Ind.: Warner Press.

Strong, Marie. 1980. *Basic Teachings from Patmos: A Simple Guide to the Basic Message of the Book of Revelation.* Anderson, Ind.: Warner Press.

Tanner, Paul A. 1959. *The Church, the Body of Christ.* Anderson, Ind.: Gospel Trumpet Company.

Tasker, George. 1924. "An Appeal to the Free and Autonomous Churches of Christ in the Fellowship of the Evening Light." Calcutta, India: Published privately.

Teasley, D. O. 1918. *The Bible and How To Interpret It.* Anderson, Ind: Gospel Trumpet Co.

Telfer, David. 1975. "Sociological and Theological Foundations for Church of God Ministry in Ethnic Minority Communities in the United States." Unpublished thesis, Iliff School of Theology.

The Church of God in Black Perspective. 1970. Proceedings of the Caucus of Black Churchmen in the Church of God (Cleveland, April, 1970). Shinng Light Survey Press.

Thorsen, Donald A. D. 1990. *The Wesleyan Quadrilateral: Scripture, Tradition, Reason & Experience as a Model of Evangelical Theology.* Grand Rapids: Zondervan.

Toulouse, Mark. 1992. *Joined In Discipleship: The Maturing of an American Religious Movement.* St. Louis: Chalice Press.

Vital Christianity. Originally *Gospel Trumpet.* Indexed at Anderson University School of Theology.

Walker, Dean. 1992. *Adventuring for Christian Unity.* Collection of Walker's essays. Johnson City, Tenn.: Emmanuel School of Religion.

Warner, Daniel S. 1880. *Bible Proofs of the Second Work of Grace.* Goshen, Ind.: E. U. Mennonite Publishing Society.

_____. 1885. *Songs of Victory.* Joseph Fischer, Ed., Warner major contributor of original material. Williamston, Mich.: Gospel Trumpet Co.

_____. 1888. *Anthems From the Throne.* With Barney Warren. Grand Junction, Mich.: Gospel Trumpet Co.

_____. 1893. *Echoes From Glory.* With Barney Warren. Grand Junction, Mich.: Gospel Trumpet Co.

_____. 1890. *Poems of Grace and Truth.* Grand Junction, Mich.: Gospel Trumpet Co.

_____. n.d. *The Church of God or What Is the Church and What Is Not.* n.p.

_____. 1894. *The Sabbath or Which Day To Keep.* Grand Junction, Mich: Gospel Trumpet Co.

_____. 1896. *Innocence: A Poem Giving a Description of the Author's Experience from Innocence Into Sin, and From Sin to Full Salvation.* Grand Junction, Mich.: Gospel Trumpet Publishing Co.

_____. 1896. *Salvation, Present, Perfect, Now or Never.* Moundsville, W. Va.: Gospel Trumpet Co.

_____. 1897. *Marriage and Divorce.* Grand Junction, Mich: Gospel Trumpet Co.

_____. 1903. *The Cleansing of the Sanctuary.* With Herbert Riggle. Moundsville, W. Va.: Gospel Trumpet Co.

_____. 1972. *Journal of D. S. Warner.* Unpublished, reprint from the original. Large portions reproduced in Andrew Byers, *Birth of a Reformation* (1921). Handwritten original now in the Archives of Anderson University.

_____. Numerous articles in the *Gospel Trumpet,* 1881-1895, and in *Herald of Gospel Freedom* and *Church Advocate* in the years prior to 1881.

Watson, Cecil. 1957. "Schismatic Tendencies in the Church of God Reformation Movement." B.D. thesis, Anderson School of Theology.

We Believe: A Statement of Conviction on the Occasion of the Centennial of the Church of God Reformation Movement. 1979. Anderson University School of Theology.

We Believe: Churches of God General Conference. 1986 (rev. ed.). Findlay, Ohio: Churches of God Publications.

Weaver, J. Denny. 1987. *Becoming Anabaptist: The Origin and Significance of Sixteenth-Century Anabaptism.* Scottdale, Pa.: Herald Press.

Webb, Henry E. *In Search of Christian Unity: A History of the Restoration Movement.* Cincinnati: Standard Publishing.

Wickersham, Henry C. 1894. *Holiness Bible Subjects.* Grand Junction, Mich.: Gospel Trumpet Co.

_____. 1900. *A History of the Church.* Moundsville, W.Va.: Gospel Trumpet Publishing Company.

Williams, Carl C. 1955. *Things Most Surely Believed.* Anderson, Ind.: Gospel Trumpet Company.

Williams, Lima Lehmer. 1986. *Walking in Missionary Shoes: A History of the Church of God in East Africa* (1905-1970). Anderson, Ind.: Warner Press.

Willowby, Richard. 1986. *Family Reunion: A Century of Camp Meetings.* Anderson. Ind.: Warner Press.

Worship the Lord: Hymnal of the Church of God. 1989. Anderson, Ind.: Warner Press.

Wynkoop, Mildred. 1972. *A Theology of Love: The Dynamic of Wesleyanism.* Kansas City: Beacon Hill Press.

Yoder, John H. 1994. *The Politics of Jesus.* Grand Rapids: Eerdmans. First ed., 1972.

_____. 1994. Michael Cartwright, ed. *The Royal Priesthood: Essays Ecclesiological and Ecumenical* (by Yoder). Grand Rapids: Eerdmans.